4.00

THE SPECTACLE OF SUFFERING

THE SPECTACLE OF SUFFERING

Executions and the evolution of repression: from a preindustrial metropolis to the European experience

PIETER SPIERENBURG

Department of History, Erasmus University, Rotterdam

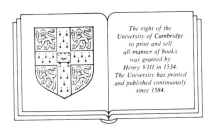

The right of the
University of Cambridge
to print and sell
all manner of books
was granted by
Henry VIII in 1534.
The University has printed
and published continuously
since 1584.

CAMBRIDGE UNIVERSITY PRESS

Cambridge

London   New York   New Rochelle
Melbourne   Sydney

Published by the Press Syndicate of the University of Cambridge
The Pitt Building, Trumpington Street, Cambridge CB2 IRP
32 East 57th Street, New York, NY 10022, USA
296 Beaconsfield Parade, Middle Park, Melbourne 3206, Australia

First published 1984

Printed in Great Britain at the University Press, Cambridge

Library of Congress catalogue card number: 84-3195

British Library cataloguing in publication data
Spierenburg, Pieter
The spectacle of suffering
1. Corporal punishment – Europe – History
1. Title
346.6'7'094   HV8609
ISBN 0 521 26186 4

CONTENTS

PREFACE

The sight of whippings, thumb-cuttings and hangings is not part of the experience of the average inhabitant of the Western world. Most people have merely a vague sense of public physical punishment as a thing of the past. Elsewhere public executions of delinquents are generally only a feature of countries with a fundamentalist Islamic regime and even there they are not applied consistently. We are told that a provincial town in Iran introduced public flogging but discontinued the practice, because the people apparently did not accept it. Death penalties in Iran are carried out within prison walls, but the distribution of official photographs makes them semi-public.[1] Where it exists today, capital punishment is hardly ever inflicted out in the open. In Europe and America its abolition or re-introduction is a much-debated issue. These discussions reflect an uneasiness about our ways of dealing with delinquents which has deep historical roots.

For a better understanding of the options open today it is necessary to possess a diachronic analysis of the developments in repression that helped shape the present. This book offers a contribution. I see my subject from the angle of the history of mentalities, rather than focusing on repression as a system of control. Throughout the preindustrial period the authorities never achieved the ordered society they were aiming for. Nevertheless, the modes of repression changed. This was an expression of changing mentalities. The 'mental history' of repression refers to notions of what constitutes undesirable behavior and how it should be dealt with.

Public executions were the most conspicuous feature of repression in preindustrial Europe (and in some countries during industrialization as well). In this book I attempt to describe their rise to prominence, continued functioning and ultimate disappearance, and to offer an explanation for this. By public executions I mean all penalties meted out in a public place. Execution originally meant the carrying out of any sentence, not only death sentences. The list which was drawn up before each 'justice day' in eighteenth-century Amsterdam, for instance, was called the 'list of names of those who are to be publicly executed', even though most received a corporal penalty. I will keep to this wider use of the word execution. It has one implicit advantage. A few authors, in discussing capital punishment during the *ancien régime*, place it exclusively in the context of attitudes towards death.[2] It should, however, also be viewed as an element of a penal system in which physical treatment figured prominently. The wider meaning of the word execution clearly refers to this system.

The word repression, as used in this book, in its turn has a wider meaning. It refers to more than punishment alone: also to matters such as prosecution policy, trial procedure and semi-judicial institutions of control. We may define repression as all means which the ruling groups employ to keep the population in line, whether these are effective or not. As noted above, it is not the effectiveness of repression that constitutes my subject, but its changing modes.

The best-known study of changes in modes of repression is by Michel Foucault.[3] He analyzes the rise of the modern prison in the nineteenth century and the era of physical punishment which preceded it. The main difference between these penal systems is twofold. The earlier one had two major characteristics which were to a great extent absent from the later one: publicity and the conscious infliction of physical suffering. This characterization is certainly valid. Foucault's study, however, remains defective in a few respects. His theoretical frame of reference is essentially that of structuralist philosophy. He conveys the picture of a sudden transition from one penal system to another, without inquiring into that transition. Moreover, the changes in modes of repression are hardly explained at all, which could be done by showing their interdependencies with other societal developments. A third criticism is that his study, especially his analysis of public executions, was not based on archival sources.

Foucault's picture of one system quickly replacing another is actually far from historical reality. The infliction of pain and the public character of punishment did not disappear overnight. Both elements slowly retreated in a long, drawn-out process over several centuries. For one thing, public executions survived in most European countries into the 1860s, when the penitentiary had already been firmly established. On the other hand, with the disappearance of serious mutilation in the early seventeenth century a major change in the direction of a decline of the physical element in punishment had already taken place. Around the same time, imprisonment was introduced. These are only the most prominent examples. There can be no doubt that the history of repression exhibits long-term processes. We need, therefore, a developmental perspective. This book was written from this perspective and attempts to construct a 'counter-paradigm' to Foucault's.[4]

A study by Rusche and Kirchheimer, published more than forty years ago, does attempt to account for changing types of punishment from a developmental point of view. Yet this book is also of limited value. Rusche and Kirchheimer provide a very general and crude overview of the development of penal systems. They roughly distinguish three phases: until the sixteenth century mutilation and death combined with fines prevailed; the seventeenth and eighteenth centuries witnessed compulsory labor in houses of correction; after 1800 this was followed by solitary confinement in penitentiaries. They offer unconvincing economistic explanations for this development. Essentially they argue that the nature of a penal system is determined by the demand for labor. In the mercantilist period labor power was valuable and hence people were put to work; but not before and after. This type of theory, however, cannot explain why non-productive punishment sometimes consisted of physical treatment and at other times of solitary confinement. That cannot be done without taking changing sensibilities into account.[5]

In this book, then, I am working out my own theory in order to explain the development of public executions in Western Europe and their ultimate disappearance. I will consider changing modes of repression as a reflection of changing sensibilities. But I will also analyze the functions which executions had for the various social groups involved. That is a necessary step towards establishing the relationship of the evolution of repression with other long-term processes in society. A model of the interrelationship between the development of mentalities and changes in human organization is provided by Norbert Elias.[6] His theory can serve as a general frame of reference, but I do not follow the model too closely. A few points need to be revised. The model does serve my purpose as far as the development of mentalities is concerned. Elias conceptualized the psychic changes he observed, first in the elites and then in broader sections of society, in terms of processes of *Zivilisation*, which might best be translated as 'conscience formation'. Two elements of this process of conscience formation are particularly relevant for the present study: first, several forms of human behavior, among which was the infliction of physical injury, came to be loaded with restraints and, second, several aspects of life became privatized, disappearing from the public arena. The development of repression, with the retreat of physical punishment

ix

and the decline of its public character, fits this model very well.

The second part of Elias' model, however, has to be handled more carefully. He accounted for the dynamics of conscience formation by relating them to the development of society in general, but within this development state formation clearly plays the major part. Two objections can be raised to this emphasis: first, state formation, although certainly of vital importance, may not be the only long-term process which explains changes in mentality. Urbanization, for instance, played its role too. The second objection is that Elias' model of state formation relies too heavily on the French development. In this sense he comes close to Foucault, who also sees the early modern state as largely identical with French absolutism. There were, however, other models of state formation in the early modern period, such as Britain and the Dutch Republic. Moreover, I would rather place the emphasis on the development of the entire network of states in Europe, than on the development of each single state. The influence of this network also reached areas which lagged behind in some ways, such as the Netherlands in the seventeenth and eighteenth centuries.[7] With this shift in emphasis state formation may still be crucial for the explanation of changes in repression. Elias' theory has, in contrast to Foucault's, the advantage of being truly historical. It suggests that the evolution of repression is part of processes involving the changing sensibilities of the upper and middle classes, and is related to the rise of states.

The conclusions of this book will be based on the evidence. Within the general framework of Elias' model, revised as indicated above, I put forward my own theory. The book's thesis is twofold: first, an original positive attitude towards the sufferings of convicts slowly gave way to a rising sensitivity, until a critical threshold of sensibility was reached in the nineteenth century. Consequently, executions played a crucial role as the most conspicuous part of the penal system, but finally disappeared from public life. Second, these developments are closely related to the rise of a network of states and the changes they underwent. Notably, the disappearance of public executions is related to the transition from the early modern state, whether absolutist or patrician, to the nation-state.

The empirical evidence for my thesis comes from Germany, the Netherlands, France and, to a lesser extent, England. The bulk, however, is derived from an investigation of Amsterdam court records and related sources. The choice of Amsterdam was not accidental: for one thing, there is an abundance of source material, which makes it possible to put together a coherent picture of the history of executions. And pre-industrial repression reached its fullest elaboration in the context of large cities. The evidence from the Dutch metropolis can be compared with the data compiled for London. There are no indications that the Amsterdam experiences deviated in any significant respect from those in Western Europe generally.

Hence the empirical evidence is composed of four concentric circles, representing a decrease in depth and an increase in scope. The nucleus consists of a comprehensive scrutiny of public sentences pronounced in Amsterdam between 1650 and 1750. The second circle is formed by a survey of other relevant court records and pamphlets pertaining to justice in Amsterdam. An investigation of published sources and literature on executions in the Northern Netherlands constitutes the third circle. The fourth, finally, is made up of cases collected from the literature on various Western European countries. This structure has, I think, a double advantage. It combines a wide geographic range with a firm base in archival material. In this way it is hoped that the construction of a counter-paradigm to Foucault's will indeed be realized. Of course the book still leaves many questions of detail open. The primary task is to elaborate the paradigm and to show its potential.

The bulk of the following chapters consists of a successive treatment of the various parties involved in executions. Of course no absolute division exists between them; it is a way of organizing the material. Although the composition of the book is largely thematic, chronology has influenced it too. Chapter one discusses the emergence of criminal justice as a function of state formation and urbanization in the later Middle Ages. Chapter two deals with the executioner and focuses especially on the rise of the office during the same period. Chapter three and chapters four and five concentrate on the 'classic' age of preindustrial repression during the seventeenth and most of the eighteenth centuries. Chapter six discusses the transformation of repression in the late eighteenth and nineteenth centuries.

This book is the result of a ten-year involvement with problems of preindustrial criminal justice. The bulk of the archival research, however, was performed during 1975 and 1976, when I enjoyed a grant from the Netherlands Organization for the Advancement of Pure Research (ZWO), which also provided funds for the correction of the present text. The original investigation resulted in a dissertation, presented at the University of Amsterdam and supervised by M. C. Brands. In those years I profited from the help of several people, whose advice indirectly benefited the present book. Of these I am especially indebted to Hans Blom, who critically accompanied the research, and Sjoerd Faber, who explained a number of intricacies of the Amsterdam judicial archive to me. His book on criminal justice in the city[8] appeared after I had completed the manuscript for this study. Lia van Wijk and Rob van der Horst assisted with the computer-processing of the data.

The first version of the present book was written during the year 1981, aided by the ample facilities provided by the *Subfaculteit Maatschappijgeschiedenis* of Erasmus University, Rotterdam. My colleagues Rudolf Dekker and Jan van Herwaarden both offered critical comments on a chapter of the manuscript. The completion of this book also owes a great deal to numerous encounters with scholars working in the field of the history of crime and justice. I should mention in particular Herman Bianchi, Nicole Castan, Yves Castan, Herman Diederiks, Gustav Henningsen, Jim Sharpe and Jan Sundin. Two successive versions of the manuscript were typed by Anneke Daniëls-de Leeuw and Tineke Huijssen, whose attentiveness saved me from a number of errors. Anne Lavelle polished my original English text and, consequently, made this into a much better book.

Chapter one

THE EMERGENCE OF CRIMINAL JUSTICE

From the way in which I have defined repression, it is obvious that its evolution should be intimately connected with the development of the state. The practice of criminal justice was one of the means by which authorities, with or without success, attempted to keep the population in line. As the position of these authorities changed, the character of criminal justice changed. However, before we can speak of criminal justice in any society, at least a rudimentary state organization has to be present. A system of repression presupposes a minimal level of state formation. Differentiation of this system, moreover, also presupposes the rise of towns. This chapter is an attempt to trace the origins of preindustrial repression. This cannot be a detailed analysis, but a short discussion is necessary for a fuller comprehension of my central thesis, and will indicate the social context for the subjects treated in the rest of the book. This chapter does not deal with changing sensibilities. It focuses on repression as a system of control, the emergence of which was a function of the rise of territorial principalities and of urbanization.[1]

At the height of the feudal age in Western Europe the state hardly existed at all. Violent entrepreneurs were in constant competition; from his castle a baron would dominate the immediate surroundings and *de facto* recognize no higher authority. His domain may be called a unit of attack and defense but not a state. Essentially it comprised a network of ties of affiliation and bondage. But in the violent competition between the numerous chiefs of such networks the mechanism was immanent which would eventually lead to the emergence of states. The first units with the character of a state were the territorial principalities which appeared from the twelfth century onwards.

As it happens, the emergence of criminal justice also dates from the twelfth century. Several legal historians have studied the 'birth of punishment' or 'emergence of public penal law'. The most detailed work is by P. W. A. Immink.[2] This author also comes closest to a sociological–historical view of the subject. He placed the origins of punishment in the context of changing relationships of freedom and dependence in feudal society. Thus he avoided presenting an analysis of legal texts alone, which can be very misleading especially for the period in question. From a sociological–historical perspective the essence of criminal justice is a relationship of subordination. This was noted by Immink: 'in common parlance the term "punishment" is never used unless the person upon whom the penalty is inflicted is clearly subordinate to the one imposing the penal act'.[3] This is the crucial point. This element distinguishes punishment from vengeance and the feud, where the parties are equal. If there is no subordination, there is no punishment.

The earliest subordinates in Europe were slaves. In that agrarian society, from Germanic times up into the feudal period, freemen were not subject to a penal system, but unfree persons were. The lord of a manor exercised an almost absolute authority over his serfs. When the latter were beaten or put to death – or maybe even fined – for some illegal act, this can certainly be called punishment. The manorial penal system of those early ages belonged to the realm of custom and usually did not form part of written law. Therefore we do not know much about it. The Barbarian Codes (*Leges Barbarorum*) were meant for freemen. They only referred to unfree persons in cases where their actions could lead to a conflict between freemen.[4]

Free persons, on the other hand, settled their conflicts personally. There were a few exceptions to this, even in Germanic times. In certain cases, if a member was held to have acted against the vital interests of the tribe, he could be expelled from the tribal community (branded a 'wolf') or even killed.[5] But on the whole, as there was no arbiter strong enough to impose his will, private individuals settled their own conflicts. A settlement could be reached through revenge or reconciliation. Vengeance and the feud were accepted forms of private retaliation, but they did not necessarily follow every injury. In a situation where violence is not monopolized, private violence is potentially omnipresent, but does not always manifest itself in practice. Notably it can be bought off. Reconciliation through payment to the injured party was already known in Tacitus' time.

To the earliest powerful rulers who represented an embryonic public authority, encouragement of this custom was the obvious road to be taken if they wished to reduce private violence. This is in fact what the Barbarian codes are all about. In every instance they fix the amount which can buy off vengeance. These sums are not fines in the modern sense, but indemnities. They were either meant as compensation when a person had been killed, wounded or assaulted (*wergeld*) or as a form of restitution when property had been stolen, destroyed or damaged.[6] Among freemen this remained the dominant system well into the twelfth century.

Criminal justice, however, slowly developed alongside this system. Its evolution during the feudal period was construed by Immink as one argument against the thesis put forward by Viktor Achter.[7] The latter had argued that punishment suddenly emerged in Languedoc in the middle of the twelfth century, from where it spread to the rest of Europe. Although Immink placed the definite breakthrough around the same time, he believed the evolution of punishment was inextricably linked with feudalism. The feudalization of Western Europe had brought about a fundamental change in the notion of freedom. This change eventually led to the emergence of criminal justice.

Before the feudal age the notion of freedom was closely connected to the allod. An allod should not be considered as a piece of property in the modern sense, but rather as an estate which is free from outside interference. Its occupant is completely his own master. His freedom implies a total independence from any worldly power and is similar to what later came to be called sovereignty. Hence the relationship of a freeman with the unfree persons subject to him, and over whom he exercises a right of punishment, is not one of owner–owned but one of ruler–ruled. The development of the institution of vassalage slowly put an end to the notion of freedom based on the allod. The Frankish kings and their successors attached freemen to themselves in a relationship of lord and *fideles*. Hence the latter were no longer entirely independent. By the time the whole network of feudal ties had finally been established, the notion of freedom had been transformed. Freedom meant being bound directly to the king, or to be more precise, there were degrees of freedom depending on how direct the allegiance was.[8]

The feudal transformation of the notion of freedom formed the basis of the emergence of a penal system applied to freemen. The king remained the only free person in the ancient allodial sense, the only sovereign. His reaction to a breach of faith by his vassal (*infidelitas*, felony),[9] usually the imposition of death, can truly be called punishment. The king himself never had a *wergeld*, because no one was his equal.[10] His application of punishment for *infidelitas* resembled the exercise of justice by a master over his serfs. When more and more illegal acts were defined as felonies, the emergence of a penal system with corporal and capital punishments applied to freemen became steadily more apparent.

The implication of Immink's analysis for the study of state formation

3

processes is evident. Absence of a central authority is reflected in the prevalence of private vengeance, the feud or voluntary reconciliation. The development of criminal justice runs parallel to the emergence of slightly stronger rulers. Originally it is only practiced within the confines of a manor; later it is applied by the rulers of kingdoms and territories. But we do not have to accept every part of Immink's story. For one thing, in his description the evolution of criminal justice and the parallel decline of the feud appeared too much as a unilinear process. This follows partly from his criticism of Achter. The latter, for instance, saw the legal reforms of the Carolingian period as a precocious spurt in the direction of a breakthrough of a modern notion of punishment. This would be in line with the fact that this period also witnessed a precocious sort of monopoly of authority. Achter considered the spurt as an isolated episode followed by centuries of silence.[11] This may be too crude. Immink, however, with his conception of an ultimate continuity, seems to go too far in the other direction, playing down the unsettled character of the ninth and tenth centuries.[12] These were certainly times when the vendetta was prevalent, despite whatever intentions legislators might have harbored.[13] On the other hand, we should not overestimate the degree of monopolization of authority around AD 800. The Carolingian Empire and its successor kingdoms were no more than temporary sets of allegiances over a wide geographic area, held together by the personal prestige of an individual king or by a military threat from outside. From Roman times until the twelfth century Europe witnessed nothing approaching a state, but there were certainly spurts in that direction.

In the middle of the twelfth century the first territorial principalities made their appearance and a penal system applied to freemen was established. The symbiosis is evident. Criminal justice emerged because the territorial princes were the first rulers powerful enough to combat private vengeance to a certain degree. The church had already attempted to do so, but largely in vain. I leave aside the question of whether its representatives were motivated by ideological reasons or by the desire to protect ecclesiastical goods. In any case they needed the strong arm of secular powers in order to succeed. The *treuga Dei* only acquired some measure of effectiveness when it became the 'country's peace'.[14] Two of the earliest regions to witness this development were Angevin England – which can also be seen as a territorial principality[15] – and the duchy of Aquitaine.

Incidentally, the South of France is also the region where, according to Achter, the concept of punishment originated. It is interesting that he reached this conclusion even though he used quite different sources and from a different perspective. Achter considered the element of moral disapproval as the essence of punishment. This notion was largely absent from Germanic law, which did not differentiate between accidents and intentional acts. If a felled tree accidentally killed a man the full *wergeld* still had to be paid.[16] Immink criticized this view and it may be another point where his rejection is too radical. He indicated, in fact, how Achter's view can be integrated into an approach focusing on state-formation processes. For the private avenger redressing a personal wrong, the wickedness of the other party is so self-evident that it need not be stated. As long as the law merely attempts to encourage reconciliation, it is likewise indifferent to a moral appreciation of the acts which started the conflict. When territorial lords begin to administer punishments to persons who have not wronged them personally, their attitudes to the law change as well. Theorizing about the law increases. The beginnings of a distinction between civil and criminal cases become apparent. The latter are *iniquitates*, acts that are to be disapproved of morally and which put their author at the *misericordia* of his lord.[17]

Thus it is understandable that a new emphasis on the moral reprehens-ibility of illegal acts also dates from the middle of the twelfth century. Indeed this period witnessed an early wave of moralization–individualization, connected to what medievalists have long been accustomed to call the Renaissance of the twelfth century. And yet we should not overestimate this spurt towards individualization, certainly not with regard to penal practice. Before the twelfth century there may have been even less concern for the motives and intentions of the perpetrators of illegal acts, but – as I will argue in other chapters – the practice of criminal justice continued to focus on crimes and their impact on the community rather than on the criminal's personality and the intricacies of his guilt. Up into the nineteenth century repression was not primarily individualized.

There is another aspect of the transformation under discussion which merits attention. When a malefactor finds himself at the mercy (*misericordia*) of a prince, the implication is that a religious notion has entered criminal justice. Mercy was an attribute of God, the ultimate judge. The relationship of all people with God had always been viewed as one of subordination. Hence God was indeed able to punish. Any wrong suffered, such as the loss of a combat, could be seen as a divine punishment, of which another man was merely the agent. Heavenly justice was never an automatic response. The Lord could be severe or show mercy. By analogy this line of thought was also applied to human justice practiced by a territorial lord.

5

Several authors discussed the 'sacred quality' of preindustrial punishment and even considered it an explanatory factor for its character.[18] According to this view, executions, especially capital ones, were a sort of sacrifice, an act of expiation. They reconciled the deity offended by the crime and restored the order of society sanctioned by heaven. This notion may have been part of the experience of executions, although there is little direct evidence for it. But it would certainly be incorrect to attribute an explanatory value to it as being in some way the essence of public punishment. For one thing, during and after the Middle Ages *every* social event also had a religious element. In the absence of a division between the sacred and the profane, religion pervaded life entirely. To note the sacred quality of executions in this context is actually redundant. If a religious view of the world has to 'explain' public punishment in any way, it should do so in a more specific sense. But the evolution which gave rise to criminal justice hardly lends support to this view. Criminal justice arose out of changing relationships of freedom and dependence in the secular world. It was extended by powerful princes at the expense of vengeance and the feud. Ecclesiastics had indeed already advocated harsh corporal penalties in the tenth century. But they too favored these merely as alternatives to the vendetta.[19] Their wishes were realized by the territorial princes of the twelfth century. Only then, when powerful lords applied a new form of justice, did notions of mercy, guilt and moral reprehensibility enter the picture; rather as a consequence than as a cause of the transformation. That clergymen should figure in the drama on the scaffold during the next centuries is only natural. As will be argued in this study, the role of the church remained largely instrumental in a spectacle which primarily served the purposes of the secular authorities.

The transformation during the twelfth century was only a small beginning. First, private vengeance had been pushed back to a certain degree, but continued to be practiced throughout the later Middle Ages. Second, generally the various courts were not in a very powerful position. Often they acted merely as mediators facilitating the reconciliation of the parties involved. A resolute practice of criminal justice depended as before on a certain measure of state power and levels of state power continued to fluctuate. But state formation is not the only process to which the further development of criminal justice was linked. A new factor entered the stage: urbanization. During the later Middle Ages the peculiar conditions prevailing in towns increasingly made their mark on the practice of justice. This situation was not equally marked everywhere. In a country such as France alterations in criminal procedure largely ran parallel with the growth of royal power. In the Netherlands, on the other hand, the towns were the major agents of change.

During the early stages of urban development the social context actually formed a counter-influence to the establishment of criminal justice. Originally, relationships of subordination did not prevail in cities. The charters of most towns recognized the inhabitants as free citizens. It has long been commonplace in historiography to note that the urban presence was encapsulated into feudal society. The body of citizens became the vassal, as it were, of the lord of the territory. The town was often a relatively independent corporation, a *coniuratio*. *Vis-à-vis* each other the citizens were equal. The councils ruling these cities were not very powerful. There were hardly any authorities in a real sense, who could impose their will and control events.

This situation left plenty of room for private violence. As the degree of pacification around the towns was still relatively low, so was the degree of internal pacification. To be sure, the vendetta might be officially forbidden. In the Northern Netherlands the prohibition was legitimized by the notion of a quasi-lineage: the citizens were held to be mutual relatives and a feud cannot arise among relatives.[20] But the fiction of lineage could never prevent actual feuds from bursting out, as the prohibitions, reiterated well into the fifteenth century, suggest.[21] Similarly, proclamations ordering a truce between parties were frequent until the middle of the sixteenth century.[22] An early seventeenth-century commentator gives a good impression of the situation. Speaking of the 1390s, he denounces the lawlessness of the age:

The people were still rough and wild in this time because of their newly won freedom and practically everyone acted as he pleased. And for that reason the court had neither the esteem nor the power which it ought to have in a well-founded commonwealth. This appears from the homicides, fights and wanton acts which occurred daily and also from the old sentences, in which one sees with what kind of timidity the Gentlemen judged in such cases: for they bargained first and took an oath from the criminals that they would not do *schout, schepenen* and burgomasters harm because of whatever sentence they would pass against them. And the most severe, almost, which they imposed on someone, was a banishment, or that the criminals would make a pilgrimage here or there before they came in [to town] again, or that they would give the city money for three or four thousand stones. They also often licenced one or the other, if he was under attack from his party, that he might defend himself with impunity, even if he killed the other in doing so. These are things which have no place in cities where the law is in its proper position of power.[23]

Apart from the fact that this situation was considered abnormal in the seventeenth century, we note an acceptance of forms of private violence

7

and the predominance of a reconciliatory stand instead of serious punishment.

Towards the end of the fifteenth century, however, this began to change. The ruling elites finally became real authorities. Patriciates emerged everywhere, constituting a socially superior group. The towns became increasingly stratified. The patrician courts could act as superiors notably towards the lower and lower-middle class citizens. In the towns of the Netherlands this development is clearly reflected in their ways of dealing with criminal cases. For a long time the main business of the courts had been to mediate and register private reconciliations. Around 1500 'corrections' gradually outnumbered reconciliations. The former were measures expressing a justice from above and often consisted of corporal punishment.[24]

Another development in criminal law which took place during the same period, was even more crucial. A new procedure in criminal trials, the inquisitorial, gradually superseded the older, accusatory procedure. This change occurred throughout Continental Europe, but not in England. The accusatory trial, when nothing else existed, was geared to a system of marginal justice. Where the inquisitorial trial prevailed, a justice from above had been established more firmly.

The contrast between the two procedures is a familiar item in legal history. Here it suffices to review briefly the relevant characteristics.[25] The inquisitorial procedure had been developed in ecclesiastical law, and was perfected by the institution which took its name from it. From the middle of the thirteenth century onwards it entered into secular law. Generally speaking, the rules of the accusatory trial favored the accused, while the rules of the inquisitorial one favored those bent on condemning him. The former procedure was much concerned with the preservation of equality between the parties. Thus if the accused was imprisoned during the trial – which was not usually the case – the accuser was often imprisoned as well. Moreover, if the latter could not prove his case, he might be subjected to the *talion*: the same penalty which the former would have received if he had been convicted. While the proceedings in the older trial were carried out in the open, the newer one was conducted in secrecy. Publicity was only sought after the verdict had been reached.

The most important element of the inquisitorial procedure, however, was the possibility of prosecution *ex officio*. The adage of the older procedure, 'no plaintiff, no judge', lost its validity. If it wished to, the court could take the initiative and start an investigation (*inquisitio*). Its officials would collect denunciations and then arrest a suspect, if they could lay hands on him. The court's prosecutor acted as plaintiff. Thus an active prosecution policy was possible for the first time. In the trial the authorities and the accused faced each other and the power distribution between the two was unequal, favoring the former. Under the accusatory procedure the authorities had hardly been more than bystanders. Consequently the rise of the newer form of trial meant a further spread of a system of justice from above.

This is also implicit in the final element to be noted. The inquisitorial procedure brought the introduction of torture. An accused who persisted in denial, yet was heavily suspect, could be subjected to a 'sharper examination'. It is evident that the principle of equality between parties under the accusatory procedure would have been incompatible with the practice of torture. Torture was not unknown in Europe before the thirteenth century. It had long been a common feature of the administration of justice by a lord over his serfs. Under the inquisitorial procedure torture could for the first time also be applied to free persons.[26] The parallel with the transformation discussed above is obvious.

The retreat of the accusatory before the inquisitorial procedure did not occur at the same pace everywhere. That the older one was originally more common is reflected in the names of 'ordinary' and 'extraordinary' procedure which the two forms acquired and often retained throughout the *ancien régime*. The gradual establishment of the primacy of the latter took place between the middle of the thirteenth and the beginning of the sixteenth century. Its use in France by Philip the Fair against the Templars paved the way for its further spread.[27] Prosecution *ex officio* increased in importance from the fourteenth to the sixteenth centuries. The growth of royal power was the main force behind it.[28] In the Netherlands, North and South, the cities formed the most important theater.[29] The formation of patrician elites facilitated the shift. But here too the central authorities confirmed it. In 1570, when the Dutch Revolt was already in the process of breaking out, Philip II issued his criminal ordinances, which clearly favored the inquisitorial trial.[30]

In the Dutch towns non-residents were the first to be tried according to the inquisitorial procedure. As outsiders they were more easily subjected to justice from above. Citizens occasionally put up resistance to it, in Malines, for example.[31] In France it was the nobles of Burgundy, Champagne and Artois who protested. Louis X granted them privileges in 1315 which implied a suspension of inquisitorial proceedings.[32] In the end they were unsuccessful. The forces of centralization and urbanization favored the development of a more rigorous penal system.

England forms a partial exception. Criminal procedure in that country remained largely accusatory throughout the preindustrial period. Nevertheless, essentially the developments discussed in this chapter can be observed there too, and in the end processes of pacification and centralization brought about a firmer establishment of criminal justice. Originally there had been plenty of room for private violence, just as on the Continent. An outlaw or 'wolf', for instance, could be captured by any man and be slain if he resisted. This right was abrogated in 1329, but as late as 1397 a group of men who had arrested and beheaded an outlawed felon, were pardoned because they had thought it was lawful.[33] Around 1400 it was not uncommon for justices to be threatened with violence by the parties in a lawsuit. The power of the courts went up and down with the fluctuations in the power of a central authority.[34] It was the Tudors, finally, who gradually established a monopoly of violence over most of England. Consequently, except in border areas, the feud definitely gave way to litigation.[35] The available literature on crime and justice in early modern England suggests that a system of prosecution of serious crimes, physical punishment and exemplary repression prevailed there, which was basically similar to that on the Continent.

Thus, the emergence and stabilization of criminal justice, a process going on from the late twelfth until the early sixteenth centuries, meant the disappearance of private vengeance. Ultimately vengeance was transferred from the victims and their relatives to the state. Whereas formerly a man would kill his brother's murderer or beat up the thief he caught in his house, these people were now killed or flogged by the authorities. Legal texts from late medieval Germany sometimes explicitly refer to the punishments imposed by the authorities as 'vengeance'.[36] Serious illegal acts, which up until then had been dealt with in the sphere of revenge and reconciliation, were redefined as being directed not only against the victims but also against the state. In this process the inquisitorial procedure was the main tool. Its increase in frequency in fourteenth-century Venice, for instance, went hand in hand with the conquest of the vendetta.[37] Private violence by members of the community coming to the assistance of a victim was similarly pushed back. In the Netherlands a thief caught redhanded could be arrested by any one. His captors were obliged to hand him over to the court, but they might seriously harass him and were often excused if they killed him. This 'right' retreated too before the increase of prosecution *ex officio*.[38]

It would be incorrect to assume that the state's arm was all-embracing during the early modern period. An active prosecution policy remained largely confined to the more serious crimes. Private vengeance had been conquered, but reconciliation survived in cases of petty theft and minor violence. The mediators were no longer the courts but prestigious members of local communities. The infra-judicial resolution of conflicts prevailed beneath the surface of justice from above. Historians have only recently come to realize this and the phenomenon has only been studied in detail in France.

This 'subterranean stream' was kept in motion from two sides. The authorities, though able to take the initiative, restricted their efforts to specific cases. Prosecution policy was often concentrated on vagrants and other notorious groups. The near-absence of a professional police force further limited the court's scope. Hence many petty offenders were left undisturbed. The attitude of local residents also contributed to this situation. Victims of thefts and acts of violence did not often take recourse to the judiciary. One reason was that a trial might be too costly for the potential plaintiff. Another reason was that numerous conflicts arising from violent exchanges or disputes over property were not viewed in terms of crime and the court was not considered the most appropriate place to settle them. Mediation was sought from non-judicial arbiters. This form of infra-judicial reconciliation survived until the end of the *ancien régime*.[39] Thus preindustrial repression was never an automatic response to all sorts of illegal acts.

Relics of private vengeance can also be observed in the early modern period. This is attested by the public's reaction to property offenders in Republican Amsterdam. The archival sources regularly make mention of a phenomenon called *maling*.[40] From it a picture emerges of communal solidarity against thieves. Events always followed a similar pattern. A person in the street might notice that his pocket was picked or he might be chasing after someone who had intruded into his house. Soon bystanders rushed to help him and the thief was surrounded by a hostile crowd. The people harassed and beat him and forced him to surrender the stolen goods. The thief was then usually thrown into a canal. Servants of justice were often said to have saved his life by arresting him, which meant getting him out of the hands of the crowd or out of the water. Memories of the medieval treatment of thieves caught redhanded were apparently still alive. The authorities tolerated it but did not recognize a form of popular justice. In 1718 a man was condemned for throwing stones at servants of justice when they were busy saving a woman, who was in the *maling*, from her assailants.[41] Comparable forms of self-help by the community against thieves existed in eighteenth-century Languedoc.[42]

At the close of this exposition I should say something briefly about the mentality aspect. As noted at the beginning, the emergence of criminal justice was not a function of changing sensibilities. These only started to play a role later. If corporal and capital penalties increased in frequency from the twelfth to the sixteenth centuries, this certainly cannot be taken as reflecting an increased taste for the sight of violence and suffering. It was primarily a consequence of the growth and stabilization of a system of criminal justice. Conversely, whatever resistance may have been expressed against the transformation – and, as I will show in the next chapter, there was resistance – did not spring from an abhorrence of violent dealings as such. Physical punishment was simply introduced into a world which was accustomed to the infliction of physical injury and suffering. In that sense it was not an alien element. The authorities took over the practice of vengeance from private individuals. As private retaliation had often been violent, so was the penal system adopted by the authorities. Similarly, as the first had always been a public affair, so was the second. Attitudes to violence remained basically the same. Huizinga demonstrated the medieval acceptance of violence more than sixty years ago and recent research confirms his view. Thus – to mention only a few – Barbara Hanawalt gets the 'impression of a society in which men were quick to give insult and to retaliate with physical attack'.[43] Norman Cohn recalls the violent zeal with which self-appointed hunters of heretics proceeded, such as the two who managed to reverse God's dictum at the destruction of Sodom and Gomorrah: 'We would gladly burn a hundred, if just one among them were guilty.'[44]

It is understandable that in such a climate of acceptance of violence no particular sensitivity prevailed towards the sufferings of convicts. This arose only later. Urban and territorial rulers had to ensure that people accepted the establishment of criminal justice. But once they had accomplished that, they did not encounter psychological barriers against the full deployment of a penal system based on open physical treatment of delinquents. By the middle of the sixteenth century a more or less stable repression had been established in most of Western Europe. It did not exclusively consist of exemplary physical punishments. Banishment was important as well and confinement would soon appear on the scene. From that time on it was possible for changing sensibilities within society to affect the modes of repression. From that time too the development of states and the ensuing pacification produced domesticated elites and changed mentalities. These would eventually lead to a transformation of repression. This is the subject of the following chapters.

Chapter two

THE ACTORS: EXECUTIONERS
AND THEIR STATUS

The social position of the executioner presents us with a paradox. In medieval and early modern Europe the attitude of most groups in society towards him was highly negative. Why should this have been so? The thesis of the present book is that a positive attitude or indifference to the sufferings of convicts prevailed throughout most of the period. Consequently, we would expect at least an indifference towards the person who inflicted these sufferings. The actual contempt bestowed upon him looks like a blow to the thesis. In fact, it is not; the paradox is only anomalous at first sight. This chapter argues why.

The first section gives a set of examples showing the negative attitude of the public. It focuses on attacks against hangmen and on the notion of infamy. Section two discusses explanations which have been put forward by other authors and ends with my own explanation in terms of the expropriation of private vengeance. The third section treats the continuing ambivalence towards executioners in early modern Europe and the reactions of the authorities. This is largely a work of reconstruction. The existing literature on the hangman is rather unhistorical. It tends to be an inventory of mentalities and customs, without posing the question of change.

I   THE PEOPLE'S CONTEMPT

The precariousness of the hangman's existence among his fellow citizens and countrymen is most vividly expressed by the custom whereby spectators harassed the actor after a less than perfect performance. A bungled execution usually implied a big risk for him. The risk was greatest during capital executions. Nothing much can go wrong with an ordinary whipping. The convict will receive his due number of lashes anyway. But if the job is to kill, and to kill quickly, then skill counts. Decapitation is the classic example. It is the executioner's 'masterpiece':

his first beheading admits him to the ranks of the masters of his craft.[1] It is a sort of initiation, a *rite de passage* for both the actor and the victim; though the ultimate one for the latter. A masterpiece should be performed well. The victim has a right to lose his head in one stroke. And no doubt this was the rule. Mistakes, however, occur in every craft, so it is not surprising that failures were reported. Popular stories about hangmen who, to gain courage, drank just a little too much, are not necessary for an explanation.

Examples of assaults by the populace on clumsy hangmen are abundant. They come from various Western European countries and cover a period from the late fifteenth to the early nineteenth centuries. Our ignorance of older cases may be just a consequence of the state of the records. The examples vary in one important respect: the degree of violence. Sometimes the populace only threw stones; at other times the executioner was killed. The majority of the cases I collected are German, a reflection of the fact that the available literature on the hangman as a whole is largely German. Let me start, however, with a few Dutch examples. In 1522 the hangman of Haarlem did a poor job on the beheading of two delinquents. He was hit with stones and injured, but rescued from the crowd by the magistrates. A year later, however, someone killed him in his own house. The murderer was caught, tried and beheaded in his turn, apparently by a strong-nerved colleague of the victim.[2] Half a century later the executioner of Nijmegen also paid for a bad performance with his life.[3] In Republican times the multitude was just as ready to act. In 1665 the Groningen executioner had the misfortune to need two strokes for a decapitation, while a second convict's head had not fallen after five. He saved his life by fleeing into a wine-house.[4] One of his successors in the city was attacked, together with his servants, in 1714 and 1717. On the first occasion the crowd managed to climb onto the scaffold. The hangman, who was busy branding, had the fire-pot thrown over him.[5] In the Southern Netherlands a chronicle of Malines tells a comparable story. In 1513 the executioner had botched a beheading and was stoned to death by 'people of diverse conditions'. The principal actors declared that it was their right to do so under the circumstances.[6]

As most examples come from the German countries, so does the oldest known. The year is 1464. The executioner of Augsburg had missed, was threatened and fled under a bridge. Nevertheless a journeyman smashed his head with an iron bar. The murderer was sent to Rome to procure an indulgence.[7] According to another chronicle, because of a bungled decapitation, five hangmen, no doubt a hangman and four servants, were supposed to have been killed on the same day in Lübeck in 1533.[8] In 1590 the executioner of Frankfurt was only maltreated for a bad performance. The council, however, decided to fire him. Very humbly he petitioned to be granted at least the office of *Stöcker*.[9] The executioner of Magdeburg, who in 1611 needed four strokes also survived. The stones thrown at the scaffold accidentally hit the two preachers.[10] In Nürnberg in 1641 the hangman's servant tried to grab the sword from his master's hand, in order to do a better job himself. The latter held on to it. The result was that militiamen saved him, his head already covered with blood.[11]

On the borders of the Empire popular attitudes were no different. A bungling hangman in Prague was assaulted in 1591. In this case the crowd waited until he had hanged three others. The executioner withdrew to the gallows, which stood on a separate structure that could be locked. It was to no avail and at last the court took him under its protection by making him a prisoner.[12] A Swiss case (Chur, sixteenth century) is represented in a picture. The executioner is evidently drunk and has already botched two beheadings. Spectators throw stones at him, while he is busy sawing off the head of a third man. A magistrate makes a helpless gesture to the crowd. Another, on horseback, points at the two bodies.[13]

France witnessed the custom too. When a Breton gentleman was beheaded in Angers in 1625, the hangman needed no less than twenty strokes. Many hit the victim's head and shoulders. The people threw stones at the executioner, grabbed him when he fled and killed him. On a similar occasion in Château-Gontier in 1719 the executioner did manage to escape from his assailants, who numbered over 200.[14] In Cahors in 1779 a hanging went wrong because the rope broke. Thereupon the executioner wanted to strangle the convict but the crowd intervened. They chased away the *maréchaussée* (constabulary), threw stones at the hangman and freed the prisoner.[15]

The last example comes from the British Isles. The city of Edinburgh witnessed the scene in 1819. The construction of the scaffold and the gibbet was so bad that the robber who was to be hanged did not drop correctly. He remained half-standing, half-suspended. Here the spectators threw stones too, but their main efforts were directed at the rescue of the convict. They stormed the scaffold, cut down the robber, restored him to his senses and took him to the streets. Police officers, however, recovered possession of the convict and in the end he was hanged anyway.[16]

These illustrations should be quite sufficient.[17] Paradoxically, the analysis of public justice starts with accounts of bleeding and dead hangmen instead of delinquents. The geographic range shows that we are dealing with a universal European custom.

I chose to treat the subject of assaults on hangmen so extensively because it makes the negative attitude towards them so abundantly clear. Nevertheless, the subject is of limited value as an illustration of the attitude in question. First, it refers only to very specific situations. Second, the examples do not cover the first two centuries when hangmen appeared on the scene in Western Europe. It is easy, however, to correct these two biases. We should shift the focus to more formal aspects of the executioner's position. The detestation attached to his function is already apparent before the late fifteenth century.

The office of executioner is not peculiar to Western Europe. Earlier civilizations such as China, India and Rome were familiar with it. The office's low status is widespread, but not entirely universal. In the Ottoman Empire, for instance, executioners reportedly had a relatively high status.[18] But, in my opinion, in the majority of cases where contempt prevailed, similar explanations for it apply. It would be beyond the scope of the present study to go into this. I will restrict myself to Western Europe and to a tentative explanation, put forward in the next section, of the attitude towards hangmen there. The thesis can be tested against the evidence from other civilizations. Even in the case of Western Europe the evidence is far from complete. Most data have been collected for Germany, where the oldest document mentioning an executioner in office dates from 1276. It is the *Stadtbuch* of the city of Augsburg. The executioner is counted among the *unehrliche Leute* (infamous persons). Consequently, a few other more or less mean tasks are entrusted to him. He has to supervise the prostitutes, to guard the corn market at night, to clean latrines and to chase away lepers.[19] The designation as 'infamous' is a clue. Hangmen have been connected with infamy from the very beginning.

The notion of infamy, again, was most influential in the German-speaking countries. *Unehrlichkeit* was a more or less formal status. It was attached to a number of different occupations, that of the executioner being only one. Those following these occupations and their families were confronted with opposition in various ways. The clearest consequence of infamy was the refusal by (*ehrliche*) guilds to accept the sons of infamous people as apprentices; an acceptance would contaminate the entire guild. The position of the guilds then, is crucial in the politics of infamy. They defined which occupations were despised. Urban authorities endorsed their regulations from time to time. Imperial laws, on the other hand, occasionally tried to limit the number of infamous occupations. Thus the Diet held in Frankfurt in 1577 ordered that linen-weavers, barbers, shepherds, millers, publicans, whistlers, trumpeters and bath-keepers and their children should not be barred from the guilds, provided that they lived an irreproachable life.[20] These lucky ones were only a minority among the infamous occupations. The implication of the Imperial regulation is that the others – including outsider groups such as Jews and gypsies – were confirmed in their infamy.

It might be argued that an encompassing theory has to be developed to account for the infamy attached to the entire spectrum of occupations. This is the position adopted by Werner Danckert, who argued for a common magical–religious explanation.[21] I will not pursue this course and doubt its usefulness. For one thing, not every occupation on the list has been considered infamous in all places and at all times. More-detailed investigations are needed on this subject. It is more likely that *Un-ehrlichkeit* functioned as an ideal type, a label available to pin on certain groups when, for various reasons, attitudes towards them changed negatively. For example, both beggars and the officials appointed to catch them, could be counted among the infamous persons. The first group came to be held in ill repute only around 1500; a change which, among other things, gave rise to the second.[22] An existing notion of infamy was superimposed on newly developed negative stereotypes. The prototype of the infamous occupation was not the job of hangman but rather that of skinner.

A second reason for caution lies in the geographical limitations of the concept. While the contempt for executioners shows remarkable similarities in several Western European countries, the notion of infamy was more particularly German. It is less easy to trace in the Netherlands. The situation in France clearly differs from that in the German countries. In the latter the bottom of society was defined as *unehrlich*, which turned the craftsmen in the guilds and all other groups into *ehrliche Leute*. In France, at least in the early modern period, the top-groups were called *honnêtes gens*, making all those beneath into an undifferentiated mass without a particular reputation to defend.[23]

Some attention should now be paid to the social consequences of the executioner's status and to popular beliefs. The expressions of the populace's contempt for hangmen can be grouped into three categories: physical harassment and insults, avoidance of contact and spatial restrictions placed on executioners.

I started with a number of examples of the first category; they can be completed by mentioning a few instances of assaults which had nothing to do with inadequate performances. Hangmen were bothered in the streets as well. Examples of this date back even further. In 1422 the council of Utrecht noted that citizens used to injure Mr Herman van Culen. They did so because he was the town's executioner. The council stated that it would prosecute anyone who continued to engage in such acts or incited his children to do so. The threat was repeated after the appointment of a new executioner in 1460.[24] We hear of similar problems in other Dutch towns around 1500. In Kampen in 1477 and in Zwolle in 1500 the council issued a proclamation against harassing the hangman and throwing mud at him.[25] When the town of Rhenen wished to borrow Utrecht's executioner in 1521, the latter city feared he would never return in one piece. It only consented on the condition that Rhenen sent a hostage plus a surety in money. The executioner was indeed severely wounded in Rhenen. Nevertheless, Utrecht released its hostage, after he paid 100 golden shields. The magistrates promised to urge those of Rhenen to reimburse him.[26]

Similar stories come from the Southern Netherlands. In Malines in 1479 five citizens intruded into the executioner's house. They threw stones at him and injured him. The furniture was destroyed.[27] More examples can be found in the literature on Germany. A journeyman from Nürnberg was banished from the city in 1457 for throwing stones at the hangman.[28] Two citizens of Freiberg had done the same at the end of the fourteenth century.[29] There are few examples of 'daily' violence against hangmen after the middle of the sixteenth century, although we do hear of executioners' servants who were harassed at night while cleaning the public latrines.[30]

The second category, that of contact avoidance, would seem to be in contradiction with the first. How can you kill a hangman without touching him? The contradiction, however, is only partial. It can hardly be a coincidence that the preferred method so often consisted of throwing objects, especially stones. In this way the attackers remained *ehrlich*. Nevertheless people occasionally laid their hands on hangmen. When it was a question of a whole multitude grabbing him, the complicity of everyone may have prevented fatal consequences. In other cases we are indeed confronted with the contradictions in popular attitudes.

In normal social life people tried to stay away from the executioner and his family (save for certain occasions, which are dealt with later, see pp. 31–2). To be touched by him meant infamy for the unlucky one, which, in popular tales, could be undone by an accolade.[31] The 'contagion' could even be transmitted through objects, notably money. In various regions it was a custom not to take the money owed by the hangman directly from

18

his hands. In the tavern he had to place it on the counter. The host blew over the coins, to 'cool them off' and then picked them up. Sometimes the hangman's glass was broken after use.[32] In the marketplace the goods were in danger too. According to another custom the hangman had to take apples from the stock first and refrain from touching any others, while everybody watched carefully.[33] It has also been reported that boatmen refused to transport him.[34] Whoever was unlucky enough to have been drinking with a stranger, not knowing that he was an executioner, was in severe trouble if it became known. Even suicides were reported as a result.[35] The infamy of hangmen did not stop at their death. There are several accounts of the guilds responsible for funerals refusing to carry their bodies to the grave.[36]

It is not surprising therefore that the hangman's touch was considered as a penalty in itself. The ensuing infamy constituted an important ingredient of the injury that punishment should be. In popular tales this touch emerges as the most dreadful of all for the condemned. Consequently, it is a means of showing mercy if the judges determined that a person to be beheaded was not to be touched by the executioner. The convict walks to the scaffold by himself, kneels down and is only touched by the sword. It depends of course on his co-operation. The judges of Frankfurt granted this privilege to a manslaughterer in 1661. But the man did not want to play the game and was tied up and led from the jail by the executioner. The later custom of hangmen to wear gloves might be connected with this.[37]

If occasional contact with the executioner is to be avoided, the more so is a personal relationship. Thus the masters of the sword often had difficulties finding godparents for their children. Magistrates occasionally acted as such out of compassion. They were apparently too secure in their position to be reproached for it. More often a colleague from another place became godfather.[38] Similar restrictions appear in the case of marriage.[39] To marry the son or daughter of a hangman was the last thing honest parents would want for their children. A young man who was so foolish as to fall in love with the master's daughter usually ended up as a practitioner of the craft himself. The matter emerges in a colorful way in connection with an ancient custom of pardon. A maiden condemned to death could be saved by the executioner through marriage. This right of pardon may or may not have existed in reality. It was a recurrent theme in popular culture. French, German and Bohemian folksongs, among others, have been devoted to it. Always the heroine prefers death to a life with the hangman or his servant. The most appropriate role for her is that of a young unmarried mother condemned for infanticide. A famous

19

Bavarian song, quoted by various authors, recalls the story of one Agnes Bernauer, sentenced to be drowned. It ends:

> *Und eh' ich will werden ein Henkersweib,*
> *So will ich lassen mein jung stolzen Leib*
> *Ertrinken im Donauwasser.*[40]
> (Rather than to be a hangman's wife,
> I will let my young and proud body
> Be drowned in the water of the Danube).

A third expression of the low status of executioners takes the form of spatial restrictions. The location of their home was often stipulated. It could be outside the city or just inside, against the wall. In other cases it stood in a neighborhood which was infamous in its own right. The hangman had his own pew in church, usually far back, close to the tower. At the Lord's Supper or Communion in Protestant as well as Catholic countries he was the last participant. Such restrictions in church have been reported in Germany and the Netherlands. A third place where the executioner had to mind his step was the tavern. A special small table with a stool – three-legged like the gallows – might be reserved for him. Sometimes his beer was brought to him in the street. In other cases only one tavern in the town was open to him.[41]

The infamy of hangmen was transmitted to his equipment and to the scaffold and everything connected with it. This aspect of the matter will be discussed in chapter four, as part of the general problem of the public's attitudes towards executions.

2 THE EXPROPRIATION OF PRIVATE VENGEANCE

A number of authors failed to notice the paradox inherent in people's attitudes towards hangmen. The explanation for his infamy was obvious to them: his 'bloody handicraft' gained him the disrespect of honest citizens. Armed with modern sensibilities towards violence, these authors apparently ignored or disregarded the standards of an earlier age. Thus contempt for the hangman appeared a natural reaction to a person engaged in violent acts for money. As late as 1966 André Lachance formulated this view splendidly: 'This cruel being, a veritable butcher of men, all stained with blood, drew the repugnance of the members of these two societies (i.e. France and New France), who, by a natural reflex of disgust, thrust him from their bosom and took care to keep him far from them.'[42]

In the German specialized literature on the executioner the negative attitude towards him is usually recognized as a problem. Originally his infamy was accounted for by connecting it to the infamy of others. Thus the hangman was supposed to have inherited it through other infamous occupations, servility, or crime or a combination of all three. There is no lack of evidence which was held to support this contention. We saw that the Augsburg *Stadtbuch* burdened the executioner with some additional tasks. The combination of executing with other infamous jobs was common in the later Middle Ages; and after, in various regions. The hangman regularly had to supervise the prostitutes, or acted as a brothel keeper himself. Sometimes he had to catch dogs, clean the streets and the public latrines, or, in the early modern period, take care of syphilis patients. Worst of all, he could be a skinner. The occupation of skinner was even more infamous than that of executioner, and the former's infamy outlasted the latter's.

But of course this merely displaces the problem. If the additional jobs explain the executioner's infamy, we would have to suppose that an originally honest craft was suddenly burdened with menial tasks. Why should this have happened? Karl von Amira already knew that the reverse order was more likely: first the hangman was infamous and, because of that, he was a convenient candidate for other low tasks.[43] A similar argument can be put forward in the other cases. It is more likely that persons of unfree descent were recruited as executioners, because this job had a servile status, than vice versa. The argument in the case of crime is based on a common practice in the later Middle Ages. It often happened that when a court, having no executioner at its disposal, sentenced a party of thieves to death, one of them was selected to hang his former colleagues. In return he was granted his life. Of course he would continue in the fateful job. In the late fifteenth century Netherlands the word *hangdief* (hanging-thief) was a common name for executioner. But again it is clear that this practice cannot explain the infamy. The court pardoned one of the criminals because it could find no one else to execute the sentence.

As noted above, the German legal historian Von Amira put forward another theory. According to him, the origins of infamy lay in the survival of pagan popular beliefs. The character of Germanic criminal law supplied the ultimate cause. To the Germanic tribes the public death penalty was of a sacred nature. It was an expiatory sacrifice to the Gods who had been offended by the crime, and its execution was a carefully regulated rite. Thus the victim and the executioner enter into a relationship, as sacrifice and sacrificer, with the deity. Through this relationship they acquire magical powers and, consequently, a taboo is placed upon them. The awe for the deity is transmitted to the executioner

21

– the one who lives on. The taboo attached to his person causes people to refrain from touching him and to fear his powers. With the decline of paganism then, as Von Amira supposed, the component of fear and contempt came to the foreground. In this way the subconscious survival of Germanic taboos accounts for the executioner's infamy.[44]

Several later authors presented a variant of this theory. Von Amira's explanation was adopted by Angstmann and Schuhmann.[45] In his various works, Von Hentig, of whom the latter was a student, also sought for explanations in terms of popular, religious and magical beliefs. Danckert, finally, presented another variant. According to him, all infamous occupations, including that of executioner, had carried a religiously loaded, positive value in pagan times. The cultural shock inherent to the coming of Christianity eventually turned things upside down. Thus a reversal of pagan values by Christianity is supposed to have led to infamy. Danckert believed that despised occupations outside Europe similarly bore the mark of a clash of religions.[46]

The custom of attacking a hangman who fails, illustrated at the beginning of this chapter, seems to fit the religious–magical type of theory very well. If the execution is considered as a sacrifice to the gods, a stroke that misses means a rejection by the deity. Consequently, the victim should be released. A second attempt by the hangman is an insult to the gods. The idea makes sense in a Christian world as well. The spectators seized the opportunity to slay Cain instead of Abel.

These magical–religious types of theory are nevertheless unsatisfactory. In fact, they are rather unhistorical. An explanation of the executioner's infamy in terms of contemporary beliefs asks the very question it attempts to answer. The problem of why these beliefs take a particular direction remains unsolved. At first sight the explanation in terms of Germanic taboos looks historical but it is a failure as well. It places the origins in a remote past, and the connection between this past and the attitudes which have to be accounted for is left in the dark. There were no executioners in Western Europe from Roman times until about the thirteenth century. One wonders how the ancient taboos survived. Similarly, the idea that attacks on failing hangmen result from subconscious notions of human sacrifice looks plausible at first sight, but there is no evidence whatsoever that the spectators harbored these notions. On the contrary, as Oppelt remarked, they often put off their assault until the victim, or even the whole group of delinquents had been put to death. So it was not always a matter of intervention. Moreover, a badly performed decapitation is usually a bloody affair. The strokes that missed, often hit the victim's skull or shoulders. Such painful maiming is not very conducive to the idea that a sign from heaven has ordered that the delinquent should be pardoned.[47]

This does not necessarily mean, however, that the idea of an obligation for pardon *tout court* was absent. In various places in medieval Europe when a capital execution had failed, it was indeed customary to grant the delinquent his life. This occurred most frequently with hanging, which was then usually done by means of strangulation. There are several known cases of persons who lived on after being hanged, like the famous 'half-hanged Smith' in England. In early modern Europe legislators found it necessary to state explicitly several times that the execution should proceed anyway. Yet in the USA in 1938 the electric chair failed and 8,000 people signed a petition for pardon.[48]

Wolfgang Oppelt's book is the most recent study on the hangman. This author came very close to solving the paradox of the people's contempt. He elaborated on an idea first put forward in an article by Joachim Gernhuber.[49] The latter supposed that a subconscious rejection of the system of physical punishment was transformed into a reaction of hatred towards its active agent.[50] Gernhuber was praised by Oppelt as 'the first to attempt to introduce psychological categories into the discussion on the infamy of the executioner'.[51] But Oppelt shifted the focus a little. Although he also seems to suppose that the public rejected severe physical punishment, he emphasized that a repressed desire to kill the delinquent with one's own hands lay behind this rejection. But private vengeance was forbidden, hence the desire to kill was directed towards the hangman instead. The result was a permanent psychic tension among the spectators, which was sometimes unleashed. Thus Oppelt realized that the hangman was a symbol of forbidden vengeance. He also noted that an executioner was needed in cases where there was no plaintiff. Finally, he placed more value than earlier authors on the fact that the hangman gets paid for his job.[52]

The combination of hangman–denial of private vengeance–prosecution in the absence of a plaintiff took Oppelt a long way. But his stumbling block was an unhistorical approach to the subject. He presents the psychological characteristics he discusses too often as timeless and unchanging. Consider, for example, this quotation: 'It remains a constant psychological law that man reacts to agression with affects of counter-agression'.[53] On various occasions Oppelt borrows similar arguments from an unhistorical psychology, or even presents a quasi-biological argumentation.[54] In doing so, he sometimes manages to reverse the order of causation. The tension 'between prescribed execution and forbidden vengeance' is supposed to have necessitated the introduction of the office of executioner.[55] Oppelt presents the repressed desire to kill as timeless, equally harbored by Germanic tribesmen. In this connection he goes so far as to relate it to 'forces within the race and the *Volksgeist*', quoting approvingly from a *Habilitationsschrift* that appeared in Berlin in 1942.[56]

We need a true historical theory, which adopts a developmental approach. Oppelt, though coming close to the clue, in the end took the wrong road. Absence of a developmental perspective also diminishes the value of other books devoted to the executioner. A few authors, for instance, did not distinguish between persons occasionally executing a sentence and professionals holding a formal office. Others did, but hardly related it to a specific periodization or failed to see its implications. Nevertheless, these authors provide the data which carry the clue.

The basic rules to be observed in this quest are twofold. First, we should not speak about *the* hangman, as something given. Instead, the story must be told in terms of the sociogenesis of the function of executioner. Second, this sociogenesis does not take place in a void. It must be related to transformations in legal practice and criminal procedure. In their turn, these transformations are part of processes of state formation.

In societies where there is no effective central authority and the feud or other forms of private violence are the dominant modes of obtaining satisfaction, there is no need for an executioner. The murderer will be killed in his turn by a relative of his victim. References to executioners outside Europe come from areas where empires existed. As argued in the previous chapter, a low degree of state formation means the prevalence of private vengeance. Of course I am dealing with an ideal type. The Hobbesian struggle of all against all, as a zero-point in state formation, never existed in reality. Even in relatively undeveloped societies authorities manifested themselves and practiced criminal justice. But this justice was marginal and did not require a special official for the execution of sentences. A few 'abominable crimes' were considered to be an injury to the whole tribe or community. Consequently, the entire community had the right to execute the death sentence: a regulated form of vengeance. A few passages in the Old Testament refer to such a practice. The blasphemer should be stoned to death by all the people. Flogging was a task for the town's elders.[57]

Similar rules applied for the Germanic tribes. The crimes in question often had the character of offenses against religion. Therefore, the reported sacredness of Germanic capital punishment is not surprising. Executions could sometimes be supervised by a priest.[58] But at the same time private vengeance reigned. This situation remained essentially the same throughout the feudal period. In most cases the injured party was allowed to take his revenge.

To be sure, during the Middle Ages revenge was also regulated. The injured party usually had to act through a court trial. His revenge was the result of a criminal process. But the trial was conducted according to the accusatory procedure. Here, the link between legal changes and the sociogenesis of the executioner's function comes in. The emergence of the formal office of executioner was a result of the rise of the inquisitorial procedure. It would probably be difficult to establish for every individual jurisdiction that a prevalence of this procedure coincided with the presence of a professional executioner. Nevertheless, the connection is unmistakable. The first hangman appeared in the thirteenth century. But the office was only fully developed and institutionalized in the first half of the sixteenth. Thus its sociogenesis took about three centuries. It is exactly the period in which the inquisitorial procedure became the dominant mode in criminal trials.

Before this period it was also possible that for some reason a plaintiff was unable or unwilling to make use of his right of execution, in which case he was usually allowed to select a substitute, whom he might pay. This custom is an obvious prefiguration of the office of executioner. The transitional period was characterized by a variety of customs concerning execution. Some jurisdictions had a hangman at their disposal; others did not. Those which did, might not necessarily have regarded the office as permanent. In many places execution by the plaintiff – presumably after an accusatory trial – remained common well into the fifteenth century, in cases of capital as well as corporal punishment.[59] The idea that it was the plaintiff's task survived in some places in a custom, whereby the hangman assumed this role on the day of the execution.[60] Another custom was to pay the hangman out of the plaintiff's pocket.[61] If there was no hangman and the plaintiff did not undertake the execution, various people could be obliged to perform the task. Sometimes it was the youngest judge; in age or in office. The German word *Nachrichter* (the 'last judge') has its origin in this custom. At other times it was an employee of the court. In the Netherlands it was regularly done by the *bodel*, a court messenger. The Dutch word *beul* (hangman) derives from this title. The task could also be required of the most recently married man in the community or of the newest immigrant. Occasionally soldiers and even clerics performed executions. The fatal chord of the famous guillotine in Halifax, England, was drawn by the multitude or by an animal. In Germany, in a few instances, laws required a condemned person to perform a mutilation on himself. This implies of course at least the threat of force by others.[62]

In all of these cases we are not dealing with a professional executioner. This is the crucial point. In all of these cases too, executing brought no infamy whatsoever to the person who performed the task. He was not held in contempt, because to a satisfactory degree, his actions were reminiscent of private vengeance. Only the professional, paid executioner, who had not been injured by the delinquent in any way, earned the people's contempt.

It is different, when the office of hangman has become established, in places where no one else has performed the task for a long time. Then the rule no longer applies; executing means 'doing the job of the hangman' and makes a person infamous as well. Even assistance at an execution becomes dangerous, as the person providing it acts as a hangman's servant. Around 1500 magistrates in the Netherlands occasionally attempted to enforce old regulations requiring such assistance. They always met with strong resistance, and obedient inhabitants were mocked by their neighbors.[63] In 1466 the court of Olst received a deputation of elders who swore that in the last sixty years three persons had been burned, a woman buried alive and four persons broken on the wheel, without any service having been asked from the peasants of Welsum.[64]

The most famous case in this respect involves a citizen of Breslau, called Hans Rintfleisch. This man, a scion of one of the leading families in his native city, was robbed by the landlord of an inn in the Polish town of Plock in 1478. Rintfleisch accused the thief, who was condemned to death. Plock, however, had no executioner; Breslau was apparently more 'advanced'. Moreover, the laws of the former town stuck to a radical interpretation of the *talion*. Hans Rintfleisch had either to execute the thief or be executed by him. His pleas to be spared this unattractive choice were of no avail. Ultimately he preferred the first option. He died shortly afterwards – presumably a natural death – but his son, Christoph, inherited the evil reputation. He procured declarations from King Wladislaw and from the consuls of Plock, but that did not put an end to it. In 1507 the Breslau consuls elected him *Schöppe*, but popular pressure obliged them to depose him again. Christoph Rintfleisch died without receiving the last sacraments.[65]

The case is clear enough. According to the modern notions current in Breslau, Hans Rintfleisch had done a hangman's job and had consequently become infamous. He had realized this when offered the choice in 1478, and later the populace treated his son accordingly. In Plock the older procedure, and the mentality inherent to it, prevailed. It was a normal case of execution by the plaintiff. The reference to the *talion* is evidence that the trial was accusatory.

The recruitment of criminals as hangmen is also typical for the transitional period. On the one hand, it presupposes that the office is not unknown and that the task is infamous, because no citizen can be found to perform it. On the other hand, it shows that the office is not as yet institutionalized. There is no hangman, so the court takes an 'emergency measure'. This happened regularly in the fifteenth century, but few instances were recorded after the middle of the sixteenth.[66] The ensuing connection of hangmen with crime also manifested itself in the reverse order. There are numerous cases, notably around 1500, of executioners accused of a crime.[67] It is clear that these circumstances are not conducive to the stability and permanence of the office. But we seldom hear of condemned hangmen after the middle of the sixteenth century. It only happened in the relatively unsettled conditions of colonial societies. In New France almost all the executioners – save for a black slave from Martinique – were former criminals. A few were accused anew when in office; sometimes together with their whole family. In 1695 the inhabitants of Quebec City were treated to the amusing spectacle of a hangman exposing his own wife on the pillory.[68]

A few references from the transitional period suggest that torture only gradually established itself as hangman's work. There may have been special officials for it originally. Thus Malines had a *tortor* in 1220. Maes calls him the city's earliest recorded executioner, but the passage he quotes speaks merely of torturing.[69] Although torture was undeniably tied up with the inquisitorial procedure, its practice was not public and could not be considered as an infringement upon the right of private satisfaction. Nevertheless, in the course of the fifteenth century it became tainted by infamy. At the beginning of that century the town of Brielle determined that torture had to be carried out by the *hanghedief*, instead of by the court's messengers. The latter were 'persons of merit' and could not be required to perform the task 'because those who do it become infamous'.[70] Frankfurt had an official called the *Stöcker*, who had originally been a porter of the court. In the fourteenth century he practiced torture, but this task was taken over by the hangman at the end of the fifteenth.[71] The 'indoor executioner' in Amsterdam (see pp. 36–8) may also originally have been a torturer. Further research has yet to confirm this development. It would be another facet of the institutionalization of the office of executioner and the infamy attached to his tasks.

We can now see very clearly how contempt for executioners originated.

The hangman is a professional who torments, maims and kills people for money. In the code of honor prevalent in societies with a low degree of monopolization of violence, the use of physical force is valued positively, but its use for a payment against someone totally unconnected to oneself is shameful. The 'bounty-hunter' of the American frontier provides a parallel. The medieval judges and messengers who executed were paid for their office in general and not for this specific task. This was one reason why they kept their honor. The valiant knight was a hero, but the mercenary never acquired his status.

The hangman's actions contradict the feudal warrior-ethos in yet another way. The knight may indulge in a violent struggle, but a relatively fair fight is expected. A warrior was shamed if he slew a defenseless person. But this is exactly what the hangman does at a capital execution, and he realized that this made him shameful, which is attested by an interesting custom in Languedoc. The hangman there often pretended to struggle with the convict. The expression 'to act like the hangman', meant either attacking persons in a sneaky way or referred to masters meting out excessive punishments to their servants.[72] The awareness that a capital execution is a struggle between unequal parties, comes to mind most vividly if the task is not performed well. Hence this would invoke the most intense expressions of hostility. We might indeed see it as a transference of revenge from the convict to the executioner.

Thus the executioner's task is diametrically opposed to the feudal warrior-ethos, which still pervaded the mentality of all strata in the relatively urbanized society of the later Middle Ages. But this is not a sufficient explanation for the contempt he incurred. We should add one more element. As explained above, the emergence of hangmen meant the substitution of public for private vengeance. The office became a necessity when authorities themselves started prosecuting, even in the absence of a plaintiff. In the previous chapter I argued that these changes in criminal procedure and prosecution policy are part of processes of state formation. They go hand in hand with attempts to arrive at a greater stabilization and internal pacification of towns and territories. Major historical changes usually generate resistance because something is lost in the course of every such change. At this stage of monopolization of violence, private vengeance, once practically an inalienable right, was lost. Formerly the knights had killed those who injured them, and local inhabitants had slain a thief caught redhanded. These practices were gradually combated. But the memory of them remained alive; the more so, because this combat was carried on with ups and downs. The authorities are of course the real actors in restricting private satisfaction.

But the hangman's actions are most clearly visible. His function symbolizes the expropriation of private vengeance. It is common for preindustrial resistance to be directed at others rather than at those ultimately responsible. Peasants attacked the steward instead of the lord of the manor; rebels denounced the king's evil advisers. To the populace, the executioner was the real actor.

3 THE EARLY MODERN AMBIVALENCE

So far the story has been a little unfair to the executioner. I have focused completely on expressions of hostility and contempt, and for an obvious reason. The central thesis of this study seemed to be threatened. The paradox emerged of an acceptance of violence in general, coupled with a rejection of the hangman's activities. I argued that this rejection was born from a resentment against the expropriation of private vengeance. The hostility towards executioners actually means a non-acceptance of restrictions on violence, an attitude which is consistent with general popular sensibilities. This solves the paradox. However, the hangman was not rejected completely. There are examples of neutral or even positive attitudes towards him. In popular culture he figured as a man of extraordinary capacities. In actual practice people visited him for medical services. The authorities, finally, had an obvious interest in raising his status: he was their servant. These aspects throw light on the history of repression too.

Thus, the attitudes towards executioners express a certain ambivalence. Most authors have noted this. They supposed that the ambivalence had been present from the start and they may be right. On the other hand, the expressions of a positive attitude, such as medical consultations, all date from the early modern period. We may suppose that they represent a particular historical stage, but this has still to be established. If the supposition holds true, the order of events is as follows: by the middle of the sixteenth century the institutionalization of the office of hangman had been completed in Western Europe. From that time on the memory of the expropriation of private vengeance fades from the minds of the people. Still the infamy of hangmen remains. It outlives the conditions which gave rise to it: 'a cultural lag', if you like. Nevertheless, popular mentalities underwent a change of accent. Outright hostility was transformed into ambivalence.

Angstmann made an inventory of beliefs about the extraordinary capacities of hangmen. She comments: 'The Middle Ages knew such compromises' (between rejection and the demands of utility).[73] But her historical examples are all early modern.[74] Other examples come from folklore and we now know that these stories, collected around 1800, do not represent beliefs and conditions from time immemorial. Making my own classification, I divide the popular beliefs into three groups: those referring to magical powers, to extraordinary capacities in general and to the art of healing.

One origin of the belief in the magical powers of executioners lay in the great witch-hunt. As the hangman was apparently immune to the sorcery of the witches he burnt, he must be a magician of sorts himself. The idea that many members of the craft secretly practiced sorcery, can be found in various popular tales. Interestingly, there is seldom talk of black magic. In part, executioners would practice the art for themselves. It was sometimes said that the money in their pocket never got used up. In other stories they helped people. They recovered lost children, or located stolen goods. In the folktales of Silesia the executioner is able to exorcize demons. One story tells how a group of hangmen came to a place where an evil spirit lived in a cave close to the road. They managed to exorcize it, although it had been attempted by many monks from the nearby monastery without success.

Strange things also happened to the executioner's instruments. The belief that the swords in his house rattled when a person was condemned to death is widespread. The sword was supposed to be longing for blood. The inevitable might be avoided by satisfying the weapon with just a drop. If it came to a capital execution, the convict's blood carried a positive value. Notably it was said to cure epilepsy. The presence of epileptics at executions was recorded as late as the nineteenth century. In general, everything connected with the hangman's activities had magical value. The finger of a condemned thief or a piece of rope were coveted items. Normally, only the executioner or his servants could supply these objects. In such cases people were apparently unafraid of contact with him, although it was often said that they visited him secretly at night. Karl Huss, an early nineteenth-century Bohemian executioner, was influenced by Enlightenment ideas and wrote a tract 'on superstition'. He postulated that honest hangmen did not sell these objects. According to him, people bought them from skinners and shepherds, who said untruthfully they had procured them from hangmen.[75]

These examples of popular beliefs are understandable as emanating from the experience of people familiar with executions. Again, there is no need to relate them to the sacred rites of Germanic times. A second category of stories about extraordinary capacities of hangmen refers more directly to their job. A few masters of the craft were supposed to have accomplished the most impossible feats, such as decapitating a standing man so fast that his head remained on the trunk and only a stripe of blood was visible. The stories about hangmen who executed a whole party of rogues in a few minutes are numerous. In one tale from Schleswig-Holstein the executioner of Hamburg beheaded seventy-nine pirates non-stop. When he had finished, the senate asked him how he felt and he replied: 'I am feeling so well that I could easily go on and do away with the entire Wise and Honorable Senate.' The senators, so it was told, lacked a sense of humor and the answer cost the hangman his own head.[76]

The medical visits to executioners, finally, are the most unambiguous examples of a positive attitude. They were believed to be able to cure various illnesses. Notably they reset broken or dislocated limbs. It is understandable that their occupation allowed them to acquire a proficiency in these areas, matching that of contemporary doctors. Someone who regularly stretches and dislocates limbs, also knows how to relocate them. People in need of this service visited him willingly. Of course surgeons' guilds protested against this infringement on their monopoly. Their repeated complaints actually constitute the main sources for the medical practices of hangmen.

An illuminating case is that of Haarlem, 1676. The provincial executioner of Holland resided in the town. He presented a petition to the burgomasters, who made their decision after consulting the surgeons' guild:

Received a petition from Tobias Ran, Master Executioner of this city, asking to become qualified by special permission, to exercise the art and practice of limb-setting (which has been taught to him, so he says, from childhood) during the time of his function as well as after he might have quit it, or will be unable to practice it because of old age. After reading the request and the reaction by the *overluyden* of the surgeons' guild within this city (in whose hands the request has been put), it has been allowed that the executioner, during this office of his as master executioner, will be allowed, by connivance, to practice limb-setting in this city after the example of his forebears, without anyone being allowed to hinder him in this exercise in any way. But, having left his charge or no longer capable of it because of old age, the requester, before continuing with limb-setting, has to direct himself again to the Gentlemen Burgomasters of this city, in order to gain permission anew, after giving a proof or otherwise.[77]

The passage demonstrates both that it was customary for hangmen to perform medical services and that the authorities were relatively favorable to him. The expression 'by connivance' means they knew that officially the surgeons' guild had a monopoly, but allowed its infringement nevertheless. The guild apparently acquiesced. In a dispute in 1694 its commissaries even ordered a certain woman to pay the executioner the money due for bandages on her arm.[78] The authorities in other places were not always so favorable to the executioner. At times they gave in to the demands of the surgeons' guild. Incidentally, the cited case also tells us that hangmen used to stop when they grew too old. It is surely a job for a person in the prime of his life.

Numerous cases of hangmen practicing medicine were recorded in the Dutch Republic from the 1590s to the 1790s.[79] Other known cases belong to seventeenth-century Flanders and to Germany from the middle of the sixteenth to the end of the eighteenth century. German executioners were occasionally allowed to perform autopsies on the bodies of the delinquents handled by them.[80] As Oppelt remarks, at the end of the early modern period the surgeons' guild may have been motivated less by deep-seated feelings of contempt than by a desire to restrict competition.[81]

It is not clear yet which groups in society overcame their hostility and consulted the hangman as a doctor. A few references suggest that it was especially the poorer sections, who were less afraid of being associated with him. Thus the executioner of Arnhem was permitted in 1642 to live in an honest neighborhood because of 'the services which he was offering daily among the poor commonalty with his cures'.[82] The association of the poor with the hangman may also have existed in Paris. According to the last executioner of the Sanson family, his eighteenth-century forefathers spent large sums on charity. A multitude of poor people were said to have followed the funeral procession of Charles II Sanson in 1726.[83]

We still have to consider the reactions of the authorities to popular attitudes towards hangmen. It is another subject on which we would like to have more data. It is possible, nevertheless, to draw the tentative contours of the evolution of official policy. During the formative period of the office the authorities probably condoned popular attitudes. They confirmed the infamy of executioners from the start. In one of the transcripts of Augsburg's charter the hangman is referred to as the son of a bitch.[84] The ecclesiastical authorities acted in line with the secular by denying him burial in consecrated ground. We can imagine two reasons why the urban rulers of the later Middle Ages should have given in to popular hostility. First, they were not strong enough to resist it. The second reason is related to this. They had not yet differentiated themselves sufficiently from the wider body of citizens to become a group with a distinct mentality and interests. To a large degree they shared popular attitudes, even if these were contrary to their interests as rulers.

To be sure, the authorities may actually have profited from giving in to the hostility of the populace. Because resentment of the expropriation of private vengeance was directed against the hangman, they were out of harm's way. Being unable to protect him, they 'sacrificed' him in order to save their own position. An interesting document from Frankfurt shows the authorities denying complicity in the hangman's actions. In 1446 the council decided that instead of being paid per execution, the executioner would henceforth receive a regular weekly salary. The motivation for this decision was stated as follows: 'so that the council is not guilty of his activities, but that he is only an accomplice and servant of the court'.[85] The council conveniently passed the predicament on to the judicial authorities. Two sentences by the court of Antwerp show very clearly how the hangman could be held responsible for his actions, despite his following orders from his superiors. It concerns infringements by the court of Bergen-op-Zoom upon the right of Antwerp's citizens to be judged in their own city. In 1425 and again in 1493 this court had arrested and tortured a citizen. The Antwerp judges did not only condemn the *schout* and the *drost*, but also the executioner. In both cases he had to go on pilgrimage.[86]

On the other hand, authorities started to protect the hangman from the violence of the populace from an early date. The above-mentioned fifteenth-century cases, in which persons were condemned for throwing stones at him, testify to it. Indeed, those examples of violence only appeared in the sources, because of the prohibitions against them. Towards the end of the transitional period the authorities became more determinate. The first half of the sixteenth century may have been a turning-point. The hostility towards hangmen was attacked on the ideological level as well. In Germany Martin Luther argued for a rehabilitation of the executioner. Among other things, he opposed the custom of apology. In Germany, but also in sixteenth-century England, the hangman at a capital execution was obliged to ask the convict forgiveness for what he was going to do to him. Luther felt offended by the custom. What the hangman did was a necessary job and no more: 'Quick, head off, away with it, in order that the earth does not become full with the ungodly.'[87] Luther compared the executioner to a father chastizing his son. In another passage he put him on a par with the authorities. Both derived their functions from the Lord. The magistrates are nothing but 'God's hangmen'. According to Radbruch, an attitude similar to Luther's was later adopted in Catholic countries too.[88] In the course of the early modern period the churches further changed their point of view. They accorded hangmen a normal church funeral.[89]

In the first half of the sixteenth century the authorities also took a firmer stand when the hangman was attacked because he had bungled. After the murder of the executioner of Malines, noted in the first section, Maximilian issued a special placard. He was particularly annoyed about the fact that some spectators had shouted that it was lawful to stone a bungling hangman. The promulgation placed the Malines executioner under his special protection.[90]

Charles V followed Maximilian's example. As Roman emperor and as Count of Holland he was concerned about orderly executions and the hangman's safety. During the series of incidents in Haarlem he issued an order to publish a warning throughout the province:

> Because we have been notified that recently in various towns and places within our country of Holland, where the master of the sharp sword failed in the exercise of justice (. . .) many and diverse persons, old and young, have proceeded to run after the aforesaid master of the sharp sword, to throw stones and to cry 'beat him to death' (. . .) which sets a very bad example, tending towards commotion, crowding and sedition, and which is directed against us, our highness and justice (. . .) therefore, we forbid everyone (. . .) to abuse, injure, run after or threaten (. . .) in any way the master of the sharp sword during the exercise of justice, whether he makes a fault in doing justice or not. Whoever shall be found guilty of trespassing against this order in any way, will be punished corporally and financially.[91]

A few years later Charles included protection of the hangman in the Carolina, the criminal code for the Empire. Article 98 ordered the *Fronbote* to warn the public before the execution: if the executioner should – 'contrary to our hopes' – not perform his task properly, no one was allowed to lay hands on him, on penalty of corporal punishment.[92]

There is one more reference suggesting that the authorities stopped using the hangman as a scapegoat during the early modern period. In various German towns it was a custom for the executioner to ask the judge if he had done the job well. It was followed by a routine answer, but in case of failure he received an evasive reply. In Frankfurt, for instance, it was then: 'I have no commission for this'.[93] But in 1672 the council of Schwäbisch Hall decided that the *Schultheiss* should always give the positive routine answer, even in cases of failure.[94] Such a change may have occurred in other places as well.

In the Dutch Republic the executioner was generally regarded as a servant of the authorities. Towards the end of the sixteenth century the humanist Coornhert associated them with each other in a way reminiscent of Luther. That is to say, Coornhert accorded a more benevolent role to the rulers than Luther and so he compared bad princes

34

and harsh executioners. Tyrants, according to him, were sent by God as 'cruel hangmen', to make the people pay for their sins.[95] We might take it to imply that wise rulers can be compared to able executioners. A more unambiguous rehabilitation of the executioner was provided by the writer Bredero in the early seventeenth century. A character in his most successful play says about the master of the sharp sword: 'You may say what you want, my dear, it is an *honest* office. He is a servant of God and holy justice'.[96] Constantin Huygens, writing in 1644, expressed a similar view: 'He is a craftsman who practices nothing but justice / the sharp and sour sauce of the bitter last judgment / the knot in the whip with which kings do strike.' Huygens also called the executioner honest; an honest murderer, to be sure.[97]

The attitude of rulers and ruled were reflected in terminology. In the countries of Continental Europe more official, neutral names for the executioner existed, next to more derogatory ones. As a rule, after the middle of the sixteenth century, the authorities always used neutral or even flattering expressions: *maître des hautes oeuvres* (France); *Scharfrichter* or *Nachrichter* (Germany); *scherprechter*, or, more solemnly, *meester van den scherpen zwaarde* (Netherlands) (master of the sharp sword). Derogatory or mocking terms belong to popular parlance: *bourreau* (France); *Henker* (Germany); *beul* (Netherlands). French executioners in the late seventeenth and eighteenth centuries even requested legal prohibition of the use of the word *bourreau*.[98] Of course popular terminology knew endless variations. Angstmann identified 109 names for Germany, of which her own is one.[99]

The evolution of the attitudes of the authorities towards executioners is also visible in the payments to them. Around 1500 we first hear of prohibitions directed against their too luxurious way of living. Thus the hangman of Kampen was warned in 1475 not to 'walk around like a nobleman or a merchant'.[100] Financially he could apparently afford to play the gentleman. Similarly, the hangman of Augsburg was not allowed to 'dress as a cavalier or play the big man'. This sort of prohibition was very common in sixteenth-century Germany.[101] Charles V prescribed a grey costume for the executioner, while variations with red were the rule elsewhere.[102] The executioners remained well dressed and rich nevertheless, such as those of Frankfurt and Hamburg.[103] In French Canada too they lived a good life materially.[104] In one instance a very high salary for the hangman was recorded at a relatively early date. In fourteenth-century Malines he appears to have earned more than the *schout* himself.[105] This, however, seems improbable and one wonders if there is a mistake in the record.

35

It is probable, that the change towards higher payments took place around 1500. It can be regarded as an expression of the general transformation in the policy of the authorities. It completed the institutionalization of the office of executioner. The authorities needed a permanent functionary for the ungrateful and at times dangerous job. A high salary was a means of committing a reliable person for a longer period.

A series of exact figures is available for eighteenth-century Amsterdam. The city had dealings with two executioners. Regular public punishment was administered by the provincial hangman of Holland, residing in Haarlem. But Amsterdam had its own official as well, called the *binnenscherprechter* (indoor executioner). The latter's main tasks were, as his title suggests, not public. They included torture and the execution of whipping indoors. The provincial hangman only came to Amsterdam when an execution was scheduled. In 1696 he was thus described by William Mountague, an English gentleman, visiting the city:

He is a spruce Fellow, and goes well in Habit, and has Servants to attend him (. . .) has a good Sallary from the Towns where he serves and lives comfortably, tho' very few are found of his Company, it being thought the worst in the World, especially if he has a Parson with him.[106]

It is not quite clear what the author means with 'Company'. The reference to the parson suggests that he might be speaking ironically. But his observations on the hangman's standard of living are unambiguous and confirm what I have argued above. The master of the sharp sword received a basic annual salary from the Court of Holland, at least from 1620 onwards. In 1765 this amounted to 500 guilders.[107] Apart from this he received payments per execution from the jurisdictions calling upon him. Table 1 shows the fluctuations in the amount of money he received from the city of Amsterdam. The amount depended both on the quantity and on the quality of the justice done. Whipping was cheaper than breaking on the wheel. A special perk was the tip of twenty-five guilders he received when a new *schout* came into office.[108] We see that the highest average occurs at the beginning of the century. Nevertheless the amounts remain considerable. Moreover, they only refer to executions in Amsterdam. The city, to be sure, was by far the most populous of the province and had the highest annual number of convicts. We may suppose that the average in all other jurisdictions combined was about as high or slightly higher. This would mean that throughout the eighteenth century the hangman earned at least 900–1,000 guilders a year. The income of a fully employed laborer was around 300 guilders a year.

Table I. Amsterdam's payments to the Haarlem executioner in four periods

A. 1708–1717

Year	1708	1709	1710	1711	1712	1713	1714	1715	1716	1717
Guilders	684	300	333	510	639	651	567	762	642	531
Number of executions	4	3	2	3	4	4	3	5	2	2

Total amount: 5619.00
Amount per justice day: 175.59
Amount per convict: 13.07

B. 1732–1741

Year	1732	1733	1734	1735	1736	1737	1738	1739	1740	1741
Guilders	216	258	225	297	378	387	204	438	381	339
Number of executions	1	2	2	2	3	2	1	2	2	2

Total amount: 3123.00
Amount per justice day: 159.10
Amount per convict: 10.92

C. 1742–1751

Year	1742	1743	1744	1745	1746	1747	1748	1749	1750	1751
Guilders	519	564	159	351	408	—	258	201	192	243
Number of executions	3	3	1	2	2	0	2	1	1	2

Total amount: 2895.00
Amount per justice day: 170.30
Amount per convict: 12.42

D. 1781–1793

Year	1781	1783	1784	1786	1787	1788	1789	1790	1791	1793
Guilders	156	221	169	121	261	380.25	183	99	235.50	189
Number of executions	1	2	1	1	3	3	1	1	2	1

Total amount: 2014.75
Amount per justice day: 125.92
Amount per convict: 9.97

Source: GA, RA I–44 for the calendar years 1708–17 and *Schoutsrekeningen* for the fiscal years from 1732 onwards

Table 2. *Payments by the* schout *to the indoor executioner*

Year	Guilders	Year	Guilders	Year	Guilders
1732	102.00	1742	52.50	1781	51.00
1733	66.00	1743	133.50	1783	48.00
1734	123.00	1744	91.50	1784	90.00
1735	120.00	1745	136.50	1786	57.00
1736	73.50	1746	151.50	1787	169.50
1737	99.00	1747	129.00	1788	99.00
1738	69.00	1748	147.00	1789	91.50
1739	97.50	1749	130.50	1790	54.00
1740	118.50	1750	88.50	1792	120.00
1741	63.00	1751	124.50	1793	121.50
Total	931.50	Total	1185.00	Total	901.50

Source: GA, RA: *Schoutsrekeningen*

His colleague, the indoor executioner, had to be content with a smaller income. Table 2 shows that he received around 100 guilders a year in payments for 'piecework'. His basic salary constituted the major part of his income. During the eighteenth century this was increased from 270 to 400 and then to 500 guilders. Hangmen in other provinces must also have earned somewhat less than the one in Holland, because of the smaller amount of justice to be carried out. They usually coveted the position in Haarlem when it was vacant. An exchange of jobs took place in 1784. The provincial hangman, Jan van Aanhout, became Amsterdam's indoor executioner. His nephew took over the office in Haarlem, on the condition that he would cede an annual sum of 300 guilders to his uncle. The next year Jan's wife died. She was buried in the second richest class.[109]

Their high wages allowed early modern executioners to employ personnel. We noted this in the quotation from Mountague. Before about 1550 there is seldom talk of hangman's servants. It is common in the seventeenth and eighteenth centuries. Consequently, the master executioner stood at the top of a hierarchy. It allowed him to shed the additional tasks and thus to acquire a sort of status within the frame of his infamy. In Frankfurt, for instance, the executioner left the tasks of skinning and collecting dung to his servants. They could also administer minor punishments, but the most honorable penalty, that of beheading, was always reserved for the master. A few authors thought that the eighteenth-century master executioners only practiced decapitation, leaving the rest to their personnel, but this is not borne out by the facts.[110]

38

Finally, the authorities proceeded to rehabilitate the executioner legally. An Imperial law of 1731 abolished his infamy and that of the other *unehrliche Leute*, the skinners excepted. The latter had to wait until 1772 (Austria) or 1783 (Prussia).[111] In France the *Assemblée Nationale* decided in-1790 that the executioners too were *citoyens*. In the euphoria of the Revolution there was even some talk of giving them the title of *vengeur national*.[112] It was an echo from the days of private vengeance by the community. The new community was the nation-state, whose enemies were the people's enemies. This attitude towards executioners did not survive the Terror.

Despite the status-raising measures by the authorities, attacks on bungling hangmen, as we have seen, continued throughout the early modern period. Still, a few areas may have been exempt from them. It seems that the executioner had nothing much to fear in a metropolis such as Amsterdam. His relative safety there dates at least from the second half of the seventeenth century. The *schepen* Bontemantel speaks of a beheading in 1669: the convict was hit a little too high and his head had to be cut off in a second attempt. Thereupon the hangman's son showed it to the people, who apparently just let him do that.[113] Bontemantel was not a man who would have omitted an account of ensuing turmoil, if there had been any. We also learn that the *schout* took his precautions. In 1720 he wrote a letter to the hangman eight days before the execution. There was to be a beheading and the executioner should consider whether he needed assistance, 'because one of the delinquents has a short and crooked neck'.[114]

Jacob Bicker Raye, who visited most executions between 1732 and 1772, saw things go wrong four times. In 1762 a person was given the punishment of the burning sword. The sword was 'not hot enough', so the hangman laid it on the convict's back twice. In 1767 a man was to be broken on the wheel. His thigh-bones were not broken and the blow on his heart was, 'as people say', too low. So the hangman proceeded to strangle him with a rope, which came loose again. Bicker Raye commented that the victim had 'a very hard and slow death'. In 1770 a burglar was hanging alive for ten minutes, because the rope had not been put around his neck properly. A year later a beheading was 'not done well'.[115] In all these cases no mention of anger on the part of the spectators is made and Bicker Raye, a lover of sensation, was even less of a man to omit such a story.

Although possibly mitigated, the people's contempt was still alive in the eighteenth century, in Amsterdam as well as elsewhere in Europe. In the metropolis a hangman's bill from 1712 came into the hands of outsiders. It was printed several times as a broadsheet, including one rhymed version.[116] The verse indicates amazement at the high amounts of money paid to the executioner. Its anonymous author refers mockingly to the proceedings on the scaffold in popular language. He sounds a bit jealous, but manages to draw a moral from it: even thieves will mend their ways when they realize the final result of their activities is the enrichment of this detestable person. 'You, Messrs thieves, who are still alive, you better put your hands to the plough (there is still time). Or do you live for the hangman?'

In the eighteenth century several sons of executioners tried to profit from the abolition of infamy by seeking admission to universities as medical students. They met with varying degrees of success. In the Netherlands the son of Groningen's hangman was refused entry there in 1750, but three years later the university of Leiden accepted him. He attained a doctorate.[117] A German case is illustrative too. Johann Michael Hofmann had been accepted as a medical student in Marburg, where his father was executioner. Next he studied in Göttingen and he received his doctorate from the university of Strasbourg. In 1766 he applied for membership of the college of physicians in Frankfurt, to which city his father had been promoted in the meantime. The doctors of Frankfurt, however, had strong objections and it came to a lawsuit. Hofmann's attorney invoked the Enlightenment: 'I cannot imagine that in our enlightened century those whom God has given the genius to study (. . .) are forced to bury their talents (. . .) because their parents belong to a rank which does not receive the highest esteem in a republic.' His opponents exploited the association of the executioner with the skinner and consequently argued that the law was (still) on their side. They attacked Hofmann's attorney personally: 'It is highly admirable that the son of a quadruple-skinner has found an attorney here, who attempts to acquire a place for him among the *doctores medicinae* in the *collegium graduorum* and hence to make him his own colleague. These are not the honors of Justinian; *O Tempora, O Mores*.'[118] Hofmann finally appealed to Co-emperor Josef. After three and a half years the town-council decided to grant him citizenship and forced the college to admit him to its ranks.

The emotional tone and the determination with which the struggle was conducted make clear that it was not just a matter of trying to shake off a competitor. The basic mentality was still there; and it was there in upper-middle class minds. Similarly, in early nineteenth-century Netherlands the writing of a naval officer shows that for him the executioner's infamy was still a reality. He felt unjustly condemned by a court martial, but amidst his complaints he expressed relief on one point. At least he had received a naval punishment, which meant that no hangman had touched him: 'Someone who has once been in the hands of the executioner is lost forever, whatever he may do.'[119]

For our present purposes it is not necessary to trace the evolution of attitudes further. The guilds always had been the strongest supporters of the notion of infamy. With their disappearance most of its practical consequences were gone. When public punishment was abolished, the hangman's tasks were restricted to the execution of death penalties indoors. He became literally less visible, which must have influenced the people's attitudes. In the Netherlands, with the abolition of capital punishment in 1870, the last executioner was made redundant.[120]

The continuity of popular contempt in the early modern period is reflected most clearly in the emergence of hangmen's 'dynasties'. In various places the office remained in the same family for several generations. The best known are the Sansons, who were the executioners of Paris from the end of the seventeenth century until the middle of the nineteenth century.[121] There was, moreover, a high degree of intermarriage. Sons and daughters of other hangmen were the only possible marriage partners. In the eighteenth century the executioners of practically all Dutch towns were in some way mutually related. Many families were of German origin.[122] The Empire, with its numerous petty jurisdictions, constituted an enormous reservoir of potential executioners. A hangman's ideal career starts in his birthplace and he assists his father from a young age. Later he moves, to become the servant of a hangman elsewhere. There he may get a chance to present his masterpiece. He then gets a job as executioner in a small town. He performs his tasks satisfactorily and is promoted to a big city. It is an excellent career: no hard work and lavish payments; a good life for someone who does not particularly value sociability. But we know that preindustrial people valued sociability highly.

There is an intriguing similarity between the upper aristocracy at the top of society's status hierarchy and the 'estate' of executioners at the bottom. Both were forced to be exclusivist. In both cases fathers passed on the heritage to their sons. Internally the group cherished close contacts. It knew a high degree of intermarriage. Too much contact with others brought contagion into the game. A marriage with a person from outside the group would have been concluded most likely for financial reasons. The crucial difference of course is that, while both groups were constrained by the pressure of social realities, aristocrats had a strong motivation of their own to be exclusivist. This motivation formed the main foundation for their social existence and, generally, they drew

41

satisfaction from it. Executioners can be supposed to have been less content with the state of affairs and some tried to change it. That is precisely the difference between an established elite and a group of outsiders.

The state of affairs in early modern Western Europe can be tentatively described as follows: after about 1550 the authorities acknowledged the hangman as their servant to the public. The office was institutionalized. Executioners were well paid. The authorities managed to grant them protection, save in cases of failure. The attitudes towards executioners were connected to processes of state formation in a new manner. The intermediate process was that of criminalization. The notion of crime too became more clearly defined after the transitional period in which the inquisitorial procedure broke through.[123] Moreover, in the course of the sixteenth century whole social groups became criminalized: beggars, vagrants, prostitutes and marginal groups, and the poor in general. Controlling these groups became the everlasting concern of the early modern states. In the meantime the notion of infamy had broadened. From the hangman it descended to the scaffold. It became connected to being subjected to justice in general. And being subjected to justice was associated with the criminalized groups (even though these were not the only ones to produce delinquents). Consequently, the notion of infamy became streamlined more clearly along the lines of stratification. For the middle classes and the 'better' workers, honor meant both not being associated with the marginal groups and not being subjected to justice. In the latter case, to be in the hands of the hangman was still the worst. Here we see the continuing source for the contempt for executioners.

The poor were probably less affected by the necessity of contempt. This is understandable, because they had no honor to lose in the first place. Fear of loss of honor was greatest among those closest to the poor: workers still in employment, small shopkeepers, craftsmen, those people who just managed to survive without stealing (at least in normal times). They were the ones, whether members of guilds or not, who most despised the executioner.

Chapter three

THE STAGERS: THE AUTHORITIES AND THE DRAMATIZATION OF EXECUTIONS

Every execution is a planned event. The wounding and killing which accompany warfare and rebellion may be chaotic at times. Homicide can be the result of a sudden flash of rage. The execution of a penalty, by definition, is the result of a decision. This is true, even of popular justice. Hence there is always some regulation: in one way or another the stage is set. But still, though chaos is not foreseen, soberness may certainly occur. A deserter at the front, for example, will be shot without much ado. A servant is beaten by his master and that's that. In this chapter I am not dealing with sobriety. Particularly during the early modern period a sense of the appropriate degree of decorum prevailed. Ceremonial was important, in executions as well as in other events in social life. Executions were dramatized in order to serve as a sort of morality play. The stagers, of course, were the magistrates. The social drama should reflect their view of the world.

I   THE CEREMONY OF DEATH

From an early date executions in Western Europe were dramas. 'They were spectacular plays with a moral', says Johan Huizinga.[1] Plays may vary with respect to the degree of improvization. Careful staging was probably less prominent in the later Middle Ages. Take one of Huizinga's few examples: 'During the Burgundian terror in Paris in 1411, one of the victims, Messire Mansart du Bois, being requested by the hangman, according to custom, to forgive him, is not only ready to do so with all his heart, but begs the executioner to embrace him. "There was a great multitude of people, who nearly all wept hot tears."'[2] The act exemplifies

43

the directness of emotions of the time and probably was not planned in advance. Yet we should not draw conclusions too rashly. Too little evidence is available to say with certainty that staging played a lesser part in medieval executions. There is hardly any detailed account of the practice of punishment in the fourteenth and fifteenth centuries, so we have to await further research.

Nevertheless, there are a few indications for my supposition. In Holland the proceedings on the scaffold were subjected to regulation in the first half of the sixteenth century. In 1526 the Court of Holland forbade children and other 'unqualified persons' to approach the scaffold during the exercise of justice.[3] A renewed promulgation in 1544 laid down more precise rules: 'Because the Court of Holland has heard that, as a consequence of the disorderliness of some people who come up to the scaffold here in a body and do not have anything to do there, the master of the sharp sword has had trouble with executing and spectators have been endangered, thus the aforesaid Court has ordained and ordains herewith, that, except for the substitute attorney-general of the aforesaid court, with the confessor, the criminal, the master and his servants, no one is allowed to approach the aforesaid scaffold, on forfeiture of one Carolus guilder.'[4]

The implication is that the authorities strived for a greater degree of orderliness in the first half of the sixteenth century. Orderliness is a necessary prerequisite for staging. Early modern ceremonial could now be developed. The chronology of this regulation is significant. It occurred at the end of the transitional period, noted in the previous chapter. In the cities of the seventeenth and eighteenth centuries, scaffolds were usually erected, as we will see, in such a way as to be inaccessible to the public.

A second indication lies in the place of execution in particular jurisdictions. Up into the sixteenth century public punishment was usually meted out at different locations. In the seventeenth and eighteenth centuries most jurisdictions knew one regular location. In medieval Worms different modes of the death penalty each had their own place of execution. Where drowning in a river was carried out, a bridge was the appropriate point.[5] The court of Amsterdam executed at three locations in the sixteenth century: on Dam Square and at the Reguliers and St Anthony Gates. Later the Dam became the regular place.[6] In a Mediterranean town, such as Seville, various locations were still in use at the beginning of the seventeenth century. Death penalties were often executed at the Plaza de San Francisco, but also at the Macarena and

Osario Gates, the roads of Carmona and San Lazaro, the Altozano de Triana and the jail.[7]

In the old days a number of penalties were specifically formulated in a way that prevented their execution on a fixed spot. Notably this was the case with various forms of exemplary, non-corporal punishment. Persons were led through their town or village or had to carry an instrument of shame. Such penalties were in use mainly for morals offenses. This peripatetic punishment knew its corporal variations as well. In Rotterdam in 1500, for instance, a person was whipped on a cart.[8] In cases of theft and violent offenses another custom was long lived: laws often required that the execution should take place on the spot of the crime.

During the last phase of preindustrial society in Europe a regular location prevailed. Notably this is true for its three biggest cities. In London executions came to be performed only at Tyburn, in Paris at the Place de Grève, in Amsterdam at Dam Square. The step towards unilocality marks the routinizing of public punishment. In this context ceremonial was worked out. The carefully planned acting-out of executions in the early modern period contrasts with the relative spontaneity and directness of medieval times. The contrast implies that the long-term process of hiding the physical and visible aspects of punishment was already under way. The ceremony was a manner of formalizing it, of raising its decorum. An Amsterdam magistrate once referred to capital executions in general as '*ontsaggelijke plegtigheeden*',[9] which might best be translated as awesome ceremonies. It illustrates the mentality of the early modern authorities particularly well.

An execution was not the only event which was accompanied by a ceremony. In early modern Europe ceremonial was an important concomitant of many events in social life. Dying a natural death, for instance, had its ideal course too. The 'grand ceremony of the last moments' was reconstructed for France by Pierre Chaunu from *artes moriendi*, testaments and iconographic material.[10] The dying person lies in bed and the entire family, including the servants, is assembled around him. Passers-by may also be present. The dying man addresses those around him with a last admonition, invoking the solidarity of the lineage and the mutual love between Christian relatives. Sometimes he makes a public confession of his sins. A priest arrives to administer the last sacraments. He carries the host and presents it with the words: 'Brother, accept the *Viaticum* consisting of the Body of Our Lord Jesus Christ, which will protect you from the malign foe and will lead you into eternal life.' Extreme unction is given when the dying man is half-conscious. The

45

priest then recites the Passion of Christ and presents the crucifix. The physician discreetly remains in the background. His main role is to certify, by his presence, that death is imminent. The dying man is presented with the blessed candle and passes away.

The character of this ceremony is overwhelmingly religious. This was only partially the case with the ceremony of imposed death and we should now pay attention to the details of the latter. I will start with a discussion of the proceedings in Amsterdam, about which we are well informed. Several descriptions enable us to trace its evolution from the third quarter of the seventeenth until the beginning of the nineteenth century. Next, I will compare ceremonial in the Dutch metropolis with that in other jurisdictions where I found information, in the Republic and abroad.

In Amsterdam capital and corporal penalties were normally executed simultaneously. Most justice days included the former, because an execution with corporal penalties only was an infrequent occurrence. So the sources for the ceremonial concentrate on death penalties. The oldest description was written by the *schepen* Hans Bontemantel. It is a passage in his voluminous manuscript treating Amsterdam's government, which refers to the situation around 1660. Then there is the so-called book of ceremonies. It contains the official description of all ceremonial occasions in which the magistrates could be involved. We find the scenario for elections and for the entry of a foreign prince. That the ceremony of criminal justice is just one among them is significant enough. The Amsterdam archive has eight versions: six in manuscript and two in print. The earliest was written by the secretary Cornelis Munter in 1683. Subsequent versions do not differ from it significantly. A few interesting variations appear in the two printed editions. These were published about 1740 and after 1746, respectively. Next there is the work of Jan Wagenaar. His history and description of Amsterdam was published in the 1760s. It contains a passage on the ceremony of execution in his days. The sixth version, finally, is again a manuscript. It was written in 1809.

Bontemantel's story serves to set the stage. He begins on the eve of the justice day, explicitly referring to it as Friday night, because the execution is usually scheduled on a Saturday. The *schout* and two *schepenen* come to visit the prisoners sentenced to death at the inner court of the town hall. There the *schout* tells them to be prepared to die. A preacher and a comforter of the sick take care of the prisoners, urging them towards a Christian and repentant end. On Saturday *schout*, *schepenen* and burgomasters arrive at the town hall wearing their 'blood-robes' with the 'blood-sash'. The word 'blood' is a plain reference to the things to come, because the robes are black. Only the sashes are partly colored red. The latter are $5\frac{1}{2}$ centimeters wide and beset with the Andrew crosses from the arms of the city.[11] In the town hall one starts by saying a prayer. Next, the capital sentences are read for the first time. After this the *schout* asks all the *schepenen* and the burgomasters in their turn, if the time is right to do justice according to old custom and the privileges of the city. Their responses being given, the prisoners have to be declared 'children of death'. This is done by *schepenen* after having asked the formal advice of the burgomasters. Their advice is given again, when the *schout* has made his demand as to the form of the death penalty. Then the secretary recites the sentences to those present. The prisoners are led into the justice-room, where the ones condemned to a lesser punishment are already waiting. The bell tolls and the 'rod of justice' is hung from a window of the town hall. The magistrates take their seats before the open window of the gallery on the second floor. These windows offer a view of Dam Square and the scaffold, which is only accessible from the second floor of the town hall. The secretary then recites the non-capital sentences to the multitude. The magistrates come into the justice-room once again and kneel in prayer, together with the prisoners and the preacher. After this they return to the windows and watch the sentences being executed. When everything is over, the rod of justice is taken in again.

This account is Bontemantel's.[12] In Munter's description we find only a few minor variations. Two days before the execution, when the sentence is usually pronounced, the *schout* asks the burgomasters' permission to have the scaffold erected. The blood-robes are now called 'robes of justice', which sounds of course less violent. One of the possible formulas by which the prisoners are declared children of death is mentioned at the end. It is the one for killers. The formula declares that God wants the blood of those who have spilled blood themselves. Moreover, such acts cannot be tolerated in a city of law and have to be punished, providing an example to others. Munter's account mentions homicide and burglary as possible offenses and sword and rope as possible ways of capital punishment. Apart from these additions, it is identical to Bontemantel's.[13]

Later secretaries occasionally added a few words in the margin. They are faithfully reproduced in the printed version of 1740. Thus we learn that *schepenen* are the only ones to decide whether the body is to be brought to the Volewijk or granted a burial. The *schout* formally asks burgomasters to join in the prayer before the actual execution. A remarkable event took place in 1697. Peter the Great, Tsar of Russia, was present among the magistrates looking out of the windows in the gallery. 'He watched the whole execution, as he watched everything he encountered in Holland.' The most interesting addition is the following: 'in 1693 only one burgomaster gave the required advice. This is all right, if all burgomasters are of the same opinion.'[14]

The second printed version is more precise about the diminishing role of the burgomasters: it has long been discontinued for all burgomasters to come to give advice. Only the most junior in rank comes now. Moreover, he only advises capital punishment and does not say anything about the form of the death sentence, leaving that to *schepenen*.[15]

Wagenaar's account contains more new points. First, it tells us that the scaffold is erected on the preceding day. On the justice day itself a guard of soldiers is posted inside the town hall as well as in the weigh-house at the north of the square.[16] The gates of the city are closed, to prevent people from outside coming in. The soldiers and their officers salute the magistrates coming to the town hall wearing their black robes, now called judges' tabards, with the sashes. Pipes and drums are played.

A few other details can be added. On their last night, the prisoners receive better food than usual and wine. Wagenaar describes the rod of justice. It is a red branch of thorns. He is also the only one to devote a few lines to the execution itself. This information will be discussed in the next section. When justice has been done, *schout* and *schepenen* come to the burgomasters' room with the preacher. There they thank the latter for his trouble. The withdrawal of burgomasters, finally, has gone a step further. The one left also refrains from watching the execution now. Only ten pillows, for *schout* and *schepenen*, are laid in the gallery.[17]

Shortly after the Batavian Revolution of 1795 there was talk of altering the ceremony. In October the Committee of Justice, as the judges were now called, commissioned two of its members to inquire if it was possible 'to simplify the ceremonies which have taken place up to now on the execution of death penalties and which are both cumbersome and awkward for the patient'.[18] We suspect this is the mentality of a new age, which placed less value on ceremonial. The ensuing report, however, was subject to some discussion and it remains unclear whether it was put into effect. Unfortunately, it is no longer extant.

At a meeting of the judges – called *schepenen* again – in 'summermonth' (June) 1809 a concept for the ceremony suddenly turns up. The detailed account can be called cumbersome indeed. Essentially the eighteenth-century proceedings are still adhered to. No mention of soldiers is made. Instead, we hear about 'refreshments', which *schepenen* allow themselves several times. The magistrates are still watching, but the process of disappearance of the burgomasters has been completed. Only the *schout*, *schepenen* and secretaries figure in the ceremonial, besides the convict and a clergyman. The latter may now also be a Catholic.[19]

So much for the evolution of ceremonial when death is involved. On justice days without capital sentences all versions are equally short. Burgomasters do not play a part then and only the bell is tolled and the prayer said. *Schepenen* do not wear the blood-robes, as is explicitly stated in 1721.[20]

The presence of the magistrates at the executions is striking, but that of burgomasters raises certain questions. They did not represent the judicial branch of the urban government. Their advice, given at various stages, symbolizes their function as the supreme authorities, supervising even those occurrences which did not properly belong to their sphere. Putting someone – anyone – to death in the city was a weighty event, which could not take place without their consent. The extra-powerful position occupied by burgomasters in Amsterdam makes their role in the ceremonial understandable. Their gradual retreat from the balcony of the town hall may have been the expression of a growing feeling that their actual presence at executions was beneath their dignity.

In discussing cases of ceremonial elsewhere, we should, therefore, pay special attention to the role of the authorities. I will treat jurisdictions in the Netherlands first and proceed with examples from other European countries.

In 1555 the magistrates of the town of Middelburg protested against the abolition of the meal they had been used to enjoy after capital executions. The document they drew up gives a few details on the ceremony. Members of the St John's guild toll the bells. The place of execution is located outside the walls. The bailiff, as attorney, and the majority of the college of *schepenen* have to be there. Burgomasters apparently remain within the city.[21] The next example takes us to two small towns in the eastern province of Overijssel. There even the hangman had a verbal function in the ceremonial. The *drost* of Salland (in Genemuiden) or the *schout* (in Kampen) presided over the execution. After the recitation of the prisoner's confession he loudly asks the hangman how one ought to punish such criminals. The executioner answers in conformity to the judgment of *schepenen*, which has been told to him in advance.[22] In Arnhem in 1703 an execution proceeded as follows: after the bell has tolled for a quarter of an hour, the delinquent is led to the court room where he hears his sentence read. This recitation is repeated before the crowd. The preacher says a prayer for the delinquent. The *rigter* (the attorney), two *schepenen* and the secretary look down on the scaffold from a balcony. The first gives a signal to the executioner to start.[23]

The magistrates of the city of Groningen ordered a secretary to make a report of the proceedings during a capital execution in 1737. It was to serve as a model for the future. He recorded, among other things, the ancient custom of the 'gallows meal', which had been discontinued at the time in most jurisdictions. The convict sat down to it with preachers and secretaries. Ceremonial largely takes place in the town hall. The *schout* and the council play their part in it. Then a procession rides out from the town hall to the place of execution, which is situated just outside the city walls. Three chariots carrying the preachers, the hangman and the convict, follow each other, led by a mounted force. Provincial soldiers guard the place of execution. The gentlemen of the court stay in the town hall.[24]

The court of a rural district in the Dutch Republic might execute its sentences in the village where the crime had been committed. This was customary in Amstelland, for instance. The Bailiwick of Schieland was heavily dependent on the city of Rotterdam, whose burgomasters even played a small part in the ceremony. The scaffold was erected in front of Rotterdam's town hall. The bailiff and the messenger and judges of the Schieland court watched the execution.[25] Ceremonial in Utrecht was described on the occasion of the hanging of a robber in 1791. In this city there was a procession too. It proceeded from the town hall to the building where the provincial court resided and thence to the place of execution. Only the attorney-general and a preacher stayed at the scaffold. The first had to deliver his report to the court.[26]

The last Dutch example takes us again to the period of the Batavian Republic. The college of justice in the town of Delft ratified a regulation for the ceremony in November 1803. As in Amsterdam, the change of regimes allowed the presence of a clergyman of any confession the convict adhered to. Two days before the execution the *schout*, the secretary and some of the *schepenen* came to the prisoners sentenced to death to announce to them that they were going to die. On the day itself the bell tolled at 11.30 a.m. If there were only non-capital sentences the small bell was used. The magistrates, including the secretary, were dressed in black. Inside the court room the sentences were read for the first time. Then *schout* and *schepenen* took their position at the windows of a lower floor of the town hall. The clergyman and the secretary proceeded to stand on the scaffold inside the railing. The first said a prayer and the second recited the sentences to the people. During this part the convict knelt on a bench just outside the scaffold's railing, held by two servants of justice. Next, *schout, schepenen* and secretary went to a higher floor of the town hall. They watched the execution from the windows, taking a position according to rank. When everything was over, they returned to the court room, where those punished non-capitally received an admonition.[27]

Ceremonial in the Southern Netherlands was probably similar. In seventeenth-century Ghent the magistrates were spectators too. The scaffold was erected in front of the *tooghuis*, which seems to have been a tavern. The grand-bailiff and *schepenen* paid the owner of the house for allowing them to view the execution from its windows.[28]

Looking for a larger contrast, we arrive in Seville around the year 1600. There the ceremony of death was characterized by more baroque pomp. It has been reconstructed by the historian P. Herrera Puga from the diary of Father Pedro de Leon. The first part took place within the walls of the *Cárcel Real*. Nevertheless, it was decidedly public. A few Jesuits arrived to prepare the condemned for death. Persons in mourning clothes (*enlutados*) accompanied them and said a last *adios*. Then a procession of more than 200 people was assembled within the building. Together with the *enlutados* they proceeded towards the reception hall. An elaborate dialogue between the condemned and their companions followed. Recurrent themes were an honorable but deserved death and God's grace. After this dialogue the company went to the chapel. Then the *enlutados* quitted the scene, while the condemned left through the gate. The route of the procession varied, depending on the place of execution. Most often, the condemned included only one under death sentence. His companions were delinquents who had to serve on the galleys. The capital convict either rode on a mule or a chariot. After arriving at the scaffold, the priest made a speech. Those present included the judicial and the executive authorities, secretaries and servants of justice. It remains unclear, however, who among them watched the actual execution.[29]

Before we take this all to be typical of a Southern mentality, we should move the focus to a German village. The year was 1820, the place was Clingen in the principality of Schwarzburg–Sondershausen (Thüringen). Clingen had 1,000 inhabitants, but the observer counted some 20,000 spectators. The previous capital execution had taken place in 1788. The sentence was recited at the marketplace. From there a procession departed for the 'gallows mountain', two kilometers outside the village. School children accompanied it, singing songs of death. On the mountain the watching crowd could not be kept outside the 'blood-circle'. As was common in Germany, the hangman asked the *Landrichter* for a judgment on the beheading, holding the blood-stained sword in

51

his hand. He was obliged to search the crowd to find the magistrate.[30]

Another German example is just a little older. In the small town of Ansbach in 1798 the place of execution was also outside the walls. Early in the morning the necessary equipment was brought there and a guard posted. The civil militia assembled on foot in front of the town hall and the 'poor sinner bell' was tolled. The participating magistrates included twelve *Schöppen*, two *Scabinen*, ten members of the council, a secretary and the *(Blut) Richter*. The latter was dressed in red, the others in black. The main part of the ceremony was played in the marketplace in front of the town hall. One of the *Schöppen* replied to the question put by the *Richter* that everyone was present. Then the executioner was requested to bring forward the delinquent. When the latter had arrived, the *Richter* addressed him and broke a staff in front of him. Then the hangman was ordered to lead the delinquent to the place of execution. In the marketplace the chairs were overturned. The procession departed to the place of execution. This procession included the civil militia, whose commanding officer led the delinquent, the *Richter* and those *Schöppen* who wished to join him. The executioner was not mentioned but presumably he went along. The execution took place within a circle formed by the civil militia. Afterwards they marched home again.[31]

It is especially relevant to compare Amsterdam with the two other European metropolises. The course of events in London has been described by, among others, Peter Linebaugh. Its most remarkable feature was the procession to the place of execution. The preparations for death took place at Newgate. Those spectators able to pay the jailer his fee had the opportunity of being present in the chapel. All the city's churches rang their bells. The procession followed a three-mile route from Newgate through the heart of the city to the gallows at Tyburn. The authorities abolished the custom in 1783, when they moved the place of execution to Newgate. Spectators, however, were still admitted. Linebaugh does not say whether magistrates were present at the hangings.[32]

In Paris there was a procession too. The condemned was drawn on a chariot with the hangman and a priest from his prison to the town hall at the Place de Grève. The scaffold there was shielded from the crowd by a wooden palissade. A *magistrat commissaire* or *magistrat délégué* looked down from the balcony of the town hall. His eventual retirement inside signified that the execution was over. When the regicide Damiens was put to death in 1757, two ministers were present to supervise. The king himself remained in Versailles. He is supposed to have wept when it was revealed to him how difficult it had been to execute the sentence.[33]

A notorious feature of the proceedings in Paris as well as elsewhere in France was the *amende honorable*. It was a formal act of penitence, usually performed in front of a church. Not everyone sentenced to death was obliged to do this, while on the other hand it could also be required from minor delinquents. The *amende* was often made during a stop in the procession to the scaffold. This was the case in Angers when an arsonist was to be burned in 1691. Bells started to ring as the procession first took the road to the church. There the convict performed his act of penitence and they went on. All the way to the place of execution the convict had a rope around his neck and a burning torch in his hand.[34]

Before the Reformation this form of penitence could accompany punishment in the Netherlands too. The condemned might be obliged to kneel before the victim of his crime or before the judges and beg forgiveness in a church or in the court room. Another variant was to walk, in some humiliating outfit, in a religious procession.[35] We notice that the custom was already half-laicized at an early date. After the Reformation its laicization was completed. Only the act of asking forgiveness in the court room remained. The delinquent had to kneel bare-headed and direct himself both to God and the magistrates. But even this penalty was no longer imposed in Amsterdam after 1600. In the Dutch countryside it had a longer life. The court of Nieuwburgen imposed it eleven times in the second half of the seventeenth century.[36]

We should be careful in drawing conclusions from this comparison of ceremonial. The evidence is still rather haphazard. Further research is necessary. Moreover, the sources are not unconditionally comparable. Ceremonial involves the formalized aspects of an execution. Witnesses may differ in their appreciations of which proceedings are part of the ceremony. Some would include the presence of soldiers, for instance, while others would consider this as belonging to the sphere of public order. A few remarkable features remain nevertheless. In France and Spain the religious aspect seems to be a little more pronounced. This may reflect a difference between Catholic and Protestant countries. The subject of penitence and the religious setting is further discussed in the next section. A second point of variation lies in the occurrence of a procession. It was customary in a few small towns and villages where the place of execution was situated outside. But it also happened, during most of the eighteenth century, in Paris and in London. Amsterdam was more sober in this respect. Still, this sobriety is not specifically Dutch, since Groningen and Utrecht had a procession too. So far there is no explanation why some jurisdictions incorporated this feature and others did not.

53

The third remarkable aspect is the most interesting. Amsterdam's burgomasters' initial role at the scaffold seems to be unique. In a few other Dutch jurisdictions burgomasters also played a part in the ceremony. But they did not watch the execution itself. As far as we can tell from the examples, in no other place did the magistrates who wielded the executive and supreme authority officially view the proceedings on the scaffold. Besides the hangman and the convict, judicial and religious functionaries were the only people featuring in that part of the ceremony. Apparently this was the normal situation. The highest authority did not associate itself directly with violent death on the scaffold. This principle can be taken as the nucleus of the later attitude which considered violent repression in general as problematic. By their gradual retreat, Amsterdam's burgomasters undid the initially exceptional situation. This retreat took place during the period when they were at the zenith of their power. In the first half of the eighteenth century they were, more than ever before, rulers of a whole country instead of just a city. It was then that they came to consider watching the execution beneath their dignity.

2 THE DISPLAY OF RIGHTEOUSNESS

The various descriptions of ceremonial are, as indicated in the previous section, not entirely comparable. Their authors may have had different conceptions of what should be left out, as not being part of the ceremony. These missing parts still reflect the staging of executions and, consequently, the attitudes of the authorities. So they need to be commented upon.

'The publicity of capital executions', F. Lebrun writes, 'only makes sense in a climate which gives to the death of others the value of an example.' The word 'example' is crucial. Exemplarity, Lebrun continues, is inherent to capital executions in two ways: punishment is shown and the possibility of a penitent and edifying death is present.[37] This also holds true, I should add, in cases of corporal penalties. The edifying aspect then lies in a punishment suffered humbly and dutifully. All this of course presupposes a society which tolerates the open infliction of pain. Only then can the authorities hope that the example will be effective.

The accounts of ceremonial do not lead us to believe that the authorities themselves had a particular revulsion to the sight of violence. In Amsterdam burgomasters gradually withdrew altogether, but *schout* and *schepenen* continued to watch the proceedings on the scaffold. Well into the nineteenth century, Dutch patricians as well as magistrates elsewhere did not shy from the spectacle of delinquents who were beaten, broken and put to death. They could still view it unambiguously as a positive event; as a manifestation of their monopoly of justice.

When medieval rulers expropriated private vengeance and replaced it by criminal justice, they were drawn into display. It served a double function. It warned potential transgressors of the law that criminal justice would be practiced and it warned everyone to remember who practiced it. The scaffold and the gallows were symbols of authority in a dual sense. In this way the relation of display and exemplarity with the early phases of state formation becomes clear. During the late Middle Ages authority was mostly vested in the hands of rulers of cities and relatively small principalities. Their strivings toward a monopoly of violence in their territory were easily challenged; from without as well as from within. There was a relatively large amount of private violence and other forms of law-breaking. The laws these authorities enacted had to be implemented visually through the public punishment of violators. The observable fact that punishments were indeed meted out constituted a necessary prerequisite for the preservation of a shaky position of authority. People had to see that 'justice reigned' in a particular city or country. And the reign of justice implied the presence of persons powerful enough to catch and punish transgressors of the law. This attitude remained prevalent during the early modern era as well.

In Republican Amsterdam exemplarity was a matter of course. It is reflected in the formulation of the sentences in cases of public punishment. They conclude with a recurrent routine statement: 'these are things which cannot be tolerated in a city of law and have to be punished as an example to others'. Such a routine conclusion was common in the Republic. The standard formula might vary a little. Some jurisdictions had 'country of law', or 'endured' instead of 'tolerated'. Others had 'mirror or example'. But the word 'example' recurred everywhere.

This was no dead letter. The magistrates' love for examples is attested by a case in 1702–3, during the opening phase of the War of the Spanish Succession. Two men accused a third of planning actions for the enemy, such as breaking the dikes. The accused, they said, possessed letters confirming this. The *schout* of Amsterdam did not know whether he should believe the story, so he asked the advice of burgomasters. The latter stated explicitly that they did not think such a plan could ever be carried out. But, they argued, it would still be a good thing if the man and his papers could be seized, as a deterrent to others. If he confessed to have made the plan, he could be duly punished.[38] It is clear that, even without the suspicion of an actual crime, burgomasters were still motivated by a

55

desire to set an example. The victim was broken on the wheel two months later.[39]

He was at least lucky not to be subjected to the most severe form of the penalty. We encounter this form a couple of times and it assigns a technical role to the magistrates, which once again points at their involvement in executions. The sentences concerned specify that the convicts should 'lie alive without receiving the *coup de grâce* for as long as Their Honors present at the execution will think proper'.[40] It testifies to the fact that the magistrates were actively stage-managing during the actual execution too. This is likewise attested by the practice of whipping in Amsterdam. The sentences never specified the number of lashes. The *schout* determined the severity of whipping on the spot. He gave a signal to the hangman when to stop.[41] The authorities also determined the order in which the sentences should be executed. On the official lists of persons who were to be publicly punished, every condemned person had a number corresponding to this order. Interestingly, the magistrates never considered offering the spectators a climax. In Republican times as well as in the early nineteenth century capital sentences were executed first, followed by the lesser ones.[42]

Exemplarity is most clearly a purpose in actions performed on dead bodies. A corpse can no longer feel the pain. Hence its punishment is meant for others. Consider the sentences for suicide. Suicide was a punishable offense well into the early modern period, although from an early date insanity was recognized as a possible excuse.[43] The last sentence for suicide in Amsterdam was imposed in 1658. The body of a seventy-two year old sailor was dragged to the gallows outside and hung with its chin in a fork-shaped stake.[44] This was the normal penalty. Although suicide apparently became decriminalized after 1658, this form of exemplarity lived on. Ordinary individuals who took their own life went unpunished. But convicts awaiting trial or execution, who managed to kill themselves in jail, were dragged to the gallows where their body was exposed. They were not really punished for suicide. Through it they had escaped the penalty they deserved; so exposure of their corpse was the only alternative left.[45]

The chronology was not the same everywhere, as is attested by an extreme case cited by Lebrun. It occurred in Château-Gontier in 1718. An unmarried woman, who was six months pregnant, had committed suicide. This amounted to murder as well. Apparently she was buried before it came to a trial. Nevertheless a sentence was passed and executed the same day. Her body was exhumed and dragged through the streets to the central square. There the hangman took the innocent child from the mother's womb. Delivered by this post-mortem Caesarean operation, it was buried in the cemetery for unbaptized infants. The mother's corpse was hung by its feet on the gallows for an hour, with a letter denoting her crimes. Then it was burnt and the ashes were cast to the wind.[46]

In general, the exposure of dead bodies was a way of securing permanence to the example. It was a possible extra punishment for those condemned to death and as such practiced in most of Europe. In Britain it was known as hanging in chains. The corpses were to be 'consumed by the air and the birds of the sky'. They were usually exposed outside inhabited areas. This is not in contradiction to their exemplary function. The site was always a conspicuous one, preferably along an inter-urban route.[47] In Germany people spoke of the 'gallows mountain'. In England the spectacle was familiar too. Ogilby's *Itinerarium Angliae* (c. 1700) mentions a standing gallows several times as a point of orientation.[48] The flat country of Holland had 'gallows fields' instead of gallows mountains. The site was still chosen with care. Amsterdam's gallows field lay on a stretch of land called the Volewijk, along the water Y which formed the city's northern border. This means that it was situated along the main shipping route to the city.

Why were corpses exposed away from inhabited areas? The recent historiography of attitudes toward death tells us of the familiarity of the living with decaying bodies. So the smell and, to an even lesser extent, a sense of hygiene are not likely to explain it. Moreover, in a few instances heads and other parts of bodies were indeed permanently exposed in towns.[49] The reason for the normal procedure, however, is very simple. It formed part of a dual system which maximized display. The actual executions could take place on the site of the standing gallows. This regularly happened – notably in Germany – in villages and small towns, where the population could easily be expected to walk to the site. In bigger towns, such as the three metropolises, the scaffold was erected in the city center. In Paris and Amsterdam – and most Dutch towns – it was done in front of the town hall; the residence of the urban government. It could also be done in a marketplace.[50] Here we see the dual system. The executions themselves were primarily meant as an example to the inhabitants. Exposure of corpses along the roads was a special warning directed at non-residents coming in.

Thus the standing gallows functioned as a permanent symbol that a place was a 'city of law'. Hence one was proud of it; it was part of the majesty of the authorities. It has been reported that soldiers were obliged to salute the gallows when passing it.[51] During the siege wars until the sixteenth century it was an obvious target. The besieging army started with a psychological attack and cut down the town's symbol of authority.[52]

The idea that the display of corpses was to discourage potential criminals was often expressed. Its most telling expression comes from Strasbourg. There the exceptional situation prevailed that corpses were cut down after a short while. In 1461 the council, deliberating on the proceedings of capital punishment, decided to discontinue the practice: 'Up to now all the corpses of those hanged have been dropped, so that the gallows has stood entirely empty, as if no thief were punished here in Strasbourg. But we think that, if those executed remained hanging there, the sight of misery would produce anxiety and fear, so that many a person would refrain from stealing because of it, from fear of being hanged too.'[53] Henceforth only citizens would have the right to be cut down, if their family requested this. The council further ordered a wall to be built around the gallows, so that no dog would take away any of the condemned's bones.[54] Such a charming care of the gallows has also been recorded elsewhere. In Zutphen in 1468 one of the four parts of a quartered man fell off the gallows. It was hanged anew.[55] In Gouda in 1628 the wind blew a corpse off the gallows. This was likewise restored to its place.[56] But in Nijmegen a fallen body was buried in 1612.[57] In various places a sort of harness was used to fasten a corpse which had been broken on the wheel in an upright position.

Although in later times the authorities may not have bothered about specific bodies, their care continued to be extended to the site of exposure. The city of Rotterdam erected a new gallows, made of white Ardennes stone, outside the Delft gate in 1655.[58] In the eighteenth century too this form of display was certainly not an anomaly. A number of German courts renovated their standing gallows in the second half of that century.[59] Wagenaar, writing in the 1760s, says the same about Amsterdam. At the time its standing gallows was made of stone. It was a triangular structure with three pillars, each surmounted by a lion bearing the city's arms. Beneath were stone pits, into which the decayed parts fell. The gallows and the pits were renovated regularly.[60] Exposure of the corpse on the Volewijk forms a clause in 214 out of 390 death sentences pronounced in Amsterdam between 1650 and 1750.

The display inherent in executions was not confined to the act itself. Pamphlets and booklets were devoted to the lives of notorious delinquents, and they did not fail to tell the story of their public punishment. The existence of broadsheet verses composed on the occasion of executions has been noted several times in recent literature.[61] Although usually written by anonymous but no doubt private individuals, these pamphlets contributed to the atmosphere of exemplarity-with-a-moral which was so dear to the authorities. They were actively sold and eagerly bought.

In Amsterdam several such broadsheets have been preserved. They date from the eighteenth and the first half of the nineteenth centuries. The content is plainly moralistic and exemplary. Some are in prose, others in verse; a few are in the form of a prayer. Some devote a few lines to the delinquents: their crimes, their character, their guilt, a conversion, or rebelliousness towards the judges. The criminals are usually mentioned by name. Sometimes the text can be sung to the melody of a popular song.[62] There was even a market for a simple list of criminals condemned to death. A booklet enumerates the names, crimes and sentences of those capitally executed in Amsterdam since 1693. It adds a few remarks about the presence or absence of penitence. There are three editions between 1748 and 1774.[63]

In a notorious case in 1703 the authorities themselves tuned in to the pamphlet culture. They did so by providing a juicy story in one of the sentences, which, as noted above, were read aloud to the public. It concerns the trials of Hiddo Grittinga and his wife Helena Knoop. Hiddo had murdered Helena's first husband with her complicity and the two had been married shortly afterwards. Hiddo's sentence just mentions the facts, but Helena's is a real story of *crime passionnel*: Hiddo told her: 'Either your husband or me has to die.' She finally consented: 'Oh God, do what you have in mind then.' On the fatal night the victim is urged by his wife to go out to visit someone. She kisses him as he leaves.[64] A booklet on the case does not fail to mention the Judas kiss. It even supposes a parallel on the scaffold: people say that, when Grittinga was led to the cross, passing the garrotte where Helena had just been strangled, he asked permission to give her one last kiss, which was refused.[65]

In the eyes of the authorities the staging of executions achieved its most beautiful form of ultimate success when it came to a kind of overall victory of the criminal. For this his co-operation was required. He had to be convinced of the righteousness of his punishment. Those whipped and branded in Amsterdam were expected, when returning to the town hall, to kneel in front of the judges and thank them for their mildness. Reverence to the magistrates and to the spectators was required. Notably those who were going to die were expected to be penitent and convinced of the wrongness of their own acts and the righteousness of their death. They had to die repenting their sins, in order to save their souls at the last moment. The execution of a disbeliever was not a perfect one.

Illustrations of this concern for a Christian death for the convict abound. In the ideal situation repentance already started during the trial, or at least immediately after the passing of the sentence. The majority of those capitally punished seem to have obliged. They wished to part from the world with a clean conscience. This is clearly expressed in the phenomenon of 'after-confessions'. After hearing their death sentence, many delinquents confessed a few more crimes. It was usually noted that they did so of their own free will to relieve their conscience. A clerk dutifully wrote these statements down. He often added that the prisoner had nothing to hope or to fear any more; in a way it made the statement more authentic. Some prisoners 'after-confessed' on the day of execution, just before going to the scaffold. The whole phenomenon gives a sort of mystical meaning to the convict's death: a confession uttered just before parting from this world is almost by definition the truth. By death a person can confirm a statement. Death seals the truth of the after-confession.[66]

An after-confession did not necessarily refer only to acts committed by the prisoner alone. Some accused others, usually when these had been accomplices. In 1663 Jacob Sieuwertsz may have wished that Gillis Paulusse had literally gone to hell. The former was to be whipped and branded on the scaffold, confined in the house of correction for four years and banished for eight years. But on the day of his execution Gillis Paulusse, to relieve his conscience, told of two burglaries they had committed together. Sieuwertsz conceded these and his penalty was aggravated accordingly. He had to stand under the gallows with a rope around his neck, his confinement was prolonged by two years and his banishment by four years. The whole course of events was recorded in the sentences of both, so that the public could be influenced by the moral of the story.[67]

In such a case, apart from the enhancement of the moral ingredient of the spectacle of suffering, the court obviously took advantage of it. There are more cases in which the authorities took action upon accusations by capitally condemned persons. At other times they recorded the after-confessions, but did not really believe them. A number of the condemned apparently needed absolute certainty that their soul was saved and confessed improbable things or events long ago. In 1660 Pieter Fredricxz told the judges that he had once bitten a servant of justice on the thumb. He thought it had caused the man's death and this was duly recorded in his sentence.[68] In 1720 two men, after hearing their death sentence, confessed that a woman they had lived with in Amsterdam, had told them that her sister had borne a child by her father, and that she had killed it in

Groningen seven years ago.[69] These are of course extreme examples. But there can be no doubt that a feeling of repentance was common. Of the 234 capitally punished in Amsterdam in the first half of the eighteenth century, seventy-nine made an after-confession.

In Bicker Raye's diary we also hear of people who displayed their penitence on the scaffold. Raye had some compassion for a carpenter's journeyman hanged for housebreaking and garden-theft in 1761. The poor man was 'very simple and not a thief by nature'. He died with great repentance, pitying the wife and two children he left behind. Despite his lack of knowledge in religious matters, the preachers and comforters of the sick were very satisfied with his behavior.[70] Six years later a similar situation occurred. A man who had murdered his wife, died penitently, reciting a line from a religious hymn. This, we are told, brought 'great joy to the judges, the preacher and thousands of people'.[71] Here Raye suggests that the spectators were indeed impressed by a beautiful death. The interest accorded to it in his diary and in the published name-list of the capitally condemned, shows that this was a keenly discussed topic.

But the magistrates were not always successful in gaining the convict's co-operation. Here Bicker Raye is our witness too. In 1736 a man who had murdered his wife died without repentance, making jokes about his penalty on the scaffold. An eighty-five year old Swedish captain, broken on the wheel in 1742, was hardly aware of what was going on. He jumped on the cross by himself and stretched his arms and legs without interference by the hangman. Despite this material co-operation, 'he died as a beast without repentance or sorrow'. Four years later a Jew received the same punishment. He also died 'as a beast'. He refused to listen to the preacher, who apparently tried to convert him to Christianity. Ascending the scaffold, he shouted 'Abraham, Abraham'. A Swiss robber, who had murdered his victim, was broken on the wheel in 1766. He happened to be an atheist. Raye calls him 'a most horrible person' who held the theory of 'death, everything death'. He mocked at the efforts to convert him. Instead, he attempted suicide, whereupon he was given two more guards besides the usual two inmates of the house of correction. They restrained him when he tried to twist off his penis. He was finally brought to the scaffold intact. It was rumored that he made an exclamation of repentance on the cross: 'O omnipotent God, have mercy on my poor soul.'[72]

In the case of this Swiss robber a speech by the *schout* was recorded. It was delivered during the ceremony on the eve of the justice day, when the prisoner was told to be prepared to die. Such speeches were apparently also publicized. The text shows how the magistrate attempted to draw a moral even from this death, by highlighting the counter-example of extreme wickedness:

Jean Hubain, the reason why I let you appear on this spot is to tell you openly that you are going to die because of committed and confessed crimes. For this purpose I summon you tomorrow at nine o'clock before the court of the Honorable Gentlemen *schepenen* (whose assistance I request), to hear my capital demand and the ensuing sentence, and thus shortly after to end your life on an erected scaffold. With such awesome ceremonies as this it is my habit to give an admonition to those condemned to death, recommending them to spend the few remaining moments of their life for the good of their immortal soul. But in what way shall I admonish you, miserable Hubain, who has already been shown the road to salvation by so many of our ministers, but who still persists in blasphemously mocking God and religion; yes, who does not even desire that people pray for you; who has even attempted to take your life and so, if possible, to cut off every opportunity of repentance. Miserable Hubain, I do not speak to you as a judge or a claimer of guilt but as a friendly adviser. Lie down at God's throne of grace; beg the Omnipotent to soften your obdurate heart with His endless powers. Take the only road of salvation offered by Jesus Christ with love, in order that, when you raise your eyes tomorrow in an awesome eternity, you may not find yourself in a place where you, worm, will never die but be tormented eternally. Then, too late, will you remember all friendly advices and true-hearted admonitions which have been presented to you here at this time. However, because human council does not avail here, I am giving you over to God's endless mercy. O, awesome Judge, look down with pity on this hardened person and perform miracles as in the days of old. Preserve this poor soul from destruction and let Your Grace conquer this miserable person.[73]

Hubain was certainly not the first in Amsterdam to mock the religious and moralistic setting of executions. As far back as 1695 William Mountague saw a corpse on a wheel on the gallows field. People told him that the man had killed a prostitute. To the preacher's request to pray for the city and the magistrates, he had replied 'The devil take 'em all.'[74] It is only natural that the authorities did not always succeed in obtaining a beautiful Christian death. Michel Bée, who gives two such examples for early nineteenth century France, argues that these are expressions of a loss of legitimacy by public executions as a consequence of the Enlightenment.[75] The earlier cases in Amsterdam prove that this thesis is incorrect. Moreover, religious feeling was still a reality experienced by a majority of people in the nineteenth century, and Christian deaths were also reported then. To give just one example: a newspaper report of a beheading in Norway in 1864 mentions the involvement of a preacher. On the scaffold the condemned embraced him and kissed him goodbye. When kneeling before the executioner, he prayed half aloud with the preacher saying the Lord's Prayer.[76]

The presence of clergymen at executions, in Catholic as well as Protestant countries, has been attested many times, so that there is no need to dwell on it.[77] In the Dutch Republic the monopoly of the dominant religion is remarkable. Only in the territories ruled directly by the 'Generality', where almost the entire population was Catholic, were non-Reformed clergymen allowed on the scaffold.[78] In Amsterdam only about half the population was Reformed. The execution of a Jew, noted above, is especially intriguing. The Jewish chronicler Braatbard devoted a few lines to the case too. He saw the condemned as a martyr, because he remained true to his faith.[79] Thus the authorities found it more important to maintain the monopoly of the established church, as far as the religious setting of executions is concerned, than to reconcile the Jewish community, whom they protected at other times. It is understandable that they would prefer the first course of action. The magistrates needed the Reformed preachers for the moralistic–religious setting of executions and could not afford to alienate them. In the Republic and elsewhere the interests of the secular authorities and the church in this matter generally coincided; the former hoped to show an edifying death, the latter wished to save the condemned's soul. Only in Sweden does there seem to have been a latent conflict between the two. Over-zealous ministers worked on the prisoner's conscience very intensively, and sometimes pressed for a delay in the execution if they thought he was not ready to die. Several royal ordinances in the eighteenth century and at the beginning of the nineteenth were aimed at defining the boundaries between the duties of church and state. A resolution in 1725 obliged the provincial governors to give the clergy ample opportunity to do their job. At the same time it stated that no capital execution should be delayed too long.[80]

A possible component of the moralistic setting is a speech delivered by the condemned person himself. This occurred notably in England. From Tudor times on the authorities actively encouraged the condemned to address himself to the public with a moralistic story, explaining how he had sinned and deserved his punishment.[81] Speeches by the convict were also recorded in Germany and in the South of France.[82] In the Netherlands, on the other hand, he was allowed to pray or sing a psalm, but not to deliver a speech. In 1800 it was explicitly denied to a robber who wished to do so.[83] More than a century earlier Balthasar Bekker, on a visit to England, had noted the custom with surprise. The convict resembled a minister on the pulpit, Bekker wrote, were it not for the rope around his neck.[84]

And yet the relief of their conscience was not the only possible motivation for the condemned to behave penitently. They might just as well do it for a more material reward. In France those broken on the wheel and burned could earn a quick, secret death. In the Dutch Republic those condemned to exposure of their corpse could earn a withdrawal of this clause.[85] Thus the authorities showed a clear preference for one of the possible expressions of the display of righteousness. They considered a Christian death more important than another exemplary body on the standing gallows.

Those hanged in eighteenth-century London, though repenting their sins, seem to have been reluctant to betray comrades in crime. Our information on this comes from Linebaugh, who simply comments that a dying person had nothing to gain by it.[86] For England this may indeed have been true. Exposure of corpses was less frequent there and the sentence seldom specified what was to happen to the body of the hanged. For France Foucault argued that the majority of the condemned did not ultimately die penitently. At the last moment they secretly cursed their judges and heaven itself. The populace at the foot of the scaffold could hear this and loved it.[87] But his source is an Enlightened advocate of penal reform and clearly prejudiced. So this remains unproved.

There is another, extreme case of spoiling the display of righteousness. A number of convicts committed impertinent acts or even resistance on the scaffold. This generally happened during the execution of corporal penalties. The judges usually responded with renewed physical punishment. The Amsterdam court records provide a few examples. In 1653 Gillis Nicaes, who had been a prisoner five times before, was whipped and branded. Instead of thanking the judges for their mildness, when leaving the scaffold, he loudly exclaimed: 'Of course I won't be good now, but will do wrong a hundred times more.' The magistrates were dismayed. It was a contempt of justice and a bad example, they noted. The other delinquents, whether simulating or not, were annoyed as well. Gillis Nicaes was immediately whipped again.[88]

Another man, after being flogged, put out his tongue at the spectators. The consequence was identical to that in the previous case.[89] In 1718 Jan Jansz van Leeuwen committed active resistance. He was exposed with a rope around his neck, whipped and branded on 4 June. On the scaffold he raged and looked at the judges with contempt. Then he kicked the executioner and his servants, while exclaiming seditious words to the people. His crime was defined as 'resistance of execution'. Jan did not receive a new punishment instantaneously. On 6 August, the next justice day, he was whipped for his crime on the previous one, and his confinement was prolonged by ten years.[90]

It may be significant that these acts of defiance were all committed by persons subjected to corporal punishment. Still, there are examples of resistance by the capitally condemned as well. One belongs to the early history of Massachusetts. In 1638 Dorothy Talbye was hanged for murdering her child. She was described as melancholic. She did not behave well on the scaffold, repeating that she preferred to be beheaded. The latter, she said, was both less painful and – which is true – less shameful. Swinging from the rope, she struggled to free herself.[91]

The ultimate fate of Hendrik Jansen was quite the opposite of Dorothy Talbye's wish. He had killed his wife during a quarrel. He was described as wicked and insensitive, but completely master of his senses. The Amsterdam judges sentenced him to decapitation in January 1803. When they looked down on the justice day from the balcony of the town hall, they saw a discouraging spectacle. Hendrik Jansen vehemently resisted his execution, so that the hangman declared he could not possibly proceed with it. The judges, however, told him, through a messenger, to attempt to handle the prisoner in a posture other than kneeling. Thereupon the executioner tried to tie the man to a chair. Jansen remained intransigent and stood upright with the chair. The hangman finally stated that the execution of this man with the sword was impossible. The magistrates withdrew to deliberate the consequences. They considered that the prisoner had been declared a child of death and that prompt action was necessary in order to maintain the respect for justice. They changed the form of capital punishment into hanging, which would not aggravate the convict's suffering. The altered sentence was recited to the people and executed immediately after.[92]

This section concludes with one more story of co-operation. The darling of eighteenth-century stagers of beautiful executions was a twenty-eight year old woman named Hendrina Wouters. Her case is among those most widely publicized in Amsterdam. Bicker Raye devotes attention to it in his diary and a booklet about it went through at least four successive editions.[93] Hendrina had been called to the house of another woman, to return some money she owed. Instead, she robbed the woman and killed both her and a servant girl. According to the booklet, Hendrina's will was broken on the rack. Torture and the ensuing confession of her crime had taken away her unshakability. Before, she had walked through the jail frankly and self-assuredly. But after, she crept and moaned. Two female guards started singing psalms and reciting from the Bible. 'Thus divine justice is able to reveal the machinations of a wicked mind after all.'[94] Apparently the rack was considered an instrument of divine justice.

From the judgment onwards Hendrina behaved in perfect conformity to the religiously loaded display of righteousness. She thanked the judges for their merciful sentence, saying she deserved a more severe penalty. On Friday, when her death was announced, she bade farewell to her husband and two children. Bystanders burst into tears. The preacher was very content. Although, while professing to be a Catholic, she proved unable to say the Lord's prayer, he declared that she would pass away as a child of God. On the justice day he concluded his prayer by expressing the wish that it might have impressed the sinner and the spectators. He asked the Lord's blessing to descend upon her and the judges. Then Hendrina begged forgiveness once more. She remained humble and kept her eyes down. Approaching the cross, she expressed no fear but became even more cheerful. The executioner broke her arms and legs, but she kept on praying until she received a cut in her throat.

3 THE PARTICULARS OF PAIN

This chapter has focused up to now on the web of ceremonial and display woven around public punishment. The task that remains is to describe its hard core, for the penalties themselves are what it was all about in the first place. A description of the details of punishment can easily slip into a catalogue of atrocities, but that is not the intention here. There are enough books to satisfy one's curiosity in this respect.[95] I have chosen to present an integral picture of the system of public punishment as it was practiced at one particular place and time in preindustrial Europe: Amsterdam in the seventeenth and eighteenth centuries. The main purpose is to arrive at some notion of the degree of physical injury and pain inflicted. First, the more regular penalties are discussed. After that the permanence of and discontinuities in mutilation are considered.

Contemporaries drew a clear line between public and non-public punishment. The former was graver and more consequential. It was registered separately and more elaborately. It was meant to humiliate those subjected to it and, usually, to inflict pain. The distinction of physical versus non-corporal penalties came close to, but was not quite identical with, that of public versus non-public penalties. The latter included one which was corporal, appropriately called whipping in-doors.[96] Likewise public penalties included only one which was not directly physical; when people were merely exposed. In Bontemantel's order of severity public penalties stand out as the most serious. Imprisonment in a house of correction, where one had every chance of a disciplinary beating anyway, ranked above whipping indoors. And simple exposure, as the lowest degree of public punishment, ranked above confinement.[97] The actual sentences often comprised more than one penalty. Notably those delinquents who were condemned to a corporal penalty on the scaffold usually received confinement and/or banishment as well.

Starting with exposure, we can distinguish two kinds. The first symbolizes a corporal penalty, while the second merely aims at showing a delinquent. They may be referred to, respectively, as symbolic and simple exposure.

Symbolic exposure was either an alternative to a corporal penalty or an additional punishment. In the former instance, it was frequently imposed on pregnant women and young offenders. The first could not be flogged and the second were sometimes the object of mercy.[98] Thus they were exposed with rods hanging over their shoulders. It signified that they deserved to be whipped, or even branded too, but were excused from it. Only rods were used in Amsterdam, although in the nearby countryside a case of symbolic branding was recorded. A pregnant woman had to walk around the scaffold twice with the branding-iron on her back.[99]

Symbolic exposure as additional punishment has the convict stand under the gallows with the rope around his neck. This implied an obvious warning. It signified that the offender had 'barely escaped death': he could have been capitally punished and would surely be the next time. At least, such was the implication when this form of exposure was combined with whipping and branding. In that case the court spoke of 'the penalty nearest to death'. It was often imposed when *schepenen* did not agree with the *schout's* demand for a death sentence. But exposure with a rope around the neck was also used as an additional warning to a sentence of only whipping (Appendix B, no. 1).

An incident in 1757 shows how carefully the symbolized corporal penalty was imitated. A woman was condemned to be exposed with the rope around her neck, whipped and branded. Unfortunately, she fainted while standing under the gallows. Servants of the court hurried to help her, but they came too late. They could do no more than carry her dead body into the town hall. The observer concluded that she had died without receiving her punishment.[100]

In cases of simple exposure delinquents were often shown with an object reflecting their crime. The object could be a part of the stolen property or the goods illegally brought into the city. It could also be an instrument with which the crime was perpetrated: a knife or burglars' tools. Male bigamists were always exposed carrying two distaffs; one recorded 'trigamist' very appropriately had to carry three.[101] A woman condemned for this offense had to carry two sticks with trousers hanging from each, although another female bigamist in 1730 got away with one pitchfork.[102] But the most common object used was simply a notice attached to the prisoner's breast. The offense for which he or she was punished was written on it.

A sentence of simple exposure could be executed on the pillory as well as on the scaffold. In the latter case the offender was tied to the scaffold railing. The penalty could then also be in addition to whipping and even branding (Appendix B, no. 2). Exposure on the pillory should not be considered as a more severe penalty than exposure on the scaffold, since in both cases it was not allowed to throw things at the condemned.[103]

The distinction between whipping indoors and in public was known in various countries. Unfortunately, we do not know whether the former was a milder penalty, expressed, for instance, in the number of lashes. As already stated, the sentences never specified the number of lashes to be given. The standard formula of a condemnation to public whipping says that the delinquent has to 'be brought on the scaffold and be severely whipped there'. Sometimes the word 'severely' is omitted, depending on the clerk's preference. When a delinquent was whipped indoors, no formal sentence was even recorded. Here again the word 'severely' was included or omitted according to what the clerk thought fit.

Convicts were whipped on their bare backs both on the scaffold and indoors. The former penalty was described by William Mountague, who visited Amsterdam in 1695. He commented:

[The prisoner was] stript to the Waist, his Hands tied, and drawn up tight with a Cord to a Post, then the Hangman took up a good handful of large Birch (like that of Ostlers Brooms) from a great Bundle which lay close by, and slash'd him as fast as he could, backward and forwards, then took up a fresh handful, and so on for six or seven Minutes; at which time the Magistrates (who look on out of the *Stadthouse* Windows) nodded to give him over.[104]

Taking a fresh bundle of birch branches is not mentioned in other sources. The back of a person who had been whipped was usually bleeding.[105]

In the middle of the eighteenth century Jacob Bicker Raye sometimes recorded the number of lashes in his diary. He counted them as he watched the execution. Raye mentioned the total for all convicts on five occasions between 1740 and 1742. The average numbers were then thirty-seven, forty-one, thirty-six, thirty-seven and thirty-eight respectively. There could be a broad range, however. Raye recorded the number of lashes given to some particular people on two of these occasions. In the second three persons, who were branded as well, received fifty-one, fifty-one and fifty lashes. In the fifth case one man received twenty-six. Raye counted the number for particular persons on three more occasions, when he speaks of (very) severe whippings: in 1737 two men received eighty-three and seventy-eight lashes respectively. Sixty were given to a convict in 1761 and to another in 1767. All these persons, who aroused Raye's special interest, were men.[106]

It is a pity that Mountague indicates the degree of severity in time and Bicker Raye in quantity. It makes any comparison speculative. Taking six or seven minutes for some forty lashes might not seem fast, which word Mountague uses, so his observations on the duration of the penalty could refer to a higher number. It would still leave the question open because he may have been talking about an exceptional case. I assume, however, that about forty lashes constituted the average amount in the seventeenth as well as in the eighteenth century. Raye also gives this amount once for a whipping indoors.[107] Flogging with thirty-nine or forty lashes is prescribed in the Old Testament.[108] The number thirty-nine returns in a sentence of whipping pronounced in 1667 in New Amsterdam.[109]

During a whipping on the scaffold objects were occasionally exposed above the convict's head. It was generally a weapon. One sentence even specified that it should be a blood-stained knife.[110] This was not only done when the major offense was wounding. It could be robbery as well, or the major offense might be burglary if the prisoner was also charged with attacking someone or merely drawing a knife.

Whipping indoors was sometimes called 'secret whipping'. This name was used in Amsterdam in the sixteenth and – in one instance – in the seventeenth century.[111] The penalty could be administered in two different ways: at the usual post or on the so-called wooden horse. The latter instrument was used exclusively for juvenile delinquents. Various sorts of instruments have been called a wooden horse in one place or another. The one in Amsterdam, unfortunately, is no longer extant, so we cannot tell what it looked like. Did it imply a milder form of whipping or was the use of a wooden horse just a way of making the young offender feel 'at ease'? The sources do not provide the necessary information. I am inclined to think that juvenile delinquents were beaten on their buttocks instead of on their back. But this is just a guess.

The next punishment in order of severity was branding. A branding scar, or mark, stigmatized its bearer as a person who had once mounted a scaffold. If he or she happened to become a prisoner again, the judges knew they were dealing with a recidivist. In the later Middle Ages convicts were usually branded somewhere on their face; either on the cheek or on the forehead. Branding on the shoulder became the dominant mode in the early modern era, as in Amsterdam from 1551. In sixteenth-century Netherlands the ear and the ball of the thumb were other possible places for the mark.[112] The gradual change from more-visible marks to less-visible ones implies a slight increase in revulsion towards this penalty, because the result of branding was made less public. It could be hidden by the convict's clothes. A proverb from the Southern Netherlands says: 'One cannot tell from the jacket who is wearing a brand.'[113] But that did not really hamper the courts. If a prisoner was suspected of being a branded recidivist, his shoulder could always be inspected. This was a task for the executioner.[114]

The practice of branding shows us a view of criminal justice resembling the pride in the standing gallows. It was not uncommon in the early modern period for a court to literally put its own mark on a convict, as American farmers would later do with their cattle. Amsterdam's branding-iron had three Andrew crosses, which figure in the arms of the city. A characteristic passage in a letter, written by the *schout* to obtain information, says: the prisoner denies being branded, 'although we find a sign on his back which seems to portray something of an angel, being the arms of Brussels'.[115] Twice we hear of a recidivist who tried to have his brand removed. In 1667 Felix Rolé confessed to having been branded in Rotterdam in the same year. He had his mark 'skinned out' by an Amsterdam doctor.[116] In 1722 a man denied being a recidivist, although the hangman, who visited him, declared he had been branded on his right shoulder. The executioner supposed that the mark was erased with certain materials.[117]

Another penalty closely resembled branding. Both sides of a burning sword were laid on the convict's back, making a scar in the form of two crossed stripes. The scar was not meant to refer to the court of Amsterdam. Only from 1763 onwards was a sword used with the arms of the city in relief in the middle.[118] A passage in a sentence from 1660 gives an impression of the physical consequences of this type of punishment. A twenty-four year old woman had been whipped and branded in Dordrecht. Four days later she stood on watch during a burglary near Schoonhoven. When the company had to flee, she was 'not able to follow them because of her justice recently received at Dordrecht'.[119] This combination of whipping and branding was very common. In Amsterdam branding was always administered in combination with flogging, which usually went first. Likewise the penalty of the burning sword was always preceded by public whipping. The 427 cases of branding between 1651 and 1750 include two where the convict was branded twice.[120]

Leaving the subject of mutilation for a while, we come to the discussion of capital punishment. A relevant division of its various forms is between those involving an instant and those involving a prolonged death. In Amsterdam the former included beheading, hanging and garrotting. Decapitation, as usual, was the more honorable of the three. It was largely reserved for those condemned for homicide. The choice between hanging and garrotting was usually determined by the convict's sex. Only seven women were hanged and an identical number of men garrotted. The hanging of women was uncommon in Continental Europe, but it was recorded occasionally outside Amsterdam as well.[121] If a man was garrotted, it could be to facilitate additional torments. The practice of this penalty is illustrated by two plates dating from the middle of the eighteenth century: the convict is tied to the garrotte, or strangling-pole, with his back against it. Behind the convict the executioner tightens the cord with a small stick. A hangman's servant is standing in front of the prisoner or behind his master's back.[122]

The standard type of prolonged death penalty in seventeenth- and eighteenth-century Amsterdam was breaking on the wheel. After 1650 other types were hardly practiced. During the wave of sodomy trials in 1730 two men were drowned. The last case of burning occurred in 1696. The victim, a servant girl, was strangled 'until half dead', before she was thrown into the flames. She had set fire to her master's house in order to cover up a domestic theft.[123] Thus burning was used as a 'mirror penalty', reflecting the crime. More often it served the function of total obliteration.[124] As such, it was imposed on heretics and witches and later still in cases of certain grave morals offenses. In France burning was not uncommon even in the eighteenth century.[125]

Breaking on the wheel had its origins in a Frankish mode of punishment, described by Gregory of Tours.[126] He tells how a convict was laid over deep tracks in the ground, fastened down and then driven over by a heavily laden wagon. In later times, when the penalty was executed on a scaffold, a reminder of the wagon was preserved in the use of a wheel. The hangman hit the convict with it until the latter was dead. It must have been very exhausting for the executioner. This mode was practiced, among others, in medieval Malines and in sixteenth-century Frankfurt.[127] In early modern Europe the penalty was usually further simplified. The convict was laid on a wheel and the hangman broke his bones with an iron bar. In Amsterdam even the wheel was out of use. The convict was always tied on a cross, but the name of breaking on the wheel (*radbraken*) was retained. If the delinquent's corpse was taken to the gallows field, it was again placed on a wheel.

The municipal museum of Gouda preserves a specimen of the cross used. Five short legs support a 'couch', on which the convict has to lie. It consists of five planks, which together form two opposing capital Y's, so that the sufferer could stretch his arms and legs. The planks are beset with tiny wooden bars, to facilitate the breaking. An etch by Jan Luyken shows the penalty being executed.[128] The construction's legs are heavy logs. The delinquent has been tied on it by his four limbs. The hangman raises the iron bar.

The exact way of execution can be learnt from eighteenth-century hangmen's bills. There were two standard cases. In the first the delinquent was hit eight times: on his thigh and shin bones and on the upper arms and forearms. Finally his head was chopped off. In the second case he received nine blows. The last, the *coup de grâce*, was to his heart. To make sure that he was dead, he was strangled afterwards. In one instance ten blows were given. This degree of standardization was not achieved everywhere. In Germany widely varying and sometimes high numbers of blows have been recorded.[129] As stated before, a possible aggravation of the penalty was to let the convict lie alive for a time between the eighth blow and the *coup de grâce*. In 1718 the notorious robber Jaco had been condemned to await his death with broken limbs for half an hour. Being a citizen of Amsterdam, he appealed to the High Court of Holland and Zeeland. The court granted him a shortening of his life by half an hour.[130]

Apart from these variations, two modes of the penalty are reported to have been in existence in Amsterdam. The sentence's formula could speak of breaking on the wheel 'from below' (or 'alive' or both) on the one hand or breaking on the wheel 'from above' on the other. The latter was the mildest way; the delinquent was put to death before his bones were broken.[131] I found no example of this variation, although a case in 1746, when a man was first strangled and then broken 'from below', looks like it despite its formula.[132] All other sentences of breaking on the wheel added the clause 'from below alive'. In that case the hangman started with the delinquent's legs.

If the sentence says 'breaking from above' the spectators know that the delinquent is killed first. Another possibility is to hide it from them. This happened notably in France. Rendering useful information to the court could earn a convict the *retentum*. This meant that the executioner received an order to strangle the sufferer before or during the blows, but secretly. It could also be done with burning.[133] The reason for this practice is obvious. The delinquent was rewarded, while the impression on the public through the display of violent punishment was not diminished. It was a solution to a problem of conflicting aims. Originally no sensitivity towards physical punishment as such was involved. This only played a part towards the end of the eighteenth century. In 1776 Maria Theresa instructed the magistrates of Brussels always to practice secret strangling. The reason for it was clearly stated: 'Humanitarianism requires that we refrain from excessively prolonging the pain of those condemned to death.' The mentality of a new age had broken through, but the early modern state was still there and it needed display: 'This favor does not serve to encourage crime by lessening the awe of such punishments in the eyes of the public.'[134]

This is the story of the standard penalties. But the particulars of pain in seventeenth- and eighteenth-century Amsterdam involved more. This needs to be reviewed to complete the picture. Two sorts of punishment remain to be discussed: first, forms of maiming or otherwise severely hurting persons who were capitally punished; second, forms of mutilation performed as a penalty on persons permitted to live on. Notably the first testify to the imagination of the judges. They usually involve killers and robbers. I present them in a schematized form. They belong to the period 1650–1750.

Year	Crime	Punishment
1651	A man was discovered committing a burglary by a nightwatchman. He fled but was stopped by another. He stabbed this nightwatchman, who died the next day.	His right hand was cut off, then he was hanged and his corpse exposed. The hand was – and remained – nailed to the pillory.[135]
1660	Because he wanted the other's money, a man killed an acquaintance by hitting him twice with an iron spade.	The hangman hit him on the head twice with that very spade. Then the convict was garrotted. His corpse was exposed with the spade standing beside it.[136]
1661	A man of twenty-one had committed nineteen burglaries. He used to bind and threaten his victims.	His hand was cut off on a log. Then he was hanged.[137]
1664	An eighteen-year old girl killed her landlady with an axe.	The hangman gave her a few strokes with the same axe. Then she was garrotted.[138]
1668	A Norwegian servant girl set fire to the house of a friend's master.	She was first garrotted. Then her face was scorched by fire.[139]

73

1673	A Scotsman came to the Netherlands in order to burn Dutch warships for the English.	He was broken on the wheel. Then his face was scorched with a bundle of straw.[140]
1699	A sailor tried to rob someone. He attempted to kill his victim with a cobble-stone.	He was garrotted. Before he was completely dead, the hangman gave him three blows on his head with the cobble-stone.[141]
1720	A woman owed money to another. She went to the latter's house and hit her three times on the head with a hammer.	She was first 'strangled until half dead'. Then her head was smashed with the hammer. Garrotting was completed after this.[142]
1730	Two men had engaged in sex with various other men for several years.	They were garrotted and their bodies were scorched.[143]
1746	A woman murdered a servant girl and the latter's mistress. She cut the girl into pieces, which she dropped into different canals. She had robbed the other woman and wanted it to look as though the servant had done it.	She was broken on the wheel. Before she was dead, the hangman cut her throat. Then her head was cut off and put on a stake. Her right hand and both lower legs were cut off and laid upon her body.[144]

These additional torments and disfigurements accompanying the routine death penalties are concentrated in the early years of the period. Six out of eleven fall into the first quarter. When we exclude the scorchings which were, after all, performed on dead bodies, this is four out of seven. But the eighteenth century compensated for the relative lack of knocking convicts down with spades in another way. Prolonged death penalties are more frequent in the second fifty years. Four persons were broken on the wheel in the second half of the seventeenth century and thirty-six in the first half of the eighteenth. Moreover, the extra severe variant, where the convict had to lie alive for a certain time between the eighth blow and the *coup de grâce*, was only imposed between 1716 and 1722. The case of burning took place in the seventeenth, but the two drownings in the eighteenth century.

These disfigurements were all performed on persons who were going to die or were already dead. Afterwards none of the people concerned had to walk around deformed. This is not the case when mutilation constitutes the main penalty. This did occur in Republican Amsterdam. Notably, cutting off an ear was considered a normal penalty in the first half of the seventeenth century. The instruction for the provincial hangman in Holland, drafted in 1607–8, gives an example of a combined corporal penalty four times. In three cases it refers to whipping and cutting off an ear; in one case to whipping and branding.[145]

Blinding is one of the most severe forms of mutilation. It was imposed once in the early seventeenth century. The case is mentioned in the summary of previous crimes in a sentence from 1617. The penalty was not executed publicly because it was punishment for bad behavior in the rasphouse. That may be the reason why no original sentence is recorded. The summary says:

He, prisoner, was publicly whipped for the second time and confined in the house of correction in 1608. On the fourth of November of that year he committed very evil acts, showing contempt of court. When *schout* and *schepenen* visited the rasphouse he threw things at them and cursed them. Therefore, both his eyes were blinded in the aforementioned house of correction. He was furthermore condemned to stay and work there for life. And since one of his eyes had not been hit very well he broke out of the rasphouse again. He was whipped for this violation of confinement and other evil acts on February 8, 1612 and his life-long imprisonment was renewed.[146]

This was the last instance of blinding in Amsterdam, according to the early nineteenth-century investigator Jacobus Koning.[147] The practice of cutting off ears continued for somewhat longer. The last case occurred on 12 November 1650. A woman had been banished, on penalty of losing an ear. When she infringed her banishment, the threat was put into effect.[148]

Some minor forms of mutilation were practiced after 1650 as well. Up until the 1730s, a slash on the cheek with a knife or razor was sometimes imposed.[149] This penalty was discussed in Bontemantel's time. A prisoner had cut somebody in the face. He was condemned to be whipped with a knife above his head. A cut in the cheek was overruled this time. Some of the *schepenen* argued that a sentence should never deform the face. Others opposed this opinion. Both parties supported their arguments by references to precedents. Two men, in 1645 and 1648, had been punished by a cut in the cheek. Four attackers had merely been whipped with a knife above their head in between those years.[150]

Cutting off a thumb was practiced five times after 1650, with the last case occurring as late as 1748. In 1766 a man who had fraudulently acquired thousands of guilders from a bank, was tried. He only received ten years in the rasphouse and a banishment for ever. According to Bicker

Raye, the *schout* had demanded a scaffold sentence involving the cutting off of the prisoner's thumb. Raye commented: 'He gets away with it well.'[151]

In the early eighteenth century one isolated case of severe mutilation was recorded. The trial is also interesting as an illustration of the limits of tolerance in the Dutch Republic. This man in 1708 had clearly gone too far. Willem Willemse de Boer, a twenty-two year old sailor, was apparently arrested following complaints by his wife and his mother. He used to demand money from them, while threatening them with a knife. He spent it on drinks and other pleasures. Once he took a couple of friends and some prostitutes home and had sexual intercourse with one of the latter in the presence of his wife and his mother. As might be expected, the women did not like this at all. His wife reminded him of God's omnipresence each time he came home drunk at night. She accused him of a blasphemous reply to one of these admonitions. He was supposed to have said: 'I shit on God; I wipe my ass with my God; the devil is my God.' He first denied, but later confessed this. There was something else. He had sexual intercourse with his wife a couple of times, 'not in the ordinary way, as a man is used and obliged', but having 'sodomitic and unnatural dirty carnal conversation'. He maintained that his wife requested this, which she denied. On the contrary, she accused him of having forced her to do it with a knife in one hand while holding her throat with the other. The judges did not insist on this point. The blasphemous utterances constituted the main offense. The *schout* demanded capital punishment, which the *schepenen* refused. They pronounced the following sentence: 'Willem Willemse de Boer is condemned to be brought onto the scaffold to be erected in front of the town hall of this city, to be exposed there for a while with a letter denoting his offense attached to his breast; to be exposed after this with a rope around his neck also for a certain time; then to be severely whipped and his tongue pierced with a burning awl; furthermore to be confined in the house of correction away from access by any people for ever.'[152]

Tongue-piercing was indeed an ancient penalty for blasphemy. This case was an isolated one. Together with the sentences of cheek-cutting, it is the only deformation of the face practiced in Amsterdam after 1650. And the latter penalty met with opposition from some of the *schepenen* in Bontemantel's time. The thumb-cuttings constitute the only other visible mutilations. Blinding and cutting off ears belong to an earlier period. I might add the practice of branding on the face, which disappeared in the middle of the sixteenth century. After 1650 it was unusual for a convict to be punished in such a way that he walked – or

76

stumbled – around the city afterwards with a visibly mutilated body. The prisoner had either to die or be injured in a less visible spot. Note that Willem Willemse de Boer was locked up for ever in that part of the rasphouse which was closed to visitors. In the second half of the eighteenth century Wagenaar was wholly unfamiliar with such penalties. He discussed pilgrimages and other 'peculiar punishments', to which he directly added the various forms of mutilation. 'These have all fallen out of use after 1578', Wagenaar commented.[153]

The implication is that revulsion against mutilation had increased between 1550 and 1650. The decline of deformations of the face and body is a trend in several European countries in the early modern period, although the exact chronology varies. In England mutilation was common under the Tudors.[154] It apparently became less so in the course of the seventeenth century. The *Parlement* of Paris reduced the frequency of sentences involving mutilation in the middle of the sixteenth century.[155] A more hesitant attitude is evident in Flanders in 1537, when a surgeon is present on the scaffold to instruct the executioner how to cut off a piece of the convict's hand.[156] In Frankfurt branding on the face continued, despite opposition, until the 1680s.[157] The trend towards the disappearance of disfigurement of persons staying alive clearly preceded the rise of an aversion against public executions in general. It forms part of the longer-term historical process of the decline of the physical content and public character of punishment.

4 REPRESSION, VIOLENCE AND THE STATE

As this chapter has been an attempt to get inside the minds of those in authority and look at the spectacle of public punishment through their eyes, it seems useful to draw up a brief preliminary conclusion on the relationships between executions and the state: between state formation and developments in repression, I should say, since my aim is to write a history reflecting change. From a static viewpoint things are clear enough. The representatives of the state saw the system of public executions as the pearl in the crown of repression. Harboring no particular revulsion against it, they considered violent treatment of delinquents who 'deserved it' only natural. From a developmental perspective the question must be put differently. What role did the staging of executions play in that phase of state formation processes in Western Europe that roughly coincided with the last centuries of preindustrial society?

Criminal justice emerged as a concomitant of the early beginnings of state formation. Nascent ruling groups expropriated private vengeance, so in the beginning there was violence. As the vendetta exercised by individual persons was violent, so was the state's revenge. Then there was exemplarity. I argued that it served a double purpose. It was supposed to frighten potential criminals and it warned against taking the law into one's own hands. Hence visible, violent repression exemplified a relative monopoly of authority. Since violence was still accepted in society to a large degree, it created no additional problems of injured sensibilities.

This all took place before the sixteenth century. The authorities in question were still relatively weak. The personal element in ruling was preponderant. This was not only true for counts, dukes and bishops governing a territory. City rulers were equally dependent on their personal prestige in the urban community. Rulers had to guarantee 'the peace' by their personal presence. This peace included a small amount of justice. Although trends towards depersonalization, with the concept of the country's peace (country meaning territory), appeared from an early date, a personal regime remained dominant throughout most of the early modern period. Changes which did take place included an enlargement of scale and a relative stabilization of state entities. But order depended on the king's peace. The prince governed his country as a *paterfamilias*. This relatively personal rule also applied to patrician states such as the Dutch and Venetian republics.

The early modern states represent an intermediary phase between the older territories and the later national–liberal states. They were more stable and pacified than those preceding them but less so than those following them. A system of justice worked but in practice it was still a marginal justice and the degree of public security, especially in the countryside, was still relatively low.[158] This makes the continued emphasis on personalistic rule and the demonstration of a monopoly of violence understandable. On the other hand, the transference of vengeance had more or less faded from memory. Revenge was no longer a primary motive in repression. Justice rather aimed at preserving the shaky balance of relative stability. Serious crimes were to a large extent defined as offending the sovereign. They impinged on the prince's peace, which was simultaneously the peace of the community. In the early modern personalistic states violent repression was considered a necessary reaction to serious breaches of the peace. Hence the emphasis was laid more on punishing crimes than on punishing criminals; more than in the later liberal states. One might say that a form of internally oriented *raison d'état* prevailed.

This *raison d'état* is expressed most revealingly in a few aspects of *ancien régime* justice which, to a modern mind, are particularly esoteric. One is the punishment of animals. Animals were put on trial and hanged, buried alive or burned by the executioner, accompanied by the normal ritual, because of specific injuries caused by them. Most known cases come from France, where they date back to the end of the thirteenth century. Before 1550 only Sardinia and Flanders enter into the picture. From the second half of the sixteenth century onwards cases were recorded in the Northern Netherlands, Germany, Sweden and Italy. The few cases after the seventeenth century are again confined to France.[159] In these trials the notion that a serious injury suffered by a member of the community should be followed by a penalty for the one causing it, who could not go unpunished, prevailed. Only gradually did the practice of fining the owner take its place. It was all very logical from the viewpoint of punishing crimes instead of criminals.

The punishment of suicide, noted in section two, springs from a similar attitude of mind. Any unnatural death implies a breach of the peace (except when the authorities themselves are the initiators as with capital punishment or in war). Even though the criminal is gone from this world the crime can still be punished. This applies to the offense of taking one's own life. Apart from the penalty mentioned for the Netherlands, the corpses of persons who had committed suicide could be burned, thrown into a river or pierced.[160]

If the delinquent has not gone from this world but is out of reach, a related problem arises. Execution in effigy is another custom deriving from the mentality discussed here. It was uncommon in the Northern Netherlands, but was practiced in several other countries, notably in France and French Canada. There the criminal ordinance of 1670 required that, when an absent delinquent was condemned to any form of the death penalty, an effigy should be fabricated to suffer the punishment at the hands of the executioner. In other cases the penalty was merely written on a board.[161]

But the Netherlands had a custom which perhaps expresses the *raison d'état* most tellingly. Courts regularly condemned persons to a simulated beheading. The penalty was executed in quite a realistic way, in imitation of the normal procedure for decapitation. The convict had to kneel on the scaffold in a heap of sand. His neck and shoulders were bare and his eyes blindfolded. The executioner waved the sword just above his head. Of course the sufferer knew this was going to happen: it was the pronounced sentence. In Amsterdam this penalty was imposed following serious physical injury, when a person had 'almost killed' another, and in a few cases of accidental death. A third type of occurrence for which sword over head could be imposed is the most interesting. The court records do not confer a name on this offense but it might be termed 'semi-homicide'. If a person was stabbed or knocked down and only died a few days later, the physicians who carried out the autopsy had to determine whether the injury caused the victim's death. Often they were not sure. In a more individualized system of justice the suspect would consequently be charged with inflicting grievous bodily harm. This was not so in Republican Amsterdam. If a person knocked down in the street later died, this constituted a serious breach of the peace. The crime had to be dealt with as homicide. Because the offender's guilt remained uncertain, he was punished for 'perhaps committing homicide'.[162] I do not want to argue that the judges thought public order depended directly on this procedure. But the triad of relative instability, personalistic rule and emphasis on the criminal act, as characteristics of the early modern state, gave rise to the mentality which produced this punishment.

These are some observations on the relationships between early modern repression and the early modern state. There is one more to be made. A salient feature of the ceremony of execution in many places was the presence of clerks and secretaries. Often they are explicitly mentioned in the descriptions. The state kept records and let it be known. It is a feature of repression which comes less into the foreground, but is still conspicuous. Having written records at its disposal enhances the efficacy of a court. This aspect of its power was also displayed, notably in the Dutch Republic where the larger cities employed a fair number of personnel but a central bureaucracy was less developed.

The ceremony and the staging of executions thus reflect a particular phase in state formation processes. The dynastic and patrician states of late preindustrial Europe needed a display of repression. They could not yet afford to hide it partly behind the scenes and to individualize it. On the other hand there was no rough-and-ready display. The ceremony implied a sense of the appropriate amount of decorum.

Chapter four

THE WATCHERS: SPECTATORS AT THE SCAFFOLD

The spectacle of suffering did not take place in a void. It would hardly have made sense for the magistrates to stage it if there were no audience. Spectators were indeed numerous. That public executions in pre-industrial Europe drew large audiences can be considered as one of the most undisputable 'facts' in history. Who were they? What did they come for? Did they play the passive and receptive part that the magistrates' scenario had accorded them? Answers to these questions would enhance our knowledge of the character of preindustrial society. But they are not easily given. As always, the sources are relatively silent on the anonymous masses. When they do speak, the reason is often an exceptional situation, such as a rebellion. Still they permit a few conclusions pertaining to the problems discussed here. The first section explores the frequency with which the public was confronted with executions. Section two treats its reactions to them in 'normal' situations, while the third discusses the relationships of executions and riots. With a few exceptions, the attitudes of the spectators will only be examined before 1750, because the emerging rejection of public executions after that date forms the subject of chapter six.

1 THE FREQUENCY OF EXECUTIONS

The degree to which individual people were familiar with executions depended of course also on the frequency with which they saw them. Three factors influence this frequency: first, the number of delinquents appearing before a court, which in its turn largely depends on the number of residents in a jurisdiction, second, the court's sentencing policy and, third, the number of persons brought to the scaffold simultaneously. Quantitative figures for these factors are available for Amsterdam after 1650. The particulars of repression form the subject of chapter five. Here I will briefly discuss the resulting frequency of executions.

Table 1. *Frequency of executions in Amsterdam, 1650–1810*

Decade	Number of justice days	Average number of convicts per justice day	Lowest number	Highest number
1651–1660	30	7.8	1	17
1661–1670	26	10.5	1	26
1671–1680	18	8.6	1	18
1681–1690	16	10.1	2	21
1711–1720	35	12.8	4	29
1721–1730	34	13.6	4	38
1731–1740	20	13.3	4	26
1741–1750	18	15.1	2	30
1751–1760	15	14.3	3	22
1761–1770	19	9.8	2	22
1771–1780	16	10.5	2	22
1781–1790	16	12.3	2	22
1791–1800	21	13.7	2	29
1801–1810	22	25.0	9	36

When an execution of scaffold punishments was scheduled in Amsterdam, people spoke of the justice day. On Dam Square in front of the town hall: that was 'doing justice'. The term was hardly ever applied by the public to the execution of other penalties, which again points to the central function of scaffold punishments. Convicts were seldom led to the scaffold immediately after their trial. Those who were additionally condemned to confinement, had already been taken to the house of correction. Others awaited their chastisement in provisional detention in cells under the town hall. The Amsterdam court 'saved up' its convicts. Hence in principle the frequency of justice days resulted from decisions taken by the magistrates.

Table 1 shows that the frequency declined between 1650 and 1690.[1] For the two decades after 1690 the sources do not allow a quantitative reconstruction. Between 1710 and 1730 the number is again high and then it stabilizes more or less at the level of the later seventeenth century. There are no dramatic contrasts. Throughout the period the number of justice days fluctuates between one and four a year. Per decade the average number of convicts mounting the scaffold does not yield a pattern at all. Before 1800 it fluctuates between extremes of about eight and about fifteen people; these averages, however, conceal the reality of a broad range. This is borne out by the last two columns. Every decade witnessed at least one 'mini-execution' with from one to four convicts. Usually it involved special cases and/or notorious people: famous robbers, a lord of a manor, rebels. Almost always they received capital punishment. The larger executions result rather from concentrations of 'normal' delinquents. Between 1750 and 1790 it looks as if the magistrates consciously held on to a maximum number of convicts. The last decade stands out as exceptional. There is no mini-execution and the average number of convicts is excessively high.

The justice day was always scheduled with great care. Two weeks in advance the *schout* of Amsterdam wrote to the executioner in Haarlem, requesting him to reserve the day. He also informed his colleague there. On the day preceding the execution he sent a servant to confirm it. According to old custom, this servant carried a note revealing whether or not the hangman was to bring a sword.[2] Bontemantel suggests that the court normally waited until it had saved up a certain number of delinquents. The day is fixed, he says, 'when the number of sentences (. . .) has reached a fair amount or when it is judged advisable for other reasons'.[3] Although many executions included one or more delinquents under capital sentence and these had usually been pronounced two days before, capital convicts could be left waiting too. Sentencing them two days before the execution was simply customary. In such cases there was often a pause of several months between their confession and the judgment. Nevertheless the desire for a justice day to include capital cases is evident. It is explicitly revealed in one of the messages from the *schout* to the executioner. On 21 April 1725 he informed the latter that an execution had been scheduled for 5 May. However, 'for this justice I will present only one delinquent for a capital punishment and if my demand is rejected, *it might be that the public justice is postponed*'. The *schout* promised to let the executioner know in that case immediately on 3 May.[4]

It is plain that any resident of Amsterdam could have witnessed many executions during his lifetime. But Amsterdam was a metropolis. Its court handled large numbers of delinquents who were to be punished on the scaffold. Even the Court of Holland had only a fraction of Amsterdam's numbers. The frequency of justice days in smaller towns and rural districts must have been much lower. There is some information on a few sample jurisdictions in the Dutch Republic. The number of public penalties was much lower there. In the bailiwick of Waterland they amounted to seventy-five between 1700 and 1811. In Wassenaar there are thirteen known cases during the same period. The actual number may have been a little higher, because in about 30% of the trials the judgment was not recorded. But Wassenaar still has the lowest number of the regions concerned. The middle-sized town of Breda had the highest number: 224 public penalties between 1700 and 1795. These were nearly always separate cases and, the numbers being so small, there can have been no point in saving up convicts. Still there were a few parties of accomplices, so that the number of justice days was lower than the total of public penalties. In Waterland, moreover, the execution took place in one of its six villages, the one where the convict had been apprehended. The spectacle of capital punishment was even rarer in these jurisdictions. The Wassenaar court pronounced no death sentence at all during the eighteenth century. That of Heerlen condemned a relatively high number of people (forty-one) to death, but this is due to robber bands operating in the area. The number of public penalties also differs according to jurisdiction, if we consider it as a percentage of the total punishments. This percentage varied from fifty in Waterland to nine in Wassenaar. Apparently the prosecution and sentencing policies of the various courts were different as well.[5]

Of course the inhabitants of rural areas could go to a town. Waterland was situated just across the Y to the North of Amsterdam. Wassenaar lay close to The Hague. No doubt executions in the cities attracted people from outside. In the second half of the eighteenth century Amsterdam used to close its gates on a justice day, to prevent an influx of people.[6] This phenomenon is not peculiar to the eighteenth century. The magistrates of Middelburg stated in 1555 that a multitude of foreign sailors would come from the harbor into the town when capital justice was done.[7] Notable executions were of course publicized in advance. When Damiens was to be executed in Paris, spectators streamed in from the surrounding villages, from remote provinces and even from abroad.[8] A newspaper in Berlin provided its readers with the details on the following day.[9]

The literature on criminality does not yield comparable quantitative information for other European countries. No doubt the situation varied, depending on jurisdictional organization and penal practices. The Dutch evidence permits us to draw one conclusion. The crowds watching executions in preindustrial Europe were mainly composed of city-dwellers; at least in the seventeenth and eighteenth centuries. We have become accustomed to regarding urban residents as the bearers of 'modernization'. Therefore it is necessary to realize that they were more familiar than rural people with a 'premodern' phenomenon such as public executions. Of course this is not to say that the latter were not familiar with them at all.

84

A few other data bear on the relationship of town–countryside. Many rural districts, for instance, did not have their own executioner. In the seventeenth and eighteenth centuries it meant he had to come from elsewhere. This could be a problem, as in the bailiwick of Nieuwburgen in the extremely severe winter of 1697–8.[10] A group of gypsies had negotiated a lodging in the village church of Mijzen. But they broke up fences and bridges to make a fire. Six were arrested, including two boys of twelve who were sentenced to exposure with rods. Four men were originally condemned to public whipping, but the hangman was unable to come because of impassable roads. So their penalty was commuted into whipping indoors, which could be done by a servant of the court.[11] The case shows that rural judges might not be persistent in having a scaffold punishment executed, which further reduced the frequency of public justice in the countryside. The larger cities in Europe would normally have an executioner at their disposal.

Amsterdam was an exception in this, but only a partial one. The city had its indoor executioner, who did not necessarily have to remain indoors. It was a logical adjustment for the metropolis. The city's executioner's main tasks were the practice of torture and the administering of whipping indoors. His public tasks included putting persons on the pillory and occasionally burning a prohibited book or dragging a criminal's corpse to the gallows field after suicide. He was also called upon for executions after rebellions (see below, section 3). Hence the court of Amsterdam could administer public justice whenever it wanted to.

A case in Danzig reveals a curious possibility for making the spectacle of suffering frequent, independent of the number of convicts. In 1663 the court condemned a thief to be whipped on the pillory at 9.0 a.m. every Saturday for the rest of his life.[12] This, however, is an exceptional case and after all Danzig was a city. One also wonders whether the man in question kept turning up each Saturday at the required time.

It should be noted, finally, that in Amsterdam the justice day was not the only occasion for witnessing public punishment. Exposure on the pillory constituted another possibility. This had once been a penalty in which the public played an important role. In the later Middle Ages those present were allowed to throw rotten fruit, mud or dung, as in a law of Dover. A cutpurse was set in the pillory there 'and all the people that will come there may do hym vylonye'.[13] It is a survival of justice by the community. This is especially clear in the cited case, where the public was also allowed to cut off one ear. Public participation had a longer history in some places. In eighteenth-century Halle (Germany) it was even said that manure was made available by order of the council. In Hamburg, on the other hand, there is no mention of public participation.[14]

Amsterdam resembled Hamburg in this respect. All sources are silent about throwing objects, from which we may no doubt infer that it did not happen, or, at least, was prohibited. Exposure had become a routine punishment. There was no block in which the condemned had to put his head. The pillory was simply a mini-scaffold attached to the wall of the town hall. The intended penal function of exposure lay in its humiliating effect. The execution of the penalty usually followed directly upon the sentence and was not accompanied by a ceremony. It does not appear to have been high ranking in the public's interest. After 1700 it was practiced very infrequently. Most sentences of simple exposure were executed on the scaffold then. In the middle of the eighteenth century those exposed on the pillory were mainly procurers, prostitutes and bigamists. Bicker Raye recorded these cases in his diary. He makes no additional comments, save on a few occasions when the condemned committed impertinent acts: one prostitute took a pinch of snuff; another lifted her skirts so high that everyone saw her bare buttocks.[15]

On some rare occasions a court martial had its sentences executed in Amsterdam. Bontemantel tells us of an occasion in 1672, when prisoners of war were probably involved.[16] In 1744 Raye recorded that a soldier ran the gauntlet in the city. 'This has not been done here in fifty years', he commented. He mentions two more such cases, in 1754 and in 1767. The latter case involved a soldier who had deserted for the third time. He had to run up and down the rows of 300 men five times, so he received 3,000 lashes, as Raye duly counted. Not a piece of skin was left on his back.[17]

Finally, there is a source suggesting that the inhabitants of Amsterdam were also mimetically confronted with corporal punishment. William Mountague says that the magistrates issued a special warning to those cherishing vandalistic or thievish plans for the nocturnal street-lights. '[They] have in several places set up on Board painted neatly, The executioner whipping some and cutting off the hands of others for those crimes, which, by this means, are rarely heard of.'[18] It is a threat, with a more severe penalty than ordinarily practiced for such an offense, which was a common policy.

The execution of punishments on the justice day remains the most important. It is there that we must look for crowds.

2 FAMILIARITY WITH EXECUTIONS

Even though the larger cities are the main objects of our attention, we should not infer from this that people outside them were unfamiliar with public justice. Most inhabitants of rural areas would witness the spectacle of punishment once or more during their lifetime. Things and events connected with it were well known. In general, we may say that preindustrial people were familiar with the existence of public executions. These were part of life for them and on the whole were not considered as objectionable.

Although this section is about familiarity, we have to start with fear. Throughout the early modern period there are reports of people being afraid of the scaffold and the standing gallows. Notably, it was held that whoever touched these became infamous. It was the same sort of fear as that regarding the executioner. I noted in chapter two that infamy was extended from the executioner to his equipment, to the scaffold and to the convict. Finally everything and everyone connected with the exercise of public justice was tainted. I also argued which mentality sustained this notion. It is not necessary to repeat the thesis. The expressions of this fear will only be touched on briefly.

It came to the surface most clearly when a new scaffold or gallows had to be built. Artisans did not want to touch the material and wished to stay away from the site of execution. Often they simply refused to carry out the charge. This attitude left the authorities with a problem. They had to find ways to force the craftsmen. One means was legal coercion. Thus Charles V's criminal ordinance of 1532, the Carolina, determined that the tasks should be assigned by lot, but this often met with opposition. A common solution in smaller places was to let every artisan participate. The idea was that if all became tainted, none were really infamous. Usually this was not enough, and the fear of those participating had to be further neutralized. So the authorities turned the construction of a new gallows into another ceremony, in which they themselves were involved. Often the citizenry accompanied it with pipes and drums, while musicians played. The site was temporarily declared 'honest' by the magistrates, who repeated afterwards that every participant had retained his honor. Such a ceremony sometimes took place even when it was merely a matter of cutting wood for a new gallows.[19]

In this way the building of a new gallows often became an occasion for festivity. Although originally those involved may indeed have wished to express their gladness at the retention of their honor, we may wonder if their great-grandchildren simply saw it as a traditional occasion for feasting. In the small town of Ansbach, for instance, in 1798 the repair work at the place of execution did not look like a serious business at all. Not only was music played for three days, but people had even danced beside the gallows. Because a number of citizens – probably from the middle classes – had complained, the Prussian government reproached the local magistrates. It was willing to forgive them for tolerating 'the ridiculous ceremonies of the artisans', which apparently had no function in the eyes of the government at the time. But the dancing constituted a contempt of justice; it was 'a subversion of the actual purpose of the death penalty'.[20] The magistrates defended themselves by saying that the ceremony, including the music, was common everywhere and that prohibition of the festivities would have caused an uproar. They denied that people had danced.[21]

Most examples of this fear of the scaffold come from the German countries. As suggested before, the notion of infamy was especially influential in Germany. In the Netherlands we hear less of it. When artisans were building a new gallows in Amersfoort in 1550 and again in 1558, there was no talk of a ceremony.[22] The same is true for Nijmegen in 1611.[23] And in Amsterdam I found no evidence of a fear of the scaffold either. It was erected on the eve of the justice day and removed afterwards. An early eighteenth-century manuscript says that it used to be built up by the city's carpenters. Burgomasters simply gave the order to carry out this task to their 'master-servant', apparently without further ado.[24] At the end of the century one Philippus Bax was regularly paid three guilders for building up the scaffold. He was one of the city's carpenters, although not the master-servant.[25]

And yet the infamy of public justice was a reality in the Netherlands too. In 1710 it became known that a Zutphen midwife had been whipped on the scaffold in Leeuwarden twenty-six years earlier. The fact caused a serious commotion. People refused her services and to restore the peace the magistrates were forced to forbid her ever to assist a pregnant woman again.[26] The notion of infamy may even have had an echo much later, on the other side of the Atlantic. The electric chair was introduced in New York in 1889. Many electrical companies protested. They argued that it would make the public think that electricity was too dangerous for ordinary use.[27] One wonders if subconsciously they feared that electricity might become 'infamous'.

More research could clarify geographical and chronological variations regarding the fear of the scaffold and the gallows. For present purposes it is enough to conclude that the existence of this fear does not contradict my thesis. It did not preclude the acceptance of violence in the form of public justice by the majority throughout most of the preindustrial period. There was a very specific fear of touching everything connected with punishment on the scaffold. But people largely appreciated what was done there. The dancing and merry-making near the gallows actually point to a familiarity with it. The festivities do not reveal a particular sense of delicacy, although the authorities regretted that the necessary awe for justice was absent.

Before we turn to a discussion of reactions to the actual executions we should consider the attitudes towards the bodies of those capitally executed. If these were exposed, the intended function was to warn potential offenders. The authorities, who in no way identified with the delinquents they hanged, thinking they deserved it, believed that others did identify. The underlying assumption is that a living criminal would recognize the corpse as 'one of his own'. He would think 'this is a thief, I am a thief; let me stop stealing so that I won't hang there too'. But we cannot be sure that this is what actually happened. Picaresque novels occasionally suggest that such a feeling did not prevail.[28] A certain degree of identification may have existed in the sense that people felt pity for an unfortunate colleague. But they also experienced gladness at not being executed themselves. A person from the underworld might think 'my dear friend, seeing you hanging there means I am still alive'.

Nevertheless, convicts did have relatives and real friends. Indeed, the humiliation which attached to public punishment was held to descend partly on their families too. This principle undoubtedly had more effect in small rural communities than in a metropolis with a large floating population. We are informed about one such metropolis, London, in Linebaugh's account of the hangings at Tyburn. The crucial question there was not whether the corpses should be hanged in chains, but whether they would go to the anatomy room. In the middle of the eighteenth century the surgeons' guild was authorized to take away a few bodies after each hanging. But it had to find its own means of getting them. The thought of ending up on the anatomy table was usually unbearable for the convict. Often he could mobilize relatives, workmates or old friends. Hence fights over the body frequently occurred between his sympathizers and the servants of the guild. People would come to the execution from afar to prevent their comrade falling into the hands of the surgeons.[29]

In England popular feelings were relatively strong on this point. In the Dutch Republic there is no evidence that it caused great concern, although it was known that some convicts were taken to the anatomy room. Bicker Raye occasionally recorded this in his diary. The Amsterdam court did not regard it as part of the penalty and hence did not insert it in the sentence.[30] The difference with London lies in the fact that at Tyburn the bodies were simply cut loose after a while and left for whoever cared to take them. In Amsterdam the executioner remained in control and either put the body in a coffin or prepared it for transport to the gallows field. In the former instance the coffin was handed over to relatives or friends for burial. It may be that the surgeons only received a corpse if no one turned up to claim it. The sources are silent on the procedure.

The most fateful thing that could happen to one's body on the Continent was its exposure on the gallows mountain or field. This could hardly be prevented by comrades. When imposed, it was part of the punishment and as such was held to constitute extra pain for the delinquent. He must have dreaded it, just as the London delinquents feared the anatomy room. Still, it seems to have been hard to mobilize comrades for a circumvention of justice. In Amsterdam I found only one reference suggesting this. In 1689 the court issued a notification that a reward awaited those whose information led to the apprehension of a peculiar brand of thieves. Unknown persons had stolen the corpse of Jacob Brouwer, executed four days earlier, from the gallows field.[31] Since the thieves were not caught, their motives are also unknown. But they may have been friends who took the body to bury it.

The extra pain for the convict lay, so it has always been said, in the infamous condition of not being buried. The thought of being 'carrion for the birds' must surely have been at least as dreadful as that of being cut up by the surgeons. Yet there may have been more to it. Recent literature on attitudes towards death tells us about the central importance of the location of the cemetery.[32] Well into the eighteenth century most people laid great value on being buried in their own community.[33] Their place of internment should be in a sacred spot within the walls of the town. The standing gallows was situated outside the walls. Hence one's body was eternally banished. This aspect of its exposure must have been dreaded as well.

Outside the circle of relatives and friends though, no one seems to have cared. Occasionally the placing of a corpse on the gallows field in Amsterdam attracted spectators too. A multitude was watching when the various parts of Hendrina Wouters' body (see pp. 65–6) were brought to the Volewijk in December 1746. It was the second notorious corpse to be placed there within a short period of time, a Jew having been broken on the wheel three months before. The crowd was treated to an unusual spectacle. One of their number had 'the audacity to come to the Volewijk and climb on the wheel where sits that *smous* broken on the wheel on September 3'.[34] Among other jokes he embraced the corpse, saying, 'How do you do?' The executioner summoned him to leave. He refused at first, but quickly slipped away when the hangman tried to fasten him to the wheel with an iron chain, along with the corpse. Since his name was known, he came into the hands of the *schout* after all. His family, it was said, made it up with the latter for money. But he was a corn-measurer and his colleagues did not want to work with him any more, because he had made himself infamous by sitting on a wheel on the Volewijk.[35]

Thus, when a person came that close to the equipment of justice, infamy entered the picture. This also emerges from a decision of burgomasters in 1759. There had been no capital execution during most of the 1750s and apparently in the meantime the hangman had managed to shed the task of transporting corpses. Burgomasters were confronted with the fact that no one was prepared to undertake this transport. They ordered the Buiksloter ferrymen to carry the bodies in the cow-boat. Transport over land was entrusted to Willem Evertsen, the city's horse-skinner.[36]

The argumentation put forward above applies to these stories. Touching can lead to infamy, but apart from that hardly anyone seems to care. According to Wagenaar, the only dwelling on the Volewijk, the toll-house, served as a tavern. Without mentioning the corpses, he speaks of the 'nice view of the city and the vessels in the Y' from there.[37] On the other side the 'new city inn' stood on a pier stretching into the Y. It offered a view of the ships and the gallows.[38] A few pictures from the seventeenth and eighteenth centuries show the Volewijk in winter. Men and women are skating on the frozen Y.[39] Along the shore of the Volewijk there are *koek-en-zopie-tenten* (stalls with cakes and drinks). The customers do not even seem to notice the gallows behind them. A few others walk at the foot of the gallows and point at the corpses. No one looks embarrassed by the sight.

The examples of people walking along the gallows field make largely for stories of indifference. They saw the corpses and did not care. It is different with the actual executions. Then the crowd came specially to watch the spectacle and did not want to miss a minute. As noted above, public justice always drew a large number of spectators. In Hogarth's picture of the 'Hanging of Tom Idle' they struggle for a good place.[40] At Tyburn lamplighters erected their ladders and allowed customers to mount them for two or three pence.[41] When a hanging in 1758 was postponed at the last minute, a brawl ensued between the lamplighters, who had already been paid, and the disappointed customers, who demanded their money back. The angry crowd grabbed a servant of the court and hanged him with a rope under his armpits on the triple-tree. Colleagues released him after ten minutes.[42]

For the Netherlands one can refer to the etchings by Jan Luyken. All of them teem with people in front of the scaffold. Dozens are sitting on the roofs of the houses and churches.[43] Bicker Raye provides verbal testimony for Amsterdam, mentioning two occasions, apart from executions, when crowds assembled: in 1743 for the funeral of burgomaster Lieven Geelvink and in 1747 for the acclamation of William IV as *stadholder*. In both cases Raye notes that 'Dam Square was as crowded as if justice were done.'[44]

It is hard to be specific about the identity of the spectators. Contemporaries who refer to them are usually middle or upper class. They employ words such as 'mob' or similar terms. Thus William Mountague commented on Amsterdam executions: 'Vast was the number of Spectators (as always is both there and everywhere else at such unpleasant Sights), beyond what we ever saw, and most Mob, or *Jean Hagel* as they call 'em, or *John Hail*, or *Canalia*, or Canals, Sinks of Filth, etc.'[45] It is a whole litany, containing pejorative expressions for a lower-class multitude in three languages. Nevertheless Mountague himself was there too, as were other elite commentators. Bicker Raye gives a tiny clue once. On a justice day in 1749 the activities of a pickpocket generated a sudden commotion. A panic ensued and many persons were trampled. There were no casualties but afterwards the square was full of hats, wigs, caps, slippers and shoes.[46] We are at the height of the 'age of wigs', but even then those who wore them were certainly not lower class. From the work of Rudé and others we know that rioting crowds, often designated as mobs by contemporaries, actually consisted of persons from various social strata.[47] This probably also applies to the crowds watching executions. But exact percentages will certainly never be known.

Apart from cases of executions following riots and of bungling hangmen, there is not much evidence that the spectators behaved contrary to the wishes of the authorities. From the silence of the Amsterdam sources we can infer that the public was usually passive. It may have been different in eighteenth-century London. According to Bernard Mandeville, the crowd at Tyburn often refused to play the game according to the directions of the magistrates. People cheered the convicts and gave them drinks on their way to the gallows. He even blamed this situation for causing a crime wave in the 1720s.[48] Another example of a reversed partiality on the part of the public comes from Seville a century and a half earlier. A boy of seventeen had been condemned to death for murder, innocently, so people thought. Public opinion was apparently feared so much that the execution was postponed. Eventually the sentence was commuted to a few years on the galleys.[49]

But the spectators in Seville normally acted in an appreciative fashion too. The assisting priest often received compliments for his speeches. Nevertheless the crowd's reaction was ambivalent in a case of intervention. When a person was capitally punished for sodomy, the priest addressed himself to the public with the following moral: of course this is a great crime, but it does not mean that men are free to sin with women. Someone in the audience felt that too many sins were denounced at once. He exclaimed: 'What is it then that you want, Father?' He added some indecent remarks. The other spectators were reported to have been indignant at this impertinence. No one, however, betrayed the interrupter.[50]

Those defying the magistrates' purposes most clearly were of course the pickpockets. It is not surprising that a large assembly of people, such as an execution crowd, would attract them. They must have been endemic at Tyburn. As related above, Amsterdam was no stranger to their activities either. The presence of pickpockets plainly suggests that the example of punishment did not intimidate every potential delinquent. The magistrates themselves knew this too. In the sentence of an Italian counterfeiter, beheaded in Amsterdam in 1676, it was noted that, when he had just arrived in the city with his plans for making false coins, a compatriot had told him about the recent decapitation of another counterfeiter.[51]

In picaresque novels the attitude towards executions is usually ambivalent as well. Characters break down the awesomeness of public justice by speaking of it lightly and in cant words. An example of the genre in the Dutch Republic is the book published in 1700 by Gerrit van Spaan, a Rotterdam baker.[52] His hero contemplated life when he saw the scaffold in The Hague, and he visited Amsterdam on a justice day. He confers his own names on various physical penalties. Being whipped becomes 'dancing the Spanish *gaillarde*'. Someone hanged 'climbs a double ladder and makes a *faux pas* on the way'. A branded person is made 'arms-bearer of the city'. The executioner practicing torture, is called a 'chimney-sweep'.[53] There is no opposition to the system of physical punishments. These are part of life, which is sometimes hard. But the hero expresses a certain degree of identification with the condemned on the scaffold, in the sense that the reader can feel him imagining how he would stand it himself. The bravery inherent in enduring a corporal penalty, when it occurred, seems to have indeed been admired by the spectators. At least they commented on it, as Bicker Raye occasionally recorded.

An author could display his irony about public justice in other ways as well. In an early seventeenth-century Spanish picaresque novel a convict climbing the ladder notices that a rung is broken. He turns to the judge, advising him to have it fixed, because not everyone has such a sharp eye. Additionally the author accuses the pastry-bakers of mixing the condemned's flesh into their pasties.[54] The use of cant, however, was the most common way. It is a feature of many European languages.[55] Linebaugh, speaking of eighteenth-century London, goes so far as to state that 'the speech of the labouring class described the hanging with irreverence, humour and defiance'.[56] Although picaresque novels were not only read by rogues and cant may have been widely known, it remains to be seen whether this defiant attitude was characteristic for the lower classes as a whole. Linebaugh's assumption, for which he gives no further proof, is apparently an attempt to bolster up the 'conflict theory of crime'.[57]

In contrast to this popular language hangmen invented words which take us to the other extreme. The executioner of eighteenth-century Hamburg described his craft in almost academic terms. Branding becomes 'making an adorning design'; the right way of torturing is 'a clever reallocation of limbs'.[58]

Picaresque literature and the language of cant belong to popular culture, a subject recently taken up by historians.[59] Peter Burke devotes a few pages to a comparison between official executions and the rituals of popular justice. Just as official justice was often meant to make the convict infamous, so the charivari implied a public defamation. In addition, there are hangings and burnings in effigy, which both systems had in common.[60] But there were more rituals than Burke notes. In the German countries popular Pentecost plays frequently included a trial and execution. In Wurmlingen the climax was constituted by the mock decapitation of the person who had been the last to get up in the morning. When a church was inaugurated in Eastern Bohemia, a ram was beheaded by an 'executioner'.[61] The intersections of public justice and popular culture still offer a promising field for research.[62] Our preliminary conclusion can be that these too point at the people's familiarity with executions.

The pamphlet and broadside culture, already discussed in the previous chapter, is usually classified among popular forms as well. Although I

94

noted that many are set in the moralistic tone of the authorities, this is not necessarily true of all. Here is another subject which still needs to be investigated more thoroughly. Speaking of broadsides in general, Much-embled argued that printed pamphlets represent the conquest of popular by elite culture. This would suggest that broadsheets and chapbooks on executions espouse the view of the established classes. Burke, on the other hand, argues that the advent of printing initially made for the very zenith of popular culture.[63]

In eighteenth-century London the market for accounts of criminals' lives was so good that the condemned often sold their biography to the highest-bidding prospective author.[64] We may suppose that the buyers wished to indulge in crime stories rather than in edification. But other pamphlets merely demonstrated the inevitability of justice.[65] A Dutch four-page broadside contains two songs. The first is about a woman, garrotted in 1788 for killing her child and was to be sung to the melody of 'O Holland beautiful'. The second is an elegy on 'His Highness William V'.[66] On the other hand, some songs about executions were apparently disliked by the authorities. In February 1703 a sailor was fined six guilders in Amsterdam for 'singing the prohibited song about the justice done to Hiddo Grittinga and Helena Knoop'.[67] This song and others may never have been printed. They were performed by wandering artists at fairs. A painted canvas, representing the execution, often formed the background. This custom was recorded in the Netherlands and Germany from the middle of the seventeenth century onwards.[68]

A special feature of the public's familiarity with executions is the possibility these offered for an indirect suicide. A person did not necessarily have to commit a capital crime to achieve this. To confess one might be enough. There were people who deliberately sought a death on the scaffold. The Amsterdam judicial archive yields two authentic cases. They came to light because the judges did not believe the stories.

In 1653 Adriaan Struis was whipped with the rope around his neck for a burglary and a few thefts. In addition, the sentence says he had 'misled justice by deceitfully stating to have committed a manslaughter'.[69] This is a slightly ambiguous case. Adriaan had later declared that he thought he would be hanged for his burglary and that he preferred to be beheaded.[70] The story of Andries Jansen, twelve years later, is less ambiguous. He was flogged as well. During his interrogation he had claimed to have stabbed a person to death in the city on a summer's night four years before. To this confession he added that he would rather die by the executioner's hands than go to the rasphouse.[71] Later he admitted 'to have said it out of desperation, because he was tired of his life'. Again it was recorded in the sentence as 'big lies' and a deceit of justice.[72] Apparently the authorities had no empathy for this sort of act of desperation. It is not quite clear what we should make of the fact that they were included in the sentences. Occasionally the court did exclude a sensational part of the confession, if the judges thought it would give people ideas or cause commotion. It may be that this form of indirect suicide was already well known as a possibility and that the court merely wished to discourage it.

It has been claimed that a number of American capital convicts in the twentieth century had deliberately sought their own death.[73] If true, these cases are different from the preindustrial ones cited. Not only do they involve real murderers, but they belong to a period when capital punishment was executed indoors. Scruples against suicide constituted the major motive. The prototype and perhaps the first to put this idea into practice – though without success – was James Hadfield, who shot at George III in order to be executed himself.[74] It is questionable whether the Amsterdam death-seekers chose this form from scruples against suicide. The indirect way was condemned by the church too. A comforter of the sick explained to Adriaan Struis that he would be 'a murderer of himself', if he were executed for a confessed but uncommitted crime.[75] It made him yield. We do not know how many persons attempted an indirect suicide in this way and were successful. The two prisoners may merely have chosen this variant because they were in the hands of justice anyway. But we should not forget that, during the period when they were public, executions must have had a greater appeal to persons contemplating suicide. Nowadays there are still individuals who choose a dramatic end to their life. The drama of execution offered preindustrial people a unique opportunity.

Familiarity with executions also found its expression in the self-evident way in which children were confronted with them. There are two angles from which we can view this phenomenon: attitudes towards violence and attitudes towards childhood. Although the two can be treated separately, in the end they belong to the same historical development. Up into the sixteenth century at least, children were not handled as special persons. On the one hand they were subject to an almost absolute authority: social distance between parents and children was enormous. On the other hand, the latter learnt about the facts of life at an early age: psychological distance between adults and the young was relatively small. From the sixteenth century onwards this situation slowly began to reverse. The historiography of the family makes this abundantly clear, so that there is no need to dwell on it.[76] What remains to be emphasized is that the evolution of the family forms part of that more general process of transformation of people's psychic make-up. Aspects of human existence such as violence, sexuality, death, bodily functions gradually came to be hidden behind the scenes of social life. The 'area behind these scenes' was not a space which had always been there and simply needed to be 'filled up'. It developed along with the hiding process itself and the domesticated nuclear family became one such enclosed space. The creation of a children's world from which emotionally laden aspects of life were largely excluded is one of the manifestations of the process whereby these aspects became problematic *tout court*.[77]

The chronological order of things is certainly not monolithic. In some areas of life the concealment from children may have been a first step towards a general closing of the curtains. In the case of executions it rather seems that children were kept away from them only after public justice had become problematic. In the eighteenth century youngsters were still confronted with physical punishment as a matter of course. Just as the authorities intended executions to serve as an example, so parents used them as an educational tool. A father would say to his son: 'Take a good look; this is what will happen to you, if you stray from the right path.' In two late eighteenth-century drawings, made by different artists and representing Amsterdam's gallows field, we see adults calling a child's attention to the hanged corpses and those tied on a wheel. I am not quite sure what I should make of a remark by Le Francq van Berkhey. He says that when Amsterdam parents reply to their children's question of where their new brother or sister comes from, they tell them: 'Mother has been to the Volewijk.'[78]

Some of the moralistic pamphlets about crime and punishment were expressly meant for children: simple broadsheets with pictures and a few lines of text. One of them treats the proceedings of justice in six plates: the court-building, the spin and rasphouses, a woman whipped for a petty theft, a recidivist branded and a persistent criminal hanged. Above it says: 'Children, read this print and learn to fear evil from childhood.'[79]

Even in the early nineteenth century Dutch books with children's verses speak of executions. The tone has changed though, because the youngsters are definitely expected to be shocked. Nevertheless, they have to witness punishment. In an undated verse by 'Uncle Diederik' a father puts his son on his shoulders to see a beheading. The boy faints.[80] Another boy in 1808 tells the reader that he watched a man being flogged. It hurt the child from the first lash to the last, but the father retorts: 'Justice, my son, is severe but by no means cruel.'[81] A book published in

97

1823 contains the verse 'the whipping', to be sung to the melody of the national anthem. Jan is quite upset by what he saw on the scaffold: the convict's moaning, his ravaged back and his blood. The author concludes that Jan 'had seen that God punishes evil terribly. And O! What was his fate. The rest of his life was honest.'[82]

Children were indeed still taken to executions in the early nineteenth century. In the Netherlands as well as in Germany schools often closed on a justice day.[83] In the previous chapter I noted that schoolchildren sang songs of death at an execution in Clingen in 1820. This may have been one of the last of such happenings. At the same time the authorities in Southern Germany were attempting to suppress this custom. But the youths were still given a proper place among the crowd to watch the spectacle. Only in the middle of the century did the magistrates advise the schools to stay open, in order to prevent the children from watching the execution.[84]

This section concludes with a few literary renderings and eyewitness accounts of executions in the Netherlands. These too point at a familiarity largely unhampered by feelings of repugnance. At the beginning of the seventeenth century there is the voice of Jacob Cats, grand pensionary and poet. He used the story of a whipped delinquent as a parable: the thief prays for mercy, not to the executioner but to the judge. Right, said Cats. In the same way, if a person slanders you, you should not direct yourself to him. He has merely been sent by God who found it necessary to punish you. The opening lines betray that Cats considered a public whipping as a self-evident event: 'A while ago I came unto where a thief had to receive his punishment / after the sentence had been pronounced against him / I saw his body being beaten with rods / and his whole back being in a bad condition.'[85]

In the middle of the century another patrician, Constantin Huygens, touched on the subject. I referred to his views on the executioner in chapter two. Incidentally Huygens denounced the spectators at the scaffold: many are stupid. Their hearts are smothered and their minds narrow.[86] Apparently Huygens disliked the eagerness with which the lower-class spectators watched the execution. This was certainly the case with William Mountague, as emerges from the quotation above. In addition he referred to the execution as an unpleasant sight. This may reflect a certain ambivalence of feeling among the upper classes, which had already taken root at the end of the seventeenth century. The question will be explored further in chapter six. Repugnance among the elites was probably concentrated on their perception of the watching crowd. Mountague's feelings must have been shared by his Amsterdam hosts, since they taught him the Dutch expression *janhagel*, which is a derogatory word referring to the lower classes.

A work specifically devoted to public justice was written by Lambert van den Bosch and published in 1698. It is about murders and executions of famous people throughout history. We meet, among others, Johan van Oldenbarnevelt and Charles I of England. The preface sets the general tone of the book: when princes and great men end up on the scaffold, this is a tragic event worthy of literary commemoration. But the existence of scaffolds as such is a matter of course which does not deserve special notice.[87] That normal executions were not tragic events was confirmed a year later by the Strasbourg merchant Johann Zetzner. He was in Amsterdam on a justice day and described the execution without being affected.[88]

In his young years Coenraad Droste found himself affected just a little. He was a retired officer in The Hague, who wrote his memoirs around 1720. He speaks of witnessing his first execution in France in 1664. A deserter was shot by a firing squad consisting of three men: 'I saw the blood flowing from the wounds not without fright / Though unaffected I have seen military men being shot afterwards / That is the difference between young and old soldier / Fear comes unto the one and does not arise in the other.'[89]

In the middle of the eighteenth century Jacob Bicker Raye was present at almost every justice day in Amsterdam. He was an observer *par excellence*, which is why he enters these pages so often. No doubt he had a particular interest in justice, but his accounts of executions do not betray any sort of special liking for them. He registers in a factual manner and hardly displays any emotion. He pitied someone only once, in the case of the man who was not a thief by nature.[90]

Raye's contemporary Abraham Chaim Braatbard appears again as a more ambivalent man. His Yiddish chronicle of Amsterdam covers the years 1740–52 and contains a few passages on executions. Braatbard employed emotional words on two occasions, when Christians were put to death. Hendrina Wouters' execution is called '*grûzam*' and in connection with the hangings after the Tax Farmers Rebellion he uses the verb '*zar*' (to shudder).[91]

Thus we see that a certain ambivalence about public justice was already present in the period between 1650 and 1750. Some people did not care at all, while others occasionally displayed emotion. But a general feeling of repugnance was absent. No one opposed the system. A more radical transformation of sensibilities had not yet taken place.

99

3 EXECUTIONS AND RIOTS

The most obvious reason why an audience was not appreciative was because the actions of another crowd had led to the execution. Public justice could follow upon all sorts of riots from relatively minor labor conflicts to full-scale and temporarily successful rebellions. These executions were always precarious events. They caused continued or renewed restiveness and harbored the danger of a flaring up of violence, if not actual resistance. Therefore they merit special attention.

The earliest forms of resistance by the public were discussed in chapter two. From the beginning assaults on bungling hangmen had alerted the authorities to the possibility that an execution could be disturbed. A book treating court proceedings in Amsterdam, published in 1700, states: in the past the *schout* always warned the public not to riot or prevent the execution; but this is no longer customary.[92] The formula appears in the eighteenth-century books of ceremonies and is said to be 'an old address to the commonalty used in former days'. It may originally have referred to attacks on inefficient hangmen. We saw that this custom outlived the conditions that gave rise to it. In various regions it continued throughout the early modern period, but merely as a traditional reaction. In Amsterdam, on the other hand, it was not recorded after the middle of the seventeenth century. To this archaic form of disturbance a new variety was added. The indignation of the spectators was raised less by the performance of the executioner than by the identity of the convict and the nature of his crime. Thus a few types of execution led to a readiness for rioting on the part of the audience. Foremost among them was the execution of rebels.

Not every participant in a riot who was arrested received a public punishment. It depended, among other things, on the seriousness of his acts and on the policy of the court. In Holland participation in tax riots was punished more severely than in others.[93] The reactions by magistrates and governments to perceived challenges to their authority constitute a distinct subject, which is not discussed in detail. A few regular patterns are simply commented on.

A frequent policy was to set an example immediately, but to avoid being too harsh. Edmund Burke formulated this response in his recommendations after the Gordon Riots of 1780. He noted that the majority of the lower and some of the middle class were sympathetic to the rioters. They might be encouraged to defy authority anew, if the courts were perceived either as unnecessarily severe or as displaying weakness. Therefore he recommended hanging only six people, but with maximum publicity. Douglas Hay calls it 'a calculated blend of terror and mercy'.[94] The same policy was pursued during the revolts raging in the South-West of France in the seventeenth century. Bercé concludes that a few hangings immediately after an uprising usually satisfied the courts. Repression was exemplary but brief.[95] The maximum of publicity, which Burke demanded in England a century and a half later, was certainly practiced. Thus the execution in 1637 of Buffarot, a rebel leader in the Périgord region, was postponed for two days to let it coincide with a fair in the town of his birth. Parts of his body were exposed at the gates of various other towns.[96]

In the Dutch Republic too this pattern can be observed. As we will see below, the Amsterdam magistrates immediately hanged a few persons after a major rebellion, but were inclined to forget about the matter later. On a smaller scale the pattern emerges in Haarlem. After a disturbance in 1690 two men were whipped on the scaffold, one with a rope around his neck. A month later another rioter was apprehended and confessed. The atmosphere was cooler now and the judges thought it better not to raise emotions again by a public penalty, so they merely confined him in the workhouse, as an observer supposed.[97]

In England the possibility of sliding into mildness might even be used as a type of blackmail. During food riots in the county of Warwickshire in 1756 the judge sentenced four persons to be hanged. Two were executed immediately. The judge announced he would recommend the other two for pardon on Monday next, but only if the rioting was over by then.[98] The game with pardons was a typical characteristic of British judicial practice. It was less common in the Dutch Republic. It was practiced there on a grand scale, however, during the major crises of 1672, 1747–8 and 1787. In those years crowd actions had contributed to the ascendancy or re-establishment of a *stadholder*, who showed his gratitude afterwards by proclaiming a general pardon for the participants, whether on trial or not.[99]

Identification is the keyword for the understanding of the public's reaction when the execution involved rebels. Many delinquents such as burglars, counterfeiters, procurers, did not bring pity to the hearts of the spectators, because the latter had no empathy for them as fellow human beings. They may have felt sorry for a few others such as smugglers or unfortunate manslaughterers. But when a rioter was punished, many of the audience really identified with him and saw him as 'one of us'. Burke was well aware of this. It is also clearly attested in the case of the riot in Haarlem. An eyewitness to the execution noted the desolation around him: one spectator showed his grief silently by his pale face and downcast eyes. Another denounced the *schout* as a coward, who needed a company of soldiers to have two harmless men flogged. A third was more ambivalent, murmuring that the case should be investigated more thoroughly.[100]

The second spectator's remark about the presence of soldiers refers to another characteristic of the execution of rebels. The authorities knew it was a precarious event and took appropriate measures. In seventeenth- and eighteenth-century Holland soldiers were always posted near the scaffold in such cases. Preventive measures in The Hague in 1748 were even carried so far that to some extent the public character of the execution was violated. The audience was kept at such a distance, 'that no one of the lower orders could get near enough to throw a stone at the scaffold'.[101] As we will see, the troops were themselves several times the unintentional cause of a fateful course of events.

The reliance on troops to ensure the smooth execution of rebels was common in other European countries as well. When plunderers were put to death on the main square of Bordeaux in 1635, the civil militia, without its artisan members, patrolled the streets. Even the Duke of La Valette, who had suppressed the rebellion, was present with his guards.[102] Occasionally we hear that this *force majeure* led some people to make more creative attempts at preventing an execution. In Poitou in the same period justice was retarded by the kidnapping of the hangman on his way to the execution.[103] Frenchmen on the other side of the Atlantic emulated this bravery a century later. After the condemnation of Fort Niagara insurrectionists in Montreal the scaffold and the gallows were stolen.[104] The protection of justice by soldiers was carried to an extreme in Rouen in 1640. In January of that year Gorin, a leader of the great peasant revolt of the *nu-pieds* in Normandy, was broken on the wheel. The soldiers were the only spectators. All residents had been ordered to stay in their houses on pain of death.[105]

In this case, unlike the example from The Hague, the public character of the execution was violated seriously. But the situation was exceptional. There had been a major revolt, put down by an army, and the execution took place as if in occupied territory. The justice practiced during or after such large revolts, almost civil wars, is not my subject. I will deal mainly with the repression following riots and smaller disturbances. In those cases it can be noted that, just as with public justice in general, the executions were a particularly urban phenomenon. The authorities in smaller towns and rural areas were often reluctant to set the apparatus of repression in motion. They had to live with the population afterwards. In quiet times they had no police force at their disposal and therefore they were more inclined towards a policy of appeasement. Thus, in the first half of the eighteenth century, the Cornish gentry petitioned the Lord Chief Justice that a rioter's body should not be hanged in chains. It would be better for the sake of the peace of the country, they argued. They particularly feared that if the body were cut down, this would be a sign for renewed violence.[106] Similar considerations applied in the Dutch Republic. Apart from Amsterdam, the local courts in Holland were often hesitant. Hence the Estates urged them towards 'rigorous justice' and 'exemplary punishments' more than once. If they failed to do so, the Court of Holland or a special provincial tribunal tried the rebels.[107] One such case in 1678 resembles the Cornish affair. Four rioters from the Zaan region were tried by the Court of Holland and hanged in The Hague. Despite a petition from local magistrates and merchants, they were hanged anew in Zaandam. After a few days the bodies had disappeared, but there was no talk of renewed violence.[108]

Thus, if we want to catch a glimpse of the crowd's feelings when confronted with the punishment of one of their own, we have to look again at the larger cities. The fullest account in recent literature of an execution following disturbances is Linebaugh's rendering of the Penlez Riots, which took place in London in July 1749. Essentially these consisted of attacks by sailors on bawdy-houses. In the end only one person, Bosavern Penlez, was to be executed. Penlez was hanged with fourteen other convicts, who also happened to be sailors. Several thousands of their colleagues were among the crowd. An armed force of 300 civil militia, led by Theodore Janssen, the Sheriff of London, escorted the condemned from Newgate to Tyburn. The danger of violence was averted, because Janssen appeased the public by determining that the bodies should not go to the surgeons. This case is a special one though. Penlez was hanged more than three months after the riot. Although more persons were tried, he was the only one executed and many doubted the testimony on which he was condemned. There had been a vociferous movement for pardoning him and his name popped up again a month after his execution: Lord Trentham, who had failed to support the movement for pardon, sought re-election as Member of Parliament for Westminster. His opponents staged a nightly procession led by Penlez' ghost in a coffin.[109]

This London occurrence constitutes a clear example of determined opposition to an execution. It should be supplemented by reconstructing the experience of another large city over a longer period of time. On the other side of the North Sea the crowds could be restive too. The Amsterdam judicial archive enables us to trace the history of riots in the town and the ensuing repression on the scaffold. I will omit the early seventeenth-century religious disturbances, which after all seldom led to public executions, and begin the story in the middle of the century.

The first riot in the series involved sailors as well. In September 1652 a number of them had refused to return to their ships before receiving their due payments. A band of seamen besieged the West Indian House, where the directors held their meeting. The magistrates called upon a regiment of soldiers, who dispersed the rioters. The court applied the policy of a mixture of harshness and mercy. The majority of the sailors were pardoned on condition they went aboard within twenty-four hours. They all could easily have received capital punishment, so the court stated, but they had blindly followed their leaders.[110] These leaders – there were two of them – were sentenced to be hanged, however. The execution was scheduled for the next day. It was rumored that several sailors had pledged each other to rescue their comrades. Hence the authorities posted three regiments of soldiers on Dam Square. During the execution the crowd was restive but took no action. The soldiers were nervous. Then a group of spectators suddenly and accidentally pressed forward. The soldiers thought the moment of action had come and fired wild shots into the multitude. Two people were killed, making the number of casualties outside the scaffold equal to that on it.[111]

This justice day set the pattern for future executions of rebels: an audience sympathetic to the convicts and nervous soldiers or civil militia. Despite rumors, there was never a real attempt to prevent the execution. But tension usually ran high and this climate often led to casualties.

A major disturbance took place at the end of the seventeenth century. In 1695 the Estates of Holland instituted a new tax on weddings and funerals. It was followed in January of the next year by an ordinance on burials in Amsterdam, which provided for obligatory official under-takers. The Undertakers' Rebellion, which broke out in early February 1696, was directed at this ordinance. Up until then undertaker had been an additional job for many and there were grievances against the new taxes as well. During the space of a few days the crowd plundered several houses. Soldiers were called in, but the civil militia managed to halt the plundering. The magistrates reacted promptly by subjecting those arrested to quick justice:

Because the present situation requires the exercise of speedy and undelayed justice and punishment upon those who are found participating in the horrible facts of plundering, rebellion and public violence, and in order to deter everyone from further disturbance of the peace and subversion of the city therefore the Gentlemen of the Court resolved according to their office and duty, to arrive at examining the prisoners without any delay and punish those found guilty as soon as possible.[112]

This is a passage from the justice-book. The secretary wrote it down to explain why no extended formal sentence was recorded for the prisoners concerned. Their names and a few short notes simply followed; they were 'examined and sentenced on their own confession without external formalities'.[113] Twelve persons were condemned to be hanged. The court neither waited for the provincial hangman nor took the time to have the scaffold erected. The indoor executioner hanged the rebels from the windows of the weigh-house at the north end of Dam Square. It is a plain expression of the magistrates' determination to apply speedy and exemplary justice. This pattern would recur in 1748 and 1787.

No resistance against the execution was recorded in this case. The public was barred from the inner circle of the square by so many soldiers that, according to one observer, no cat or dog could go there.[114] Apart from the condemned, the bodies of four rioters who had been shot in the streets, were hanged by their feet on the gallows field.[115] A month later a minor participant was imprisoned in the rasphouse, awaiting a flogging, when three women mobilized a crowd demanding his release. These women were arrested as well and the four were whipped on 21 April. Soldiers took their stand again and in the tense atmosphere several spectators were trampled.[116] After this execution the situation calmed down. A year and a half later the court thought it better not to recall the matter to the public's attention. When a burglar, who was to be whipped on the scaffold, confessed to have helped to drink away money obtained from the sale of goods acquired through plunder during the rebellion, they erased it from the sentence.[117] In 1699, however, they thought it safe again: Hendrik Bernse, alias 'Sera Death', was hanged for six burglaries and twenty-five thefts. In addition, the sentence mentioned he had plundered five houses 'during the latest tumult'.[118]

This takes us into the eighteenth century. A riot in 1740 again involved seamen. This time the East India House was their target. In the cold winter there were few jobs for sailors. A number of the unemployed besieged the building on 18 January, demanding money. One was caught and sentenced on the 21st. The justice day had already been scheduled for the 23rd. A manslaughterer was beheaded and sixteen persons were whipped. The sailor figured among the latter, with a rope around his neck. He received the highest number of lashes. Bicker Raye, who watched and counted, makes no mention of commotion among the audience.[119] Nevertheless, this was not an isolated incident. It occurred in the midst of a troubled period: between September 1738 and August 1743 the court issued a warning against 'insolence perpetrated by sailors in front of the East India House' four times.[120]

The last years of the decade were turbulent throughout the country. In May 1747, following an adverse course in the War of the Austrian Succession, a popular movement brought William IV to power in the classical manner. This time the tension did not fade away with the appearance of a *stadholder*. In Amsterdam the town hall was the target of a riot in November, and one of a party ramming the doors of the burgomasters' room, a master carpenter, was apprehended. He was sentenced to be hanged and a justice day was scheduled for 27 January 1748. The carpenter's wife, however, went to the *stadholder* in The Hague with a petition for pardon signed by more than 100 citizens. Consequently, the whole execution was postponed.[121] The pardon must indeed have been granted because the justice day, which was finally held on 18 May, involved no death penalties.

A few weeks later a nation-wide rebellion broke out. In most cities and some rural areas the houses of tax farmers were plundered. In Amsterdam the disturbances took place towards the end of June, although by the 26th the civil militia had mastered the situation. They had shot one rebel and arrested a man and a woman. Speedy justice was applied in a similar fashion as in 1696. We have an account of the execution by Braatbard. Unfortunately for the historian of public justice, Bicker Raye was ill during the rebellion.

The two persons caught were hanged on the 28th. Again this was done from the windows of the weigh-house by the indoor executioner. Ten regiments of the civil militia were posted on Dam Square. The front rank had loaded their guns with blank cartridges, although the audience did not know that. When the prisoners were led from the town hall to the weigh-house, drummers started beating a roll so loud that no one on the square could hear himself speak. Braatbard thought they did so in order to prevent people from hearing the woman's cries. Nevertheless, she was reported to have shouted 'revenge' all the while until she was hanged. This must have heightened the nervous tension. When some of the spectators pressed forward to see the hanging of the man, the civil militia shot with the blank cartridges. Thereupon everything got out of hand. A general confusion arose, with everyone seeking a refuge. Many people were pushed into the canal and drowned. Braatbard assumed that the corpse of the rebel who had been shot was to have been hanged from the weigh-house too and that the panic made the court decide to refrain from doing so. All the archival sources, however, confirm that the dead rebel was only condemned to exposure on the gallows field.[122] Anyway, the three bodies were quickly transported to the Volewijk. The magistrates were now completely occupied by the task of restoring order and proclaimed that lost possessions could be recovered from the town hall on the following day. That night, and even later, bodies were fished out of the canal.[123]

From the second half of the eighteenth century there are no elaborate accounts of the execution of rioters. Bicker Raye was present on a justice day following riots in 1754, but he simply noted that everything ran its course in good order. A few regiments of the civil militia had been posted in the New Church this time, while fifteen more had been ordered to be ready at hand.[124]

The last two decades of the century were fraught with disturbances resulting from a political antagonism between the Patriots and the adherents of the *stadholder*. Public justice followed several times, but there is no information on the public's reaction. The major year of rebellion was 1787 and the traditional scenario was repeated. One rioter was hanged from the weigh-house on 2 June and the corpse of someone who had been shot was dragged to the gallows field. Ferryman Cornelis de Jong of the cow-boat received no less than twenty-five guilders for the transport across the Y. When Prussian armies had restored the stadholder, however, the latter proclaimed an amnesty and consequently the indoor executioner removed the body again on 7 December, to hand it over to relatives.[125]

After the restoration there was still some unrest. In May 1788 seven 'disturbers of the peace' were punished on the scaffold.[126] When the Batavian Republic was instituted in 1795, the Orangists had a hard time. In 1799 a printer was publicly whipped for calling upon the populace to take the side of the expelled *stadholder* and the British.[127]

The study of riots following executions remains to be discussed. It was noted above that several sorts of justice could lead to restiveness and disturbances. The Amsterdam sources, however, reveal only one case of a riot that started as a result of an execution. The penalty that outraged the audience was administered to a domestic servant, accused of theft from her employer. It took place in 1732.

Anna Pieters had originally been arrested on suspicion of having stolen a jewel from her master, a physician named Rijnestijn. She denied the accusation but confessed to thefts from three former employers. This extraction of other confessions satisfied the court. She was condemned to be whipped on the scaffold for the three earlier crimes. But spectators who knew about her arrest, assumed she was being punished for stealing from Rijnestijn. In addition, rumor held that the jewel had meanwhile been rediscovered amidst the laundry. It raised the indignation of part of the audience. After the execution a crowd set out for Rijnestijn's house on the Herengracht. They besieged it and destroyed property, causing 4,000 guilders' worth of damage, before the civil militia dispersed them.[128]

The people besieging the physician's house were referred to as belonging to the lower orders. The action against the middle-class master of a servant girl suggests that a feeling of solidarity with 'one of us' was the motivation. In this case the belief that the woman was innocent apparently triggered off a riot. It leads us to assume that public penalties for domestic theft were always viewed with mixed feelings by the lower-class spectators, because in this crime and its repression class tensions were particularly evident. Moreover, if it did not come to a trial, domestic servants were easily dismissed on charges of theft, against which there was little defense.

Executions for domestic theft were especially notorious in France. In that country the crime could carry the death penalty, which was indeed occasionally imposed. In such cases it led to widespread indignation. This has been noted by Foucault. He discussed the types of justice that were potential causes of rioting and identified five of them. Two have just been treated here. The others are: cases of 'class justice' (when one of the common people received a severe penalty for which an aristocrat or richer man was usually punished more mildly); cases of severe justice in general (when the offense – e.g. burglary – was considered not serious enough for the penalty); cases of minor offenses (e.g. petty theft, vagabondage, begging, mere complicity in theft). In this connection, Foucault speaks of the 'political danger' immanent in public executions, which he considers the real cause of their eventual disappearance.[129]

But Foucault's argument is not well founded. For one thing it has no base in archival research. If we accept his five categories at face value, we would have to suppose that almost every execution led to a riot. The Dutch evidence hardly points in that direction. Foucault bases his argument mainly on publicists writing in the second half of the eighteenth century. By that time public justice had come under attack. This forms his second basic flaw. From his structuralist perspective he is describing a system and it is irrelevant to him which particular point in time one picks to investigate that system. In fact it is not irrelevant. From a less unhistorical perspective we can see that a possible 'political danger' of public executions was not the main cause for their disappearance.

There is a point in arguing that class tensions crystallized around public justice to a greater degree in the eighteenth century. This is certainly the thesis of Linebaugh. In Amsterdam the magistrates' concern at the execution of rebels may have had an echo during 'normal' justice days. In the previous chapter I noted that Wagenaar, writing in the 1760s, says that soldiers were always present. The books of ceremonies from the first half of the century do not mention soldiers, but this may simply be because their presence was not regarded as part of the ceremony. Bontemantel, writing around 1670, does not mention them either and this can be taken as evidence that the military was absent. It means that the armed protection of justice was introduced after the 1670s. If the silence of the books of ceremonies can be taken as evidence as well, the introduction dates from the middle of the eighteenth century. In that case it may have been a continuation of policy after the Tax Farmers Rebellion.

But we should not make too much of this. After all the soldiers present on a justice day in Amsterdam normally played a rather ceremonial role. They play pipes and drums and salute the magistrates. This does not look like a tense situation. Of course the public punishment of offenders was more often related to class antagonisms. But these cases also occurred in the seventeenth and eighteenth centuries. And if public justice did trigger real turbulence, it was largely confined to the execution of rebels. The Amsterdam evidence shows that the 'political danger' inherent in executions after riots has a longer history too. The authorities knew about the danger but they did not give in to it. Exemplary punishment of a number of rioters was necessary in their system of justice, of which display was so important a part and particularly on those occasions. When the authorities gave in to the situation in the nineteenth century, it was because their conceptions of justice had changed.

A developmental perspective offers a better view of historical reality. The practice of public physical punishment was a characteristic of the early modern personalistic stage of state formation. This is highlighted by the fact that the authorities took so much trouble to have the due proceedings run their course in such difficult situations. Therefore the execution of rebels particularly reveals the nature of repression by the early modern state. The nineteenth-century state eventually punished offenders indoors – whether they were rioters or common thieves. The change should be explained with reference to state-formation processes. This will be attempted in chapter six.

Chapter five

THE VICTIMS: DELINQUENTS AND THEIR PENALTIES IN REPUBLICAN AMSTERDAM

The preceding chapters may perhaps have conveyed the impression that the offender himself, for whose punishment the stage was set, hardly mattered. Among the magistrates bent on arranging for an exemplary ceremony; spectators eager to watch the painful happening for their own reasons; the servant whose fateful task it was to execute the judgments of others; among all these parties the men and women punished seem almost to disappear, as if they were incidental victims. On the other hand, the final section of the preceding chapter made clear that the identity of the victim did matter. This also holds true for the regular acts of routine repression. Although the authorities largely controlled the spectacle of suffering, they were not omnipotent. They could not merely pick people off the streets and put them on the scaffold to be whipped or branded. The selection of delinquents to be punished on the scaffold was also determined by general notions of what constituted crime and what appropriate penal options were. Of course these were changing as well. But on the whole they functioned as constraints, setting the limits within which the magistrates could operate.

Thus, we should pay attention to the delinquents on the scaffold and their penalties. Throughout this book I have viewed the drama of execution from different angles, always looking for the social forces that found an expression in it; whether these were in collision or streamlined and reinforcing each other. Social forces are not extra-human; they consist of the interdependent actions of millions of individuals. A minority among these individuals, on the other hand, occupy strategic positions, so that their influence is greater. The punished delinquents made up a social force as well, but they did not usually occupy a strategic position. In this sense their characterization as the victims seems relevant. If left to themselves, most of these men and women would have preferred to stay out of this system through which the early modern state sought to perpetuate and stabilize itself. Whether they were passionate murderers, mean and calculating robbers, common crooks, poor and desperate petty thieves or even rebel heroes, they paid for it with the skin of their backs, with their necks, or, if with nothing else, the loss of their honor.

The characters of many individual delinquents and the circumstances surrounding them have been described by historians such as Richard Cobb and Olwen Hufton with a happy combination of realism and force of imagination.[1] Several other investigators devoted attention to specific groups of criminals, their motives and the social setting in which they operated. These studies belong to the historiography of crime. The subject under discussion here, though obviously related to it, is different. Moreover, the variety of types of delinquents who were subjected to public punishment precludes a more individualizing approach. In the sources most of them appear as part of an anonymous mass: even their names, usually consisting of a Christian name, a patronym and the place of birth, do not tell us very much. Therefore a largely quantitative approach is called for, and this enables us to find out something about the social identity of the delinquents after all.

A quantitative investigation is necessarily a case-study. The alternative would be a sample of publicly punished offenders from various jurisdictions and that approach would be too problematic. The differences in prosecution and sentencing policies between various courts preclude an accumulation of cases, even if we only consider the penalties. Since my study is based on the Amsterdam court as far as archival material is concerned, this city is the location of the case-study. It has the added advantage of a large number of cases, which makes a quantitative approach indeed possible.

The analysis of public punishment in Amsterdam must be restricted chronologically. To take a period of 100 years seems a viable option, as it is long enough to identify possible trends. The choice naturally fell on the period 1650–1750, during which the routine application of the system of public punishment reached its height. By 1650 the proceedings of justice had become more or less standardized in Amsterdam. The more serious forms of mutilation had ceased to be practiced. On the other hand, there was no general sensitivity towards public executions, apart from a few expressions indicating a slight uneasiness. More widespread opposition only emerged in the second half of the eighteenth century. Thus the period 1650–1750 is the last century in preindustrial times when the system of public punishment largely went unquestioned. In Amsterdam it coincides with three distinct periods in the city's political history. Between 1650 and 1672 there was no *stadholder* and the Amsterdam patriciate accepted the ascendancy of the grand pensionary John de Witt. The latter, however, usually pursued a policy which was in line with that of the city. During the next thirty years Amsterdam grudgingly yielded to the regime of William III. Between 1702 and 1747 the city reached the zenith of its power and its burgomasters actually ruled the country.[2]

The main questions are: which crimes were punished on the scaffold? Did the proportions of the different public penalties for specific offenses change in time? What was the social identity of the delinquents? If trends are found, how are they to be explained? Section one, on the punishment of crimes, addresses itself to the first two questions. A trend towards an increased use of the more serious penalties is demonstrated. Section two discusses the data on the place of birth, age and sex of the scaffolded delinquents. It concludes with the treatment of Jews and gypsies as distinguishable minorities among them. The third section, finally, seeks explanations. It explores the social context: Amsterdam and the Republic.

Exact information on the sources and the method of investigation is given in Appendix A. Suffice it here to say that here are considered a complete series of publicly executed sentences between 1650 and 1750 (though with a gap from 1706 to 1709). These amount to nearly 3,000. The existence of several parallel series made a cross-check possible, which ensured that, apart from the brief gap, we have all the public cases. Next, three samples covering three consecutive periods of thirty-three years were taken from the non-public sentences. This contrasts the scaffolded with the non-scaffolded delinquents. The two bodies of data are referred to as 'scaffold series' and 'sample' respectively. Both series contain only those offenders who were held in detention during their trial. The 2,991 scaffold cases include one sentence which was not in fact executed. Marcus Jansz Vinck was condemned to be branded for participation in burglary on 9 July 1676. In the margin was written: 'not executed, because the prisoner, having been broken out, was hanged in Monnikendam fourteen days later'.[3]

I   THE PUNISHMENT OF CRIMES 1650–1750

On the most general level of observation the question is that of the percentage of public penalties. Table 1 gives the approximate totals of all penalties imposed and the number of scaffold cases per decade. Apart from the drop in the totals, which will be discussed briefly in section two,

Table 1. *Approximate total of punishments and number of public punishments*

Decade	Approximate total	Scaffold cases	% of scaffold punishments
1651–1660	4320	254	5.9
1661–1670	4340	300	6.9
1671–1680	5260	188	3.6
1681–1690	4400	208	4.7
1691–1700	5110	358	7.0
1701–1710	3200	(188)	(8.4)
1711–1720	2100	468	22.3
1721–1730	1470	467	31.8
1731–1740	1350	280	20.7
1741–1750	1060	280	26.4

a remarkable feature is the variations in percentages of public cases. Their proportions range from 3.6% to 31.8%; but not in a chaotic manner. It is plain that the period 1711 to 1750 has consistently higher proportions of public penalties than the preceding decades. It suggests that in the first half of the eighteenth century the judges were quicker to impose these than in the second half of the seventeenth. This is a very global observation which calls for more-detailed analysis. On the other hand, it provides an assurance. If we find that in the scaffold series the use of the more serious penalties increases, this development is not offset by increasing proportions of non-public penalties.

Because of the near-symbiosis of physical punishment and the scaffold, we should pay special attention to the corporal among the non-public penalties. I noted in chapter three that in Amsterdam delinquents were also whipped indoors. It turns out that application of this penalty did not function as a counter-trend to the developments in the scaffold series. The proportion of corporal penalties in the sample was never high. It was lowest (4.0%) in the second of the three thirty-three year periods. The percentage was 6.6 in the first period, while the last had the highest proportion (12.8%).

In both series trials often ended in combined penalties. This is notably so for the public ones. Banishment and/or confinement could follow the execution of a non-capital scaffold punishment. Thus it might happen that a (long-term) confinement was combined with a relatively mild corporal penalty and was therefore an alternative to a more severe one. In fact this was very uncommon. The terms of confinement tended to

Table 2. *Correlations between severity of scaffold punishment and length of confinement per decade (Kendall correlation coefficients)*

Decade	Correlation	Decade	Correlation
1651–1660	0.4459	1701–1710	0.5475
1661–1670	0.4664	1711–1720	0.4672
1671–1680	0.4728	1721–1730	0.2984
1681–1690	0.5021	1731–1740	0.2689
1691–1700	0.5650	1741–1750	0.2124

become longer in relation to the degree of severity of the corporal penalty. The tendency was not strong and had almost disappeared by the end of the period, but the correlations of table 2 show that it was certainly not the other way around.[4] A confirmation of the thesis that the judges tended to link the severity of the added penalties to that of the proceedings on the scaffold, can be found in the case of Jacob Sieuwertz and Gillis Paulusse, noted in chapter three. When the former confessed to two more burglaries, all three components of his sentence were aggravated proportionately: a more serious scaffold punishment and a prolongation of confinement and banishment. Thus the delinquents who mounted the scaffold received additional penalties largely as an aggravation of their burden of punishment. In the following discussion I will restrict myself to the public part of these sentences.

In the sample the variety is greater still. The preindustrial period was characterized by a wide array of penal options and Amsterdam is no exception in this. Apart from whipping indoors, imprisonment and banishment, a fine could be imposed, and the Amsterdam court pronounced all kinds of other, minor sentences (Appendix B, no. 5). There were judgments restricting a person's freedom of movement: prostitutes were 'denied access to taverns and whore-houses', occasionally also to coffee-houses. Some petty pickpockets were forbidden to enter Dam Square; *schaben* (insolvent bidders at auctions) to enter the stock exchange. Other measures were formulated as an order: to move from a neighborhood or to sign on a ship. Sometimes the 'penalty' was simply the order to obey an already pronounced banishment. Most of these judgments functioned mainly as police measures, facilitating easier control in case of recidivism. But there were still more minor penalties. Various prisoners who were thought to be not entirely innocent were released *cum capitulo*; a few with the threat that their fate would be worse if they committed the offense again. The judgment on a few juvenile offenders was 'given back to their parents', with the implication that the latter would apply their own correction. All non-public penalties are grouped into eight categories (see Appendix A). Although the existence of this variety of penal options should always be kept in mind, the scaffold remains my primary subject.

The offenses for which the prisoners were condemned do not pose particular problems. An Amsterdam sentence is the opposite of an English indictment. The latter only contains a formal definition of the offense in terms of a statute or other criminal law. There is no description of the illegal acts in question. In contrast, the Amsterdam sentences seldom refer to a legal definition of crime or a particular law at all, but simply say what happened. A burglar's sentence would contain accounts such as 'he, prisoner, arrived at the Prinsengracht last Thursday at 11.0 p.m., broke a window and took away a tablecloth and a candlestick, while his accomplice stood on watch'. Such accounts merely concluded with the statement that the acts were wicked, horrible or pernicious and in any case not to be tolerated in a city of law. The composition of the sentences offers the investigator obvious advantages. He can make his own classification and be sure that theft in 1650 was the same as theft in 1750.

But the legal definitions of crime do not constitute an entirely spurious factor. A few sentences did refer to a particular *keur* (city-ordinance) or to a *plakkaat* (placard: provincial law). Also, even without these references, we can assume that the judges took them into consideration. Therefore the relevant criminal legislation (see Appendix A) will be discussed as well. As a guide to the standards of punishment, however, it is of lesser importance. We will see that the choice of the appropriate penalty was often left to the judges, and in cases where a particular penalty was prescribed, the Amsterdam court often preferred and imposed its own judgment anyway. This was notably true for property crimes. The penalties were set in a 1614 placard but the actual punishments were on average always milder. Criminal legislation, especially by the city, was largely incidental. The main function of these laws and ordinances was to serve as threats and warnings. They did not guide the practice of punishment.

This practice should be related to the specific crimes. Although the scaffold series generally contains the more serious offenses, it is not restricted to one or more particular types. The crimes can be classified into four groups, which appear in both series. The groups are: violence and damage, morals, versus authority, versus property. The third is more or less a residual category, containing the offenses that do not belong to the others. Nevertheless, these are all transgressions of various social regulations designed or upheld by the authorities. Let me further discuss crime and punishment taking each group separately.

Violence and Damage

In most societies killing another human being is considered one of the gravest crimes. A distinction between (first-degree) murder and homicide is made in many legal systems including that of early modern Amsterdam. The first rarely figures in the trials. Special cases include infanticide and suicide. A sentence for suicide was only recorded once between 1650 and 1750. Trials for homicide are more frequent.

Most persons condemned for homicide were not habitual criminals. The immediate cause of the act was often a tavern quarrel. The course of events, retold in a sentence, would often be like this: 'He, prisoner, entered a tavern and ordered a drink, which was given to him. He sat down with some of the company, of which he knew one man. They ordered some more drinks together. Then differences of opinion arose as to who was to pay for them. He, prisoner, quarreled about it with Jan Gerritsen. The quarrel resulted in a fight which was transferred to the street. Suddenly he, prisoner, drew his knife and cut in the direction of the said Jan Gerritsen. Thereupon the latter drew his knife too. But he, prisoner, stabbed him, Jan Gerritsen, in his breast. The latter fell down and died on the spot. Seeing this, he, prisoner, fled away and threw his blood-stained knife into the canal.' The stories of most cases of homicide are like this. They reflect a world of passion. They begin with common lower-class sociability and end with a fatal act committed in sudden rage. In a sentence from 1739 an inn-keeper is reproached for not having taken enough precautions against the incidence of injuries and homicides, 'which so often occur in this city at the moment'.[5]

No formal laws were enacted against murder or homicide in the seventeenth and eighteenth centuries. But they were in cases of less-serious forms of violence, such as wounding, attacking, fighting or merely threatening with the use of violence, especially drawing a knife. A *keur* in the year 1614[6] is directed against wounding and drawing a knife without distinction. It says explicitly that these offenses are especially committed by the 'common people, as being within a guild or without it'. The threat of punishment includes six guilders 'above the normal fines', but a suspension from work is also prescribed: for six weeks when the offense is committed for the first time, twelve weeks for the second time and for ever for the third. In the last case those outside a guild were to be arbitrarily corrected. A new law was promulgated in 1659, which made a distinction between drawing a knife and wounding.[7] The former offense has to be punished by a fine of 100 guilders if committed during daytime and 200 if committed at night. The fine for wounding, at least if blood flows, amounts to 300 guilders. The alternative penalty in case of failure of payment is confinement for three (drawing a knife) or six months (wounding).

The Amsterdam court also promulgated *keuren* on special occasions. In 1627 the magistrates were concerned about fights between groups of youths in the city. They threatened banishment, whipping 'or otherwise',[8] which were more severe than the penalties in the *keuren* discussed above. Another occasion was in 1685. A publication of the court made mention of a violent company of 'vagabonds and hooligans' threatening and attacking people in the streets at night. These disturbers of the peace had apparently chosen a name for themselves. They were called the 'laberlots'.[9] This would suggest that they formed some sort of gang. It is the only reference to a more or less organized band operating in Amsterdam during the period investigated. It is not clear whether they were also robbers or just attacked and chased people for fun. The court's publication is rather vague on the subject. It merely promises a reward to those bringing in a laberlot. Apparently no one ever did. I found no sentences referring to membership of this illustrious company.

Another piece of incidental legislation dates from the second decade of the eighteenth century. There was great concern about persons who troubled other passengers on the horse-drawn boats. A *keur* was enacted three times, in 1710, 1711 and 1717. In the first the 'trouble' amounted to drawing a knife. The penalty was 'as the matter requires, even by whipping or other corporal punishment'. The second explicitly accused soldiers and sailors of being the offenders. The 'trouble' amounts to wounding now. The *keur* threatens corporal punishment, 'yes, even death'. But the last *keur* is less tough again. It is a copy of the first.[10] The three laws show that severity in cases of violence offenses could also be prescribed on occasion.

A special form of violence, finally, is constituted by the sailor's revenge. Notably, eighteenth-century sentences refer to it. Numerous sailors finished overseas voyages in Amsterdam and enough had been whipped or otherwise punished while on board. Some of them thought the punishment undeserved and when ashore went looking for the responsible superior to beat him up. It is understandable that they thought the changed circumstances granted them impunity. But the scaffold could await them if the Amsterdam court got to hear of it and caught them.[11]

Thus, considerable variety existed in offenses of a violent nature as well as in the possible modes of punishment. The latter is confirmed by the actual penalties, to be discussed below (pp. 119–21). For a classification of offenses, I have only made a distinction between wounding/attacking and threatening/drawing a knife. The sentences do not permit a further subdivision. The gravity of an inflicted wound must have influenced the degree of severity of punishment, but in most cases this cannot be unequivocally determined. Sentences sometimes speak of mortal danger or blood flowing, but on the whole they are not that explicit.

A special kind of violence offense, which has elements of a morals offense as well, is constituted by rape. The few recorded cases hardly permit an assessment of contemporary perceptions of what constituted rape. A sentence from 1724 sheds just a little light on the question. Antony Antonisz had made a proposal accompanied by threats to the victim several times before. The girl replied, 'that she had heard one could get a whore for money'. But Antony retorted that he wished to have a *fatsoenlijke* (decent/honorable) woman. His mother, who was present in the room, tried to persuade him to let her go; but without success. When Antony proceeded to rape her the girl struggled and he cut her with a knife. Afterwards he wanted his mother to take her to a barber. She refused and Antony took her himself. However, when the barber said he would only bandage the wound if he knew who had inflicted it and the girl told him, Antony refused to pay and left.[12]

We can assume that the word *fatsoenlijke* is crucial. Any woman who did not count as honorable would be considered close to a whore anyway, and the court would not bother. The threat with a knife was not essential. Other rapists who had not used a weapon were punished as well. The cited case was probably only reported because of the barber's insistence. We may suppose that infra-judicial reconciliation was practiced for rape as it was for other forms of violence and for theft.

Those offenses which can be classified as causing damage are relatively infrequent. No laws refer to them. A number of persons were tried for damaging tavern property or similar brawls. A more serious form of damage is arson, of which the records contain three cases. Arson is more typical of rural areas, where it was part of the game of extortion.[13] In Amsterdam three servant girls set fire to their master's house, in order to cover up a theft.

Are there any general conclusions to be drawn from the sentences in the violence/damage group? They show that Amsterdam witnessed persons killing and attacking others, as it had done before and still does today. This is not a surprising conclusion. But one thing is especially remarkable: the ubiquity of the knife. This weapon dominates the sentences of wounding and threatening almost exclusively. Carrying a knife was apparently a normal practice. If, during a quarrel, one person drew a blade, others immediately followed suit. We can infer from the sentences that only the first person to do so was punishable. Carrying a 'naked knife' was prohibited. Possession of the weapon, as a means of self-defense, was permitted. On the other hand, possession of firearms was prohibited. It is sometimes mentioned as an additional offense. These cases, which involved robbers armed with a pistol, are more exceptional. The majority of the male population, walking around the streets of the city and frequenting the taverns, found it necessary to carry a knife for protection. The community was less protected by agents of a central government, by a police force, than it is today. Consequently, public safety was at a lower level and for their defense people had to rely more on their own strength. This is one conclusion we can draw from the sentences and records of examinations in cases of crimes of violence.

The punishments following upon the offenses in this group varied widely. When the victim of the crime had died, the judgment was normally capital. Homicide was generally punished by beheading. As the honorable mode of capital punishment, it was reserved for those who had killed their opponent in a fight. Others, who were hanged, garrotted or even broken on the wheel, already belonged to the criminal world and were charged with other offenses as well (Appendix B, no. 6). A road of escape from capital punishment was open to those considered too young and those whose guilt could not be satisfactorily established. Thus, five out of sixty-eight persons tried for homicide were allowed to live. They included a fifteen-year old boy in 1662 and a sixteen-year old in 1681. Both had the sword waved over their head, and the former was also whipped on the wooden horse.[14] A man in 1655 simply did not confess, although he did not deny it either. Use of torture was to no avail. His toughness allowed him to get away with just the sword over his head.[15] This penalty had also been imposed three years before on someone who had quarreled with his wife. He had pushed her from a bench, and she accidentally fell into the cellar and died. Not the push but the ensuing fall was seen as the cause of her death.[16] The fifth case involves a sailor in 1742, who actually successfully pleaded self-defense. However, because he did not cry for help in spite of the proximity of others, and because the victim attacked him without a weapon, the judges still thought fit to expose him on the scaffold and have the sword waved over his head.[17] The fourth case especially borders on the offense of semi-homicide discussed in chapter three. This occurs five times and sword over the head is the penalty. It was likewise imposed on two men who had killed another by accident.

The combined categories of murder, complicity in murder, attempted murder, and infanticide make up thirty cases. The death penalty was always exacted except in one instance: a twenty-eight year old servant girl having attempted murder in 1734 got the burning sword, thereby being the only woman exposed to this penalty.[18] Two persons were beheaded, one was hanged, nine were garrotted and seventeen broken on the wheel. The latter was the common penalty for premeditated murder. Most of the others put to death also received the complementary torments discussed in chapter three. Trials for infanticide are few, because this offense was so difficult to prove. This has also been noted in the literature on crime in early modern England and France. In these countries there was a period when even having a stillborn child without the help of a midwife and not reporting it was a capital offense. The Amsterdam court did not go that far. Nine servant girls, who had borne dead babies in this way, were tried, but it was condemned rather as a form of neglect than of infanticide. In all instances the penalty was public whipping.

Thus all forms of killing were always considered equally serious, so that we do not have to look for a trend in punishment. Assault may be a different matter. Wounding or attacking was the major offense in 159 cases in the scaffold series (Appendix B, no. 7). The figures are rather ambivalent. Percentages for branding and the burning sword taken together suggest a relative severity in the eighteenth century compared to the seventeenth. But a few cases of cheek-cutting – which was usually preceded by whipping – traverse this picture. The first thirty years can be considered the mildest. Absolute numbers for exposure (including two whipped indoors afterwards), whipping and more severe penalties for these three decades are twelve, sixteen and six respectively. Just one sentence of exposure, combined with whipping indoors, was pronounced in the next seven decades. But, in a way, the relative mildness of the years 1651–80 is misleading. Severity is low from the viewpoint of violence in punishment, but not from that of scaffold penalties in general. The table does not include sword over head as an additional penalty. This was imposed on ten offenders, five of whom were further only exposed. These cases all fall into the first thirty years. Four were also whipped on the scaffold and one indoors on the wooden horse. In five of these cases the sentence explicitly marked the inflicted wound as 'very dangerous'. The implication of the chosen penalty is clear: the convict was 'almost beheaded' for 'almost killing someone'. As in the cases of semi-homicide, the judges preferred this mode of punishment to a heavy corporal penalty.[19]

Wounding/attacking was not a typical 'scaffold crime'. It entered into the sample by 6.4, 4.8 and 6.6%, respectively, in the three periods. A corporal penalty was only imposed in the third period.

Those charged with drawing a knife, or threatening someone in another way, were less liable to mount the scaffold. Eight of them were whipped and two branded over the whole period. They were concentrated in the four decades between 1701 and 1740. Two persons were publicly punished for damaging a publican's property. They were both whipped. Threatening and damaging are typical offenses for a non-public punishment. They are represented in the sample, although in declining numbers. A corporal penalty was exceptional, while percentages for other types of punishment fluctuate (Appendix B, no. 8).

Rape and arson are the two remaining crimes in the violence/damage group. The latter does not need much commentary. One of the three servant girls involved was the person who was burned in 1696. The other two – accomplices in the second decade – were garrotted. Rape too is present in the scaffold series only. There are eight cases, two in the seventeenth and six in the eighteenth century. As noted above, it is likely that the identity of the victim determined whether forced sex was prosecuted as rape. On the other hand, when it came to a trial, leniency did not prevail. Whatever one may think of its punishment today, in Republican Amsterdam it was certainly not a matter of male judges partly excusing the offenders. The penalties were whipping, the burning sword, beheading and hanging. Each was imposed on two rapists. Those whipped, however, were merely accomplices; they held the victim's legs apart for a comrade.

Morals

Transgressions of sexual and moral standards were seldom punished publicly. The majority of the delinquents in this group make up the counter-example of offenders who did not mount the scaffold. Still a few did. In both series the group of morals crimes largely consists of cases of prostitution and procurership. The history of prostitution in the Dutch Republic still requires a separate investigation. The prosecution policy of the authorities would constitute an important subject within such an undertaking. It is clear that numerous brothels existed in early modern Amsterdam. In 1578, when a predominantly Protestant patriciate took over, they became illegal, but were soon tolerated in practice. Foreigners visiting Amsterdam in the seventeenth century commented on how unlucky the prostitutes in the spinhouse were, since so many of their colleagues walked around freely.[20]

Before 1578 the authorities themselves exploited the brothels. Notably the *schout*'s servants kept them. Historians are of the opinion that financial interests also accounted for the relative toleration of prostitution after 1578. The *schout*'s assistants would visit an inn, knowing that it also served as a brothel. They would not make arrests as long as they were paid a certain sum. However, the *schout* himself sometimes needed money too. Then he ordered his servants to raid a few brothels, so that his income from fines could be raised. The result was that the servants arrested those who did not want to pay and left the others undisturbed. Likewise the *schout* did not bother as long as he had enough money.[21]

But this argument is hardly confirmed by the penalties recorded. No fine was imposed in the majority of cases of prostitution and procurership. It is possible that the prisoners involved were not able to pay anyway. But I think a different motive lies behind the raids on brothels. They provided an opportunity for a much more lucrative business: catching adulterers. Searching a brothel not only led to the discovery of prostitutes: their customers were discovered as well. And some of these customers were married, so that they had committed adultery and were liable to prosecution. And again some of these adulterers were rich, which is what the *schout* was after in the first place. These people rarely came to trial because of the system of *compositie*, whereby official prosecution could be bought off for a certain sum of money. That is the reason why these cases were not recorded among the sentences in the archival sources. The unlucky customer, whose night of pleasure had been spoiled, was usually prepared to pay right away, if he could. It prevented publicity and spared him a trial in which he might be additionally punished by being declared infamous. Bontemantel informs us of a letter from the *schout* to *schepenen*. It says, among other things: 'Last night we found a married person on a bed with a whore. Because he didn't want to be known for several reasons, we finished the case off for 630 guilders, which he immediately paid.'[22]

Compositie should not be confused with infra-judicial resolution of conflicts. In the latter practice the parties involved were not prepared to spend large sums of money. Moreover, *compositie* is evidently judicial and the very initiative lies with the court. In a recent article Hovy defines it as 'the opportunity offered to or pressed upon an offender, to bargain with the public prosecutor in order to evade further prosecution'.[23] It was also practiced in minor cases of violence and fiscal offenses. The predominance of *compositie* in cases of adultery can be inferred from events in and after 1677. In that year the Estates of Holland prohibited the use of the system for this offense. However, they had to suspend the measure two years later. The reason was an almost complete halt to prosecution for adultery in Holland. No prosecuting officer bothered any more. They excused themselves by stating that proving guilt in this matter was difficult, and the judges would only condemn on very positive proof.[24] Indeed, no proof was needed for *compositie*, just willingness to pay. The events show that the magistrates were not primarily motivated by a concern for the morality of the citizens.

The game of catching adulterers also explains why some brothels were left undisturbed. The sentence of Trijn Nagels in 1677 explicitly mentions the following facts: 'She is forty years of age and a "whorehostess". She has always kept to the right path, because she used to perform services for the court by bringing in one or the other. But now she cheated. She rented a room to a drunk married man and laid a whore in bed beside him without his knowledge. Then she sent for the deputy-*schout*.' The condemnation involved a banishment for three years and exposure; hence a public punishment, which also meant that the sentence was read aloud to the public.[25] So people knew that prostitution was not always prosecuted. It is not surprising then that Anna Jans, banished for procurership in 1658, was only arrested because of a petition by all her neighbors.[26] She was living in too decent a street. Luring people into trouble with the police was also recorded in the eighteenth century. All the inhabitants of a brothel were questioned about such a case in 1739. They had set up a joint venture with a deputy-*schout* and some of the servants to lure as many married men as possible into parting with their money. The *schout* himself remained ignorant of this. When he found out he had them all arrested, including his deputy.[27] Such acts of illegal provocation were also recorded elsewhere in Holland.[28]

Prostitution, finally, was also considered a problem of public order, notably if it took the form of street-walking.[29] Most girls going around at night, earning only a little money, were probably arrested. Sometimes we hear of nightwatches finding them engaged in sexual intercourse in some nook.[30]

The city did not promulgate *keuren* on morals offenses during the seventeenth and eighteenth centuries. The one from 1580,[31] just after the change in government, remained officially valid. It decreed the following penalties, providing opportunity for adultery was punished with exposure. The same penalty was set for procurership, although this was only done because of 'the corruptness of the time', the crime officially being capital. Recidivists were to be whipped and banished. Prostitution was punished according to the discretion of the court. Other offenses for which the penalties were left up to the judges were adultery, incest, rape, seduction of a minor, sexual intercourse between a male domestic servant and his widowed mistress or the master's daughter and between a guardian and the orphan girl entrusted to him. Offenses for which I found sentences, but which were not included in the *keur*, are sexual intercourse between Jews and Christians and sodomy. The first was prohibited when a Jewish community was established in Amsterdam in the early seventeenth century.

Again, criminal legislation was not a guide to punishment. As said before, the group of morals offenses represents the type of crime considered the least serious. It accounts for a mere 3.8% of the offenses in the scaffold series, while the percentages in the samples are 25.8, 29 and 26.8, respectively. The overwhelming majority of cases concerns prostitution. Mainly prostitutes (17.2, 20.8 and 17.4%) and to a lesser extent procurers (5, 5.2 and 4.6%) make up the morals offenders in the samples. Among the 115 representatives of the morals group who were publicly punished, procurers outnumber prostitutes by eighty-three to fifteen.

Considering the chronological distribution of prostitutes and procurers in the scaffold series (Appendix B, no. 9), we note that punishment was aggravated around 1720. Just one representative of each offense was publicly punished before that year. All other cases fall into the last three decades. Prostitutes are even concentrated in one (the eighth) decade and not represented in the last. The conclusion seems warranted that the authorities were moved by a desire to set an example around 1720. This toughness somewhat decreased when the decade was over, since whipping again became rare then and public punishment concentrated on procurers. In the sample the latter were hardly treated more severely.

Adultery was never publicly punished; nor was simple fornication, or 'carnal conversation' as the Dutch sources call it. On four occasions heterosexual intercourse outside the proper matrimonial bonds entered the scaffold series. These cases concerned seduction of minors. Sexual intercourse between Jews and Christians made up 0.5% of the sample. Four cases were publicly punished.

The heavy penalties for sodomy provide an exception, compared to the relatively mild punishment for morals offenses as well as to the general climate of relative tolerance in the Dutch Republic. Persecution of gay men suddenly broke out in 1730 and the phenomenon returned in successive new waves during the remainder of the eighteenth century.

Nine sodomy trials – excluding those conducted by default – took place prior to 1750. Only one person involved escaped death, because of his youth.[32] He was exposed with the rope and whipped. Afterwards he was to be confined in the 'secret place' in the rasphouse for forty years. His partner was hanged. Of the others five were garrotted and two drowned.

Diderik van Hogendorp, writing in 1752, stated the legal base for these penalties: 'Sodomy has always been capitally punished in this country. It has often been done by secretly strangling the convict and throwing him into the sea, in order to prevent remembrance of such evildoers. A public punishment should not make an unnatural crime well-known to those unacquainted with it. But when commission of this crime became the habit of many in 1730, a public death penalty was instituted.'[33] The last remark is true. When the chain of trials had just been set in motion, the Estates of Holland issued a placard against sodomy. Amsterdam sentences did not refer to it. Neither was sodomy listed among the morals offenses in the 1580 *keur*. The story about secret strangling is rather unconvincing. On the other hand, if it were ever done, it is unlikely that it would have been recorded.

To explain the sudden proliferation of trials in the Republic in 1730 would require a separate study. Of course Van Hogendorp's view of an increase in actual practice only serves to illustrate contemporary justifications. There is enough evidence to show that around 1700 the authorities did not care about gay sex.[34] But when prosecution had started, the public were quick to consider it as one more serious crime. A broadsheet on the Amsterdam justice day of 16 September 1730 portrays the sodomite Laurens Hospanjon alongside the thief Pieter Linsman.[35] We see the public watching when the first is garrotted and the second hanged. The moralistic verses, put into the mouths of both are almost interchangeable. Linsman: 'Man, O vain child; how can thou be so blind, that thou always take thy steps onto an evil road, to commit vile thefts and thus to stain thy soul'. Hospanjon: 'How disturbed is my soul; how tormented my heart (. . .) Alas, too rash I started to commit the evil of Sodom: where have I been led to?'[36] Both verses can be sung to the melody of 'Of the Spanish Rider'. As an interesting detail, Hospanjon is unmistakably dressed and coiffured as a woman.

Thus the sodomy trials stand more or less apart in the morals group. It should be noted, finally, that morals offenses are mentioned in a greater number of sentences in the scaffold series than the 3.8% discussed here. I restricted myself to the cases where they are the major – and often only – offense. But they also regularly occur when the major offense is something else, notably a property crime. If a person who had committed, say, three burglaries and ten thefts, also had a concubine, it could be brought as an additional charge against him. Likewise wounding is sometimes mentioned as an additional offense to a number of property crimes. In these cases there can be no doubt that the delinquents were actually prosecuted for offenses against property. Apparently the judges did not always bother to find out whether the thief was living in concubinage or not. The sentence would read, 'and he, prisoner, had the stolen goods sold by his wife, or concubine'. The judges took it for granted that few proper marriages occurred in the thieves' milieu. For women, living in concubinage was especially reprehensible if the partner was a reputed thief. One woman managed to be successively the concubine of three men hanged in different cities in Holland. Also, in some of the cases of illegitimate intercourse in the sample, prosecution actually started for a property crime which could not be proved.[37]

Against Authority

In the scaffold series as well as in the sample two offenses make up about half this group. They are smuggling and infraction of banishment. Notably the first is of crucial importance. Smuggling was an offense which was not really considered a crime by a large section of the public. In this the Netherlands were no exception within Europe. In France and England too, smuggling was endemic and the smugglers enjoyed widespread sympathy or even support.[38] In this matter early modern states everywhere found it difficult to secure the loyalty of their lower and lower-middle class subjects. These felt themselves to be hard pressed by the taxes on consumption goods. Thus evasion of this tax by smuggling brought them a little relief; at least when it was a matter of internal tax barriers. The taxation system in the Dutch Republic was indeed decentralized.

The Republic had one general tax, mainly consisting of duties on import and export. Its weight was only felt by the merchants.[39] More important was the taxation by the province of Holland.[40] Before 1749 the taxes were farmed out to the highest-bidding candidates. Although they had been instituted by the province, collection was organized locally. Within each jurisdiction the taxes were farmed in the presence of the local court. The farmers obtained the title of 'impostmaster'. As they had to guarantee to pay their due amount, the authorities guaranteed them protection. Thus farmers and local magistrates co-operated neatly.[41]

There can be no doubt that the burden of taxation was high for the majority of the city population. Items of food, fuel and beer formed the majority of articles taxed in Holland. A few concrete data confirm this. Around 1700 bread, meat, beer and peat accounted for most of the tax burden on a family's budget.[42] Holland's 1720 tax-income was largely based on grains and fuels.[43] For 1750 meat should be added.[44] Naturally, tax riots occurred. In Holland they increased in frequency from the 1670s onwards.[45] The chronology may not be incidental. When war with France and England broke out in 1672, Holland's treasury was nearly empty, although according to official calculations it should have contained 9 million guilders.[46] The Estates reacted by reorganizing taxation. Between 1674 and 1680 legislation grew to enormous proportions and several new taxes were instituted simultaneously. In 1683 all taxes were raised by 10%.[47]

Before 1674 fraud appears mainly to have involved evasion of the beer tax. The Estates had already promulgated a placard against the practice in 1620, and this was renewed in 1633 and 1640. It provided for a fine as penalty, but if this were not paid within three days, the offender could be publicly whipped.[48] We will see that the court was relatively mild around 1650. The *schout* often merely forbade suspect bartenders to tap for a certain time. In 1669 *schepenen* opposed this practice: if the bartenders were known smugglers, they should be prosecuted normally. But a few months later *schepenen* aroused the anger of the *schout* by releasing some smugglers he had arrested.[49]

Evasion of the tax on foodstuffs, especially grains, became the main concern of the authorities after the 1670s. On 29 March 1680 the Estates promulgated a placard against fraud in connection with the grain tax, to which Amsterdam sentences up until 1748 constantly referred. It threatened a fine of 1,000 guilders, public whipping and banishment from Holland, 'even' for first offenders. The evaders were to be considered thieves, who stole from the country.[50] Evasion came to be commonly called '*sluikerij*': smuggling in an underhand way. The servants of the impostmasters usually performed their checks at the entrances to the city. When flour coming from a mill or other rural products coming from farms passed into the city, taxes had to be paid or proof that they had already been paid had to be presented. Tax evasion took the form of trying to pass the impostmasters' servants unnoticed. The latter had the authority to apprehend those who attempted this. The smuggler could be the miller himself or a baker who had bought the flour. At the end of the seventeenth century they increasingly employed a third. In 1707 the Estates reacted with a warning: 'In order to better prevent the smuggling of bread and flour, we decide that nobody involved can claim that he himself is not the actual smuggler.' Anyone giving orders to a third and anyone directly or indirectly receiving the articles was punishable according to the placards.[51] The majority of the Amsterdam sentences remained concerned with the actual smugglers.

The sympathy of a large part of the city's population was with the smugglers. In 1682 a *keur* was promulgated against resistance of impostmasters and their servants in the course of their duties; notably when they captured smugglers. The same prohibition was repeated in 1688, 1694, 1702 and 1707.[52] In 1703 the court offered a reward for information leading to the capture of some fugitives. The latter had maltreated a deputy-*schout* and his servant when they were arresting a smuggling miller.[53] In 1711 the Estates took up the matter. They threatened anyone resisting the impostmasters with branding.[54] The tensions connected with smuggling only increased. An incident in 1742, recorded by Bicker Raye, makes this clear. A baker and his servant were arrested, because a home-made mill had been found in the bakery. By secretly grinding their own corn, they evaded the flour tax. Both were condemned to be whipped on the scaffold. It was rumored that a former servant, who had left after a quarrel, had betrayed them. This man happened to come back into the neighborhood. When the baker's wife called him an informer, neighbors rushed to the scene. 'Moved by pity', they attacked the ex-servant and killed him. According to Raye, his brains lay on the street.[55]

This violent, hostile reaction needs no further commentary. Tensions culminated in the Tax Farmers Rebellion of 1748. After the uprising farming was abolished and provincial collectors took the place of impostmasters and their servants. The hostility of the populace remained. In Amsterdam a collector was maltreated and, consequently, a new *keur* against resistance was promulgated in 1750.[56]

With this I have started the discussion of another crime in the authority group: resistance to police functionaries. A second case where we often hear of aggression concerns the arrest of beggars. This is also an international phenomenon. In Amsterdam catching beggars was a task for the almshouse-provosts. Warnings against resisting these officials or the servants of justice assisting them, were repeatedly issued throughout the seventeenth and eighteenth centuries. They number eight in the period 1650–1750.[57] In 1670 and 1713 it was explicitly guaranteed that policemen would go free if they killed anyone attacking them.[58] Those arrested were rarely helped if they had committed crimes other than smuggling and begging. The *keurboeken* contain just one case: a reward was promised in 1721 after unknown persons had rescued a man who was being taken in for homicide from the hands of the *schout*'s servants.[59]

The promise of a reward was of no avail, since the silence of the court records makes clear that the assailants were not discovered. The actual sentences confirm the picture of the *keurboeken*. Nine persons were publicly punished because they had resisted police functionaries when these were arresting a third. The third party was a smuggler in five cases, a beggar in two and an unspecified offender in one case.[60] The remaining case is unclear: the arrested person, on whose behalf someone attacked a servant of justice, had done something against the East India Company. Thus accounts of trying to help smugglers and, to a lesser extent, beggars, were prevalent among the sentences as well. One more attempt to rescue a smuggler entered the second sample. In another case in this period the crime of the arrested person receiving help is likewise unknown. In one case in the third sample, finally, the crime was illegal trading (by a Jew).

The occupations listed for the assailants are suggestive, although – as explained in section two of this chapter – listed occupations do not always refer to actual employment. For the persons helping a beggar no occupation is given. They may have belonged to the marginal population. An occupation is mentioned for those helping smugglers: boatman (twice), wool-seamstress, cobbler, porter and knitting-woman. We may suppose that they belonged to the settled population. The solidarity with smugglers should be located especially in the lower-middle and working classes. The first sentence in the series (1699) actually says that the condemned 'led the commonalty who wanted to rescue smugglers'.[61]

I grouped these acts of solidarity under 'resistance to authority'. This offense entered the scaffold series in another twenty-eight cases. These all concerned resistance on one's own behalf or that of one's companions in crime. If a delinquent resisted his apprehension and his original crime was not that serious, resistance to authority ended up as the major charge. A few such cases entered the sample too.

Begging itself and vagabondage were usually illegal as well. These offenses were hardly ever punished on the scaffold. They are tied up with the history of confinement, which is not my subject. No legislation was devoted to most of the other crimes against authority. Only abandonment of children figured in the *keuren* twice. In 1654 banishment, whipping or a more severe penalty were prescribed. The same penalties were repeated in 1682.[62]

One more type of authority crime should be discussed briefly. Violation of a freedom-restricting measure imposed as punishment was considered a contempt of court. Escape from prison does not constitute an offense in its own right in most modern legal systems, but it did in the Dutch Republic. The majority of cases in Amsterdam only amount to an attempt to escape. It was usually punished disciplinarily, but sometimes a formal trial resulted. Sentences for infraction of an imposed banishment are more frequent. The offense was easy to commit and those who did were 'contemptuous of justice and disobedient to the orders of the Gentlemen of the court'. The infringed banishment was usually one imposed in Amsterdam. But if, as sometimes happened, the judges had information that a prisoner had been banished from the province of Holland in, say, Rotterdam, they charged him or her with infraction as well. The sentence would duly mention disobedience to the orders of the gentlemen of the Rotterdam court. There were no prescribed penalties for escape from prison and infraction of banishment. A sentence involving banishment sometimes specified what would happen to the prisoner if he returned before his term was over, but usually it did not.

Let me start the discussion of punishment with the last-mentioned offense. Infraction of banishment is the most frequent offense in this group. Only those sentences are considered in which there was no other charge. Since 43% of the penalties in the sample and 97% of the non-capital ones in the scaffold series included a banishment, recidivists had often committed infraction of banishment as well. Often it was then explicitly mentioned as an additional offense, but not always. In cases where it was the only offense, other crimes – suspected but not confessed – could play a part as well. Persons were seldom arrested just because they were recognized as banished delinquents. Simple infraction of banishment was usually not publicly punished. Table 3 shows the penalties in the sample. Note that whipping indoors has the highest percentage in the first period. This is also the period in which the offense is most frequent. Percentages in the sample are 14.4, 10.4 and 6.6, respectively.

Thus, physical punishment was decreasingly imposed in the sample. This trend is offset, however, by the figures from the scaffold series. There the offense is concentrated in two periods of thirty years. Public penalties disappear from the scene between 1680 and 1710 and are still few in number in the next decade. Before that period whipping was the usual and – if we exclude the three death penalties – most severe punishment. These two cases of beheading and one of garrotting actually form a category apart. They involved persons who were captured in Holland after having been banished from the province by default in a homicide trial. They were banished on penalty of capital punishment. So in the second trial infraction of this banishment was the official offense.

Five cases, three of which involve gypsies, emerge again on the scaffold after 1710. Infraction trials of gypsies are also a category apart, and will be ·discussed in section two. That is why the table focuses on non-gypsies

Table 3. *Infraction of banishment*

A. *Sample. Numbers of observed punishments*

Penalty	1651–1683	1684–1716	1717–1749
Corporal/confinement	2	1	2
Corporal/banishment	5	—	—
Corporal only	4	2	—
Confinement/banishment	7	8	13
Confinement only	16	27	10
Banishment only	30	13	4
Minor punishment	8	1	4
TOTAL	72	52	33

B. *Scaffold series. Absolute numbers of punishments; gypsies excluded*

Penalty	1651–1660	1661–1670	1671–1680	1711–1720	1721–1730	1731–1740	1741–1750
Exposure	6	1	1	—	—	—	1
Exposure and whipping indoors	—	—	1	—	—	—	—
Whipping	27	4	16	2	42	13	36
Branding	—	—	—	—	7	5	3
Capital punishment	—	3	—	—	—	—	—

only. Percentages for these and for the total of offenders do not differ significantly. After 1720 punishment of infraction of banishment on the scaffold is again common. Branding, which had never been used before, was also employed.

Smuggling is the only other offense in the authority group which is frequent enough to permit a diachronic analysis of punishment. Table 4 shows what happened. Before 1680 the offense was seldom punished publicly. It was nevertheless frequent, making up 8.4% of the first sample. As explained above, most of these cases refer to *smockeltappen*: tapping beer on which the excise had not been paid. A fine was the usual penalty. After the reorganization of the tax-system and the 1680 placard a higher number of smugglers suddenly appears on the scaffold. In the decade 1681–90 they make up nearly 8% of the delinquents punished publicly.[63] Between 1690 and 1710 public punishment of smugglers

Table 4. Smuggling

A. Scaffold series. Absolute numbers of punishments

Penalty	1651–1660	1671–1680	1681–1690	1691–1700	1701–1710	1711–1720	1721–1730	1731–1740	1741–1750
Exposure	4	1	13	4	1	6	—	—	1
Exposure and whipping indoors	—	—	1	—	—	—	—	—	—
Whipping	—	—	2	1	—	31	31	8	6
Branding	—	—	—	—	—	—	1	—	—

B. Sample. Numbers of observed punishments

Penalty	1651–1683	1684–1716	1717–1749
Confinement only	—	1	1
Banishment only	6	4	2
Fine only	34	14	4
Minor punishment	2	1	4
TOTAL	42	20	11

declines. The offense makes up 4% of the cases in the second sample. In the third this is a mere 2.2%. Then it generally involved persons who were excused from a scaffold punishment for some reason. In the meantime a public penalty had again become common. From 1711 to 1730 many smugglers mounted the scaffold. It is plain that punishment was more severe then than in the decade 1681–90. In the earlier period exposure was the usual penalty; in the later period whipping. The latter remains the most frequent penalty on the scaffold after 1730.

In both periods sentences refer to the 1680 placard, regardless of which penalty was used. Originally this reference served mainly to justify the amount of the fine, which was imposed together with the scaffold punishment.[64] But in the second period the judges sometimes explicitly stated the legal base for their whippings too. Then the sentences mention that 'the placards of the country plainly determine that smuggling can also be punished by whipping'. The fines had always been high, but they were increased after 1680. Most offenders probably could not pay them, often they amounted to workingman's annual wages or more. In a case of banishment in 1677 and one of confinement in the workhouse in 1686 the sentence stipulates that the penalty replaces the original fine which the prisoner was unable to pay. In 1699, however, a smuggler is exposed on the pillory because he cannot pay 300 guilders.[65] In 1704 banishment is again mentioned as the alternative in case of failure of payment, but in 1720 a sentence – a fine combined with banishment from Holland – threatens the scaffold for the same reason.[66] It might be that the judges were more inclined to think of the scaffold as an alternative after 1710, or possibly earlier still, because an increasing number of offenders could not pay the fines. So eventually they pronounced scaffold sentences straight away, in which the fine was still formally included.

Of the remaining, less frequent, offenses against authority counterfeiting and rioting were the most risky adventures one could engage in. Sixteen participants in major riots were put to death, while seven minor rebels escaped this penalty. Thirteen out of fifteen counterfeiters were capitally punished: ten by beheading, two by hanging and one by garrotting. The other two received the 'penalty nearest to death', but they had merely clipped coins. Four persons tried for spending counterfeit money were only exposed.[67] Begging and vagabondage (Appendix B, no. 11) do not need much commentary. Beggars were usually confined in the workhouse without a trial or sentence. Those officially prosecuted were largely recidivists or described as impertinent. Only a few mounted the scaffold, concentrated in the period 1701–20. The twenty publicly punished vagabonds were all gypsies. The remaining offenses against authority (Appendix B, no. 12) are infrequent as well. Two persons were capitally punished for undertaking actions for the enemy in wartime.

In the case of one of the above-mentioned offenses we possess an account of the judges' deliberations. They concern a counterfeiting trial. Bontemantel, who recorded it, was one of the participants. The year was 1669. Bontemantel seems to overstress his own role in the proceedings, but we should not forget that he was president of *schepenen* at the time. One Jannes Christiaans confessed to having coined false ducats. The *schout* demanded, 'that he should be brought onto the scaffold in front of the town hall of this city, his right hand be cut off, then punished with the sword until death follows, his body laid upon a wheel and his head put on a stake to be eaten by the birds and consumed by the air'. President Bontemantel asked Christiaans if he could say anything which would excuse him, but the latter just fell on his knees asking for a merciful sentence. When the prisoner was led outside, the president requested the advice of burgomasters, who agreed to the *schout*'s demand. After this advice it was the turn of the nine actual judges to state their opinion. Bontemantel asked the second presiding *schepen* for his, but the latter preferred the president to speak first. Bontemantel then continued: 'Various criminal lawyers wrote about the penalty for counterfeiters. Some say they should be boiled in oil, some think they should be burned. Still others argue for cutting off a hand followed by hanging or beheading. The old laws of Friesland favor the first, those of Utrecht the second penalty.[68] In Holland no law on the subject is known. Therefore it is best that we act according to the custom of this city, which is shown by two sentences in 1620 and one in 1636. The counterfeiters involved were simply beheaded, so that we should refrain from having the prisoner's hand cut off. But some of his instruments might be broken before the eyes of the people.' After this the other *schepenen* stated their opinion. Corver agreed, except for the public breaking of instruments, which, according to him, would confuse the hangman. Roetert Ernst wanted a hand cut off followed by garrotting. Geelvink and Backer favored the sword, while the second also wanted the instruments to be broken. Cloek argued for cutting off a hand, garrotting and scorching the convict's face. Grotenhuize and Blauw advised beheading, Graafland garrotting. The president concluded that the majority favored beheading without prior mutilation, while the public breaking of instruments was outvoted. The convict's body should be laid upon a wheel and his head put on a stake on the gallows field. The sentence was approved accordingly.[69]

This account is the only example of deliberations in a trial leading to a scaffold punishment that I found in the period investigated. It is interesting for two reasons. First, it provides an illustration of the level of sensibilities. Apparently the judges did not bother to discuss the forms of killing and mutilation carried out on their behalf. The debate even gives an impression of carelessness, although this might be a consequence of Bontemantel's brevity (on the others' arguments) rather than a reflection of the actual proceedings. Second, the account confirms the relative independence of actual punishment from criminal legislation. In this case no placard even existed. The discussion as such was not exceptional, because Bontemantel inserted it as an example of a standard case.

Against Property

In contrast to offenses against authority such as smuggling, property crimes were not usually viewed as permissible by the popular classes. This was shown by the phenomenon of *maling*, discussed in chapter one. Property offenses form the largest group. Crimes against property are notably frequent in the scaffold series. References to laws in the sentences are very rare. Occasionally we hear that the recited evil acts are 'contrary to the placards of the country' ('the country' meaning the province of Holland). Only one placard, dated 19 March 1614, can actually be meant here. It officially remained in vigor throughout the *ancien régime*. I will briefly discuss the text and the commentary by Diderik van Hogendorp in 1752. The latter was a Rotterdam patrician and a lawyer. He inserted his commentary in his translation of a book by another lawyer, the German Benedikt Carpzov.[70]

The placard makes a distinction between qualified and non-qualified thefts. This distinction was known in other countries too at the time, but opinions varied as to the demarcation of the two categories. The Amsterdam sentences do not usually mention whether a theft is considered qualified or not. They just tell us what the offender did. But three offenses can generally be counted among the qualified thefts: those accompanied by breaking-in, by violence or when cattle is stolen. These three are discussed by van Hogendorp and the placard focuses mainly on them, although it mentions some other conditions making for a qualified theft as well. The latter are commission of the crime at sea, making use of fire or deceit and stealing from a church, mill, bridge or sluice. In contrast to English law, legal opinion in the Dutch Republic did not attach much importance to the value of the stolen goods. Piracy does not figure in the Amsterdam sentences. I listed theft under cover of fire as arson. It does not appear that cheating or theft from churches and the like were considered more serious than simple theft in Amsterdam during the period investigated. But large-scale swindling or fraud could be so considered sometimes. Here the value, without being specified, apparently did matter. Van Hogendorp says that the penalty for swindling is arbitrary and usually involves corporal punishment followed by banishment. Only the Court of Holland sometimes imposes a death penalty.[71] He makes the following comments on theft from a church: it is qualified according to the 1614 placard, but in fact the penalty is arbitrary. Capital punishment is possible, but, unless there is a break-in, this is seldom done in this country, 'where there is not so much concern for the sanctity of the churches and their goods'.[72] Theft from a church or synagogue occasionally figures among the Amsterdam sentences. It does not seem to be considered as something special.

The placard provided for the following penalties: simple theft was to be punished by whipping and branding. When it was committed for the second time, a banishment from Holland should be added. The thief had to be hanged when caught for the third time. Moreover, the judges were authorized to impose the death penalty on the first or second occasion if they thought the theft too enormous or the number of repeated thefts too high. Qualified thefts, however, were to be capitally punished at all times. The usual mode was hanging, but the judges might also impose a more severe one, if they thought the prisoner deserved it. This was valid for those caught during an attempt as well. Receivers of stolen property ought to be considered accomplices of the thieves. But they had to be treated more severely; whipping, branding and banishment from Holland were prescribed for first offenders and recidivism carried the death penalty.

In practice the severity of the placard was never reached in Amsterdam. Van Hogendorp commented that the daily practice of law had allowed for an arbitrary treatment of the crime of theft. He approved of leaving it to the opinion of the judges. It was 'not advisable' to execute the placard to the letter. But he did argue for hanging in cases of qualified theft.[73]

The following property offenses can be distinguished in Amsterdam: theft accompanied by a break-in, theft accompanied by violence and theft of cattle. These make up the qualified property crimes. I will further refer to them as burglary, robbery and stealing cattle, respectively. Burglary involves breaking into houses, shops, warehouses, shacks, ships and other locked or enclosed places, as both the placard and Van Hogendorp specify. Robbery also includes theft or extortion under threat of violence. Cattle are specified as horses, oxen, sheep, lambs and pigs. The other property crimes are receiving, swindling and simple theft. A few variants can be distinguished. Cheating the East India Company is one of them. Sailors signing on one of the company's ships received two months' wages in advance. If they did not show up at the stipulated time, they were liable to punishment. A few persons cheating the West India Company or the Society of Surinam in this way were listed under the same offense.

Domestic theft constitutes another special case. It involves stealing from someone who lives in the same house. The thief is usually a domestic servant, but she or he can also be a lodger. As we saw, domestic thieves could meet with solidarity. It is an obvious exception among the property crimes. If a person stole from the house of his employer or from his place of work, I listed it as theft from employer. A last variant is the offense called 'undressing children', a crime typical of a past age. The offender – usually a young woman – would meet a small child in the street and lead it with sweet words to some quiet place. She took the child's clothes or ornaments and left it there. The targets were probably children of relatively rich parents, so that the value of the clothes and – if worn – the ornaments was considered worth the risk. Those arrested for the offense were often recognized and accused by the child itself. But few people today would risk punishment for a bundle of clothes.

This is the interesting characteristic of property crimes. The proceeds of a theft were hardly ever really big. Most of the stolen goods appear to be small things of relatively low value. The offenders stole anything they could get. A pickpocket would be content with a handkerchief if there was nothing else. A burglar would break a window just to take away the curtains. A thin person would squeeze himself between the lattice bars of a cellar to reach for a cheese. In our eyes there is an enormous discrepancy between the spoils of crime and the risk of punishment. Various historians have argued for necessity as the most prominent cause of criminality in the early modern era. Correlations between frequencies of prosecuted property offenses and corn prices have been offered to confirm this. I think the 'voracity' of *ancien régime* thieves provides an even clearer substantiation of the thesis. People who take the risk of corporal punishment and more for a wooden plank or old trousers, steal because they have to. They cannot even wait to plan a careful operation to lay their hands on something big. In our society junkies are a comparable set of thieves.

Stealing practices are also illustrated by the few *keuren* about property offenses promulgated in Amsterdam during the period investigated. Again they represent an incidental legislation. In 1679 the court directed itself against persons breaking off metal gratings from the city sewers and

137

the cylinders around some of the trees. Public whipping was to await them.[74] Apart from exceptional times of extreme scarcity, as in war, such acts would nowadays primarily be referred to in terms of vandalism. But the offenders were considered thieves at the time and indeed their motive was to sell the gratings and cylinders as old iron. A *keur* from 1706 prohibited theft of staves or other pieces of wood lying in the street.[75] These were usually gathered for fuel. Stealing anchors, buoys or buoy-lines from ships was forbidden in 1716.[76] One *keur* was directed against a probably more lucrative business: cheating jewellers was forbidden in 1696. Those so doing were to be 'corporally punished as the matter requires'.[77]

The sentences provide little information about the thieves' organization, a subject which would require another type of investigation. Most thefts were committed by small groups comprising from two to five persons. These groups were usually formed for the occasion, often in taverns, and their membership underwent frequent changes. Some areas in the city had the reputation of being thieves' neighborhoods. The offenses figuring in the sentences were committed both in Amsterdam and elsewhere. The system of inducing the thieves to betray each other facilitated knowledge of distant crimes. Many thefts were committed in other cities or the countryside in Holland. Some took place in other provinces of the Republic and a few as far away as Frankfurt, Leipzig or Flensburg.[78] Indeed many property offenders were wandering people. They operated throughout the province of Holland. Some of them happened to be caught in Amsterdam and were, therefore, punished there.

Bigger bands of robbers and burglars must have operated in the province too. The archival sources in Amsterdam do not provide information about them. They may have escaped capture in the city to a high degree. Only in the second decade of the eighteenth century was a network of bands rounded up and tried in Amsterdam. They had operated in the countryside in most cases, in Holland as well as in other provinces. Several of them, who of course figure among those punished for homicide or murder, were charged with killing the victims of their robberies. The notorious Jaco was one of the leaders of this network. His execution was not included in the figures, because his eventual sentence was pronounced by the High Council.

The sentences in the property group offer excellent possibilities for a diachronic analysis of punishment. Most crimes occur frequently enough. This group accounts for, respectively, 29.4, 34.8 and 39.6% of the offenses in the samples. In the scaffold series the percentage is 67.9.

Table 5. Robbery

Scaffold series. Punishments for robbery alone

Penalty	1651–1660 %	No.	1661–1670 %	No.	1671–1680 %	No.	1681–1690 %	No.	1691–1700 %	No.	1701–1710 %	No.	1711–1720 %	No.	1721–1730 %	No.	1731–1740 %	No.	1741–1750 %	No.
Whipping	—	—	56	10	71	5	41	7	30	5	18	2	6	2	18	4	33	3	—	—
Branding	50	1	39	7	14	1	18	3	18	3	—	—	19	6	23	5	22	2	33	1
Burning sword	—	—	6	1	—	—	18	3	12	2	9	1	—	—	—	—	—	—	—	—
Cheek cut	—	—	—	—	—	—	—	—	—	—	9	1	—	—	—	—	—	—	—	—
Hanging	50	1	—	—	14	1	24	4	41	7	55	6	47	15	46	10	33	3	67	2
The wheel	—	—	—	—	—	—	—	—	—	—	9	1	28	9	14	3	11	1	—	—

Changes in punishment do not show a clear pattern when we look at the whole group (Appendix B, no. 13). We have to distinguish between more and less serious offenses. Judging from the percentage of death penalties, stealing cattle is the gravest crime. However, this percentage is derived from only six cases. One person was whipped, two were branded and three hanged. The next gravest offense is robbery. If those sentenced for participation in or attempted robbery (table 5) are excluded, the percentage of death penalties is 45.6. Absolute numbers in the first and last decades are too low to arrive at a statistically significant percentage. But we can take decades one and two together and decades nine and ten. Then the percentage of death penalties is 5 in the first and 50 in the last twenty years. Capital punishment remains at a relatively low level until 1690. It rises to 41 % in the fifth decade and above 50 in the next, at which level it remains. Moreover, breaking on the wheel is only practiced between 1701 and 1740. Note that the most severe decade also contains the highest number of robbers. This was the period when the network of bands was rounded up. Otherwise there is no connection between severity of punishment and number of offenders. The second decade harbors more robbers than the fifth, but no death penalties at all. When we include the sentences for participation in and attempted robbery (Appendix B, no. 14), a similar pattern emerges. The only difference is that the average severity of punishment is lowered and the number of offenders raised. One case of exposure involved a woman who actually denied the charge of participation in a robbery. She only confessed to having drunk with the others beforehand.[79]

Burglary is likewise first considered without the categories of participation in and attempt at. Table 6 shows that the highest percentages of death penalties are reached between 1701 and 1730. Save for the ninth decade, which contains a mere four cases, capital punishment is more frequent in the eighteenth than in the seventeenth century. If we contrast the two fifty-year periods for percentages of whipping and exposure combined, the first contains the higher percentages. Note that the fourth and fifth decades are already slightly more severe than those preceding. The fifth contains one of the few cases of breaking on the wheel. In the case of burglary too, inclusion of the categories participation and attempt (Appendix B, no. 15) preserves the general pattern. The ninth decade stands out even more as an isle of mildness, but its nine cases are not serious either.

To conclude the qualified thefts, let us look at the table for them all (no. 7). A development in the direction of more severity can be observed again. Whipping is higher in the seventeenth century and death penalties

Table 6. Burglary

Scaffold series. Punishments for burglary alone

Penalty	1651–1660 %	No.	1661–1670 %	No.	1671–1680 %	No.	1681–1690 %	No.	1691–1700 %	No.	1701–1710 %	No.	1711–1720 %	No.	1721–1730 %	No.	1731–1740 %	No.	1741–1750 %	No.
Exposure	7	3	—	—	—	—	7	4	2	2	—	—	—	—	—	—	—	—	—	—
Exposure and whipping indoors	—	—	—	—	—	—	—	—	3	3	—	—	—	—	—	—	—	—	—	—
Whipping	37	16	38	12	43	9	39	24	32	28	14	3	21	9	26	6	25	1	36	4
Branding	33	14	41	13	43	9	25	15	32	28	14	3	25	11	22	5	75	3	27	3
Cheek cut	—	—	—	—	5	1	—	—	—	—	—	—	—	—	—	—	—	—	—	—
Non-prolonged death penalty	23	10	22	7	10	2	30	18	29	25	71	15	52	23	52	12	—	—	36	4
The wheel	—	—	—	—	—	—	—	—	1	1	—	—	2	1	—	—	—	—	—	—

Table 7. All qualified thefts

Scaffold series. Percentages and absolute numbers of punishments

Penalty	1651–1660		1661–1670		1671–1680		1681–1690		1691–1700		1701–1710		1711–1720		1721–1730		1731–1740		1741–1750	
	%	No.	%	No.	%	No.	%	No.	%	No.	%	No.	%	No.	%	No.	%	No.	%	No.
Exposure	5	3	1	1	—	—	4	4	1	2	2	1	—	—	—	—	—	—	—	—
Exposure and whipping indoors	—	—	—	—	—	—	—	—	2	3	—	—	—	—	—	—	—	—	—	—
Whipping	41	24	50	38	60	25	50	51	39	55	24	12	25	31	27	20	55	11	25	4
Branding	36	21	38	29	29	12	21	22	28	39	18	9	27	34	24	18	25	5	38	6
Burning sword	—	—	1	1	2	1	3	3	3	4	2	1	1	1	—	—	—	—	—	—
Cheek cut	—	—	—	—	2	1	—	—	—	—	2	1	—	—	—	—	—	—	—	—
Non-prolonged death penalty	19	11	9	7	7	3	22	23	27	38	51	26	37	46	45	33	15	3	38	6
The wheel	—	—	—	—	—	—	—	—	1	1	2	1	10	12	4	3	5	1	—	—

in the eighteenth. But we have to admit now that the ninth decade is milder than those preceding. Since in the tenth decade death penalties remain below the level of the years 1701–30, we can conclude that the judges became a little milder again towards qualified theft after 1730. This partial return of mildness coincides with a significant decrease in the number of offenders.

Confessing a qualified theft rarely led to a non-public punishment. Robbers and cattle thieves did not enter the sample, but a few burglars did (representing 0.6, 0.6 and 0.2%). Five of them were under twenty, but the other two (in the first period) were twenty and twenty-four years of age.

In the case of simple theft we can neglect the differences between degrees of complicity. The categories of attempt and participation make up about 15%, but they are not punished more mildly. Table 8 gives the figures for all cases of simple theft in the scaffold series. Exposure, whipping and branding are the three main penalties. Whipping is by far the most frequent. Indeed the combination theft–whipping constitutes the modal sentence (514 out of 2991 cases) of the entire scaffold series. The relative frequency of the penalty fluctuates over the decades. Changes in severity can be inferred from the distribution of the other two. The turning point is around 1710. Exposure almost disappears from the scene then, while branding increases markedly. If we take the few death penalties into consideration, the more severe period starts ten years earlier. The ninth decade is the least mild. It contains no cases of exposure at all, while the percentage of death penalties is the highest and that of branding the next highest still. The third decade is the mildest.

Inclusion of theft from employer and undressing children (Appendix B, no. 16) preserves the general pattern. Significantly, it lowers severity. The percentages for theft from employer alone over the whole period are: exposure 25.8 (including 6.7% whipped indoors afterwards); whipping 64; branding 10.1. The corresponding percentages for undressing children are 25.9 (whipped indoors: 6.5), 61.3 and 12.9 respectively. Regarding the latter crime we have to note that all but one of the offenders were women and that most cases fall into the seventeenth century. Mainly men (seventy-seven out of eighty-nine) stole from their employers, while cases are represented in all decades in about the same proportion. The relative mildness in punishment for the two offenses is probably due to the pettiness of the theft in most cases. The total number of thefts was usually rather low and the stolen goods few. On the other hand they are more typical scaffold crimes than simple theft. They hardly ever enter the sample.

Table 8. Simple theft in the scaffold series

Punishments for simple theft, including participation in and attempted simple theft; theft from employer and undressing children excluded

Penalty	1651–1660		1661–1670		1671–1680		1681–1690		1691–1700		1701–1710		1711–1720		1721–1730		1731–1740		1741–1750	
	%	No.	%	No.	%	No.	%	No.	%	No.	%	No.	%	No.	%	No.	%	No.	%	No.
Exposure	7	5	10	9	17	8	8	2	17	8	15	6	3	3	2	2	—	—	2	1
Exposure and whipping indoors	1	1	1	1	—	—	8	2	2	1	—	—	—	—	—	—	—	—	—	—
Whipping	86	65	78	73	79	38	80	20	73	35	77	30	78	93	60	59	69	51	79	50
Branding	7	5	12	11	4	2	4	1	8	4	5	2	18	21	33	33	24	18	19	12
Capital punishment	—	—	—	—	—	—	—	—	—	—	3	1	3	3	5	5	7	5	—	—

The year 1710 emerges again as a turning point in the special case of domestic theft. It is most convenient to present the figures in absolute numbers (table 9). Branding was not only increasingly used after 1710, but the number of scaffold punishments *per se* increased significantly. The number of cases of domestic theft in the sample dropped from the first to the second period and then rose again slightly (1.8, 0.4 and 1%). Use of a corporal penalty increased (33.3, 50 and 60%), but this is based on very few examples. If we realize that the 1% in the third sample refers to a relatively low number of actual trials (approximately one per year), we can conclude that the offense of domestic theft was increasingly 'scaffoldized' in the eighteenth century. Severity, however, did not reach the level already advocated in 1682 by an anonymous author. Impressed with the thievishness of servants, he regretted that some persons thought theft was never punishable by death.[80].

We still have to consider the figures from the sample for the other cases of simple theft. The offense was never exclusively characterized by a scaffold punishment, as with the qualified thefts. The crimes of theft, attempt at/complicity in theft, being found in the company of thieves, theft from employer and undressing children together make up 14.2, 14.2 and 11.6%, respectively of the samples. As already stated, the latter two are just a tiny portion. Penalties for the others combined (Appendix B, no. 17) also constitute a remarkable trend. Corporal punishment is least frequent in the second and most in the third period. These figures again indicate an increase in severity at some point in the first half of the eighteenth century. An increasing portion of thieves were punished publicly, since the offense remains represented at about the same level in the scaffold series, while the percentage – and therefore the absolute number even more so – in the sample decreases. And this lesser number of thieves faces a higher frequency of whipping indoors in the third period.

Swindling (Appendix B, no. 18) is a rather ambiguous offense, because of the relatively great variations in seriousness. I noted that it could be considered as qualified theft. A death penalty was imposed on eight persons and these had certainly performed large-scale operations. Four thumbs were cut off, when the delinquents had acquired large sums through forgery.[81] In the remaining cases it is still noteworthy that exposure declines after 1700, while branding is used increasingly. In the sample, swindling is seldom punished corporally. A special form of the offense is the collection of money under false pretexts. Typically, those engaging in it would declare that the money was for rebuilding a burned-down church in some German town, using false papers as identification. A number of them mounted the scaffold in the eighteenth century. The

Table 9. Domestic theft

Scaffold series. Absolute numbers of punishments

Penalty	1651–1660	1661–1670	1671–1680	1681–1690	1691–1700	1701–1710	1711–1720	1721–1730	1731–1740	1741–1750
Exposure and whipping indoors	—	—	—	—	1	—	—	—	—	—
Whipping	4	15	6	1	7	4	36	27	29	26
Branding	—	—	—	1	—	—	2	5	4	12

sentence then specified that the executioner should burn the forged papers on the scaffold. He did so in the fire-pot, which stood ready for branding anyway: a sort of recycling in punishment.

The remaining property crimes do not need much comment. Cheating the East India Company (Appendix B, no. 19) was usually followed by a non-public penalty. The reverse is true of receiving, but cases are few.[82] It should be noted, finally, that the sample contains a number of non-confessed property crimes. As a rule delinquents could only be condemned to a public penalty if they had confessed. If the prisoner persistently denied a charge the court considered proven another judgment normally followed. Most of the time this was banishment (Appendix B, no. 20). A minority of these delinquents had endured torture. Significantly, the non-confessed property offenses increased in proportion (7.4, 8.2 and 13.8% of all offenses in the samples). As more property crimes were punished on the scaffold, the unconfessed ones made up a larger portion of the non-scaffold cases.[83]

Up until now only one factor contributing to the degree of seriousness of the charges has been considered: the nature of the major offense in the sentence. It is the main factor, but there are others. The judgment could also be influenced by the personality of the delinquent. If juveniles and women were treated more mildly and they were present in smaller proportions in the eighteenth century, this might explain the increase in severity of punishment. Section two will show that this was not so. More important still are two other variables: recidivism and the total number of confessed illegal acts in a sentence. Their implications will be discussed briefly.

In fact both factors decline in score (Appendix B, no. 21). The percentage of first offenders in the scaffold series fluctuates between 40 and 45 up to the year 1690. In the next four decades it stays around 60, while it rises even higher after 1730. The percentage of 'obdurate recidivists' is highest in the third decade. Then it suddenly drops and gradually decreases further, save for a small peak between 1720 and 1730. Consideration of the total number of offenses is especially important in the group of crimes against property. Sentences enumerating large lists of transgressions of the law are concentrated there. And with some exceptions, averages are lower in the eighteenth than in the seventeenth century.

The conclusion must be that the increase in severity towards various crimes continues in spite of a decrease in recidivism and in the average number of offenses for which a penalty was imposed. It implies that the contrast between the seventeenth and eighteenth centuries becomes even greater if we include these two factors in our analysis. This is done in tables 10 and 11. I preferred to compare two periods of equal length, although the contrast would probably be greater still if 1710 were chosen as the dividing line. Absolute numbers of trials are only high enough in the group of property offenses. I considered all qualified thefts and all non-qualified ones. The factor of total number was divided in two: one to four offenses in a sentence and five or more. The factor of recidivism was simply divided in first offenders and recidivists.

The tables so obtained do not need much commentary. A genuine increase in severity of punishment can be inferred from all of them. In table 10 the greatest contrast is to be observed in the most serious category. Death penalties for the combination qualified thefts/five or more offenses jump from 29% in the seventeenth to 64.7 in the eighteenth century. And among these cases of capital punishment breaking on the wheel jumps from an insignificant 0.4 to 7.6%. The most serious category in table 11 is not the one with the greatest differences in severity. The greatest contrast is to be found in the recidivists who committed simple theft. Penalties more severe than whipping jump from 9.6% to 47.2%. And in the seventeenth century these penalties only include branding, while 5.6% of capital cases figure among them in the eighteenth. Sentences of exposure are notably frequent among the first offenders committing simple theft in the seventeenth century. If we include those whipped indoors afterwards, the percentage comes to 36.1, more than a third of the total. It drops to 2.2% in the next fifty years. A parallel change can be observed in the category non-qualified thefts/one to four offenses in table 10, but it is less marked there.

At the end of this section it is possible to give an answer to the first two questions posed in the introduction to the chapter. In terms of their crimes, we know the identity of the delinquents who mounted the scaffold. In the first place they were killers, condemned for murder, homicide or infanticide. Second, and much larger in number, are the serious property offenders: robbers, burglars and large-scale swindlers. These were the only frequent offenses that were almost always punished publicly. This was also the case for a number of more infrequent ones: arson, rape, seduction of a minor, sodomy, bigamy, treason, rioting and counterfeiting. The main offense which was punished both on the scaffold and non-publicly was simple theft. Here other factors such as the delinquent's personality – the value of the stolen goods was almost always low – apparently determined the choice. Wounding, smuggling

Table 10. *Punishment of property offenders with higher and lower total number of offenses in their sentences*

A. *Nature of major offense: simple theft (including participation in and attempt at) domestic theft, theft from employer and undressing children*

Penalty	1651–1700		1701–1750	
	%	No.	%	No.
Exposure	16	43	3	13
Exposure and whipping indoors	3	9	—	—
Whipping	76	210	77	390
Branding	5	13	19	97
Non-prolonged death penalty	—	—	2	8

Total number of offenses in the sentence: 1–4

B. *Nature of major offense: as A.*

Penalty	1651–1700		1701–1750	
	%	No.	%	No.
Exposure	1	1	—	—
Exposure and whipping indoors	1	1	—	—
Whipping	83	63	57	29
Branding	15	11	31	16
Non-prolonged death penalty	—	—	12	6

Total number of offenses in the sentence: 5 or more

C. *Nature of major offense: qualified theft*

Penalty	1651–1700		1701–1750	
	%	No.	%	No.
Exposure	2	3	1	1
Exposure and whipping indoors	1	1	—	—
Whipping	66	124	40	63
Branding	20	38	25	39
Burning sword	3	5	1	1
Cheek cut	1	1	1	1
Non-prolonged death penalty	8	15	32	50
Breaking on the wheel	—	—	3	4

Total number of offenses in the sentence: 1–4

Table 10 (*cont.*)

D.   *Nature of major offense: qualified theft*

Penalty	1651–1700		1701–1750	
	%	No.	%	No.
Exposure	3	7	—	—
Exposure and whipping indoors	1	2	—	—
Whipping	30	69	8	8
Branding	36	84	27	28
Burning sword	2	4	1	1
Non-prolonged death penalty	29	67	57	60
Breaking on the wheel	0	1	8	8

Total number of offenses in the sentence: 5 or more

and infraction of banishment likewise entered both series, together with a score of more infrequent crimes. Morals offenses such as prostitution, procurership, adultery and carnal conversation were seldom, if ever, punished on the scaffold.

The question of changes in the imposition of specific penalties receives an unambiguous answer. There was a trend in the direction of increased severity – severity meaning use of the more serious penalties. The trend can be summarized as follows: the first thirty years were on the whole the mildest, with the earliest signs of an increase in severity emerging after 1680. Attackers were less often exposed, with or without the sword over their heads. Likewise a larger number of them received a penalty more severe than whipping. Smuggling, hardly a scaffold crime before, faces a jump in public punishment in the fourth decade. Most offenders are exposed. Burglars are also treated slightly more severely after 1680. The percentage of capital punishments rises. In the fifth decade the percentage of death penalties for robbery increases likewise. Punishments for both qualified thefts further rise in severity after 1700. Breaking on the wheel is introduced for robbery. For the first time capital punishment is imposed for simple theft. The seventh decade faces a new spurt in the direction of severity. Smuggling, which had almost left the scaffold around the turn of the century, returns. And for the first time whipping becomes the most prominent penalty. Branding for simple theft increases markedly. Many thieves were non-publicly punished during the period, but the proportion of scaffold-cases increases. And the percentage of

Table 11. *Punishment of recidivist and non-recidivist property offenders*

A. *Nature of major offense: simple theft (including participation in and attempt at) domestic theft, theft from employer and undressing children. First offenders*

Penalty	1651–1700		1701–1750	
	%	No.	%	No.
Exposure	28	40	2	9
Exposure and whipping indoors	8	12	—	—
Whipping	62	89	88	356
Branding	2	3	9	38
Non-prolonged death penalty	—	—	1	3

B. *Nature of major offense: as A. Recidivists*

Penalty	1651–1700		1701–1750	
	%	No.	%	No.
Exposure	5	13	3	5
Exposure and whipping indoors	1	2	—	—
Whipping	84	201	50	99
Branding	10	23	42	82
Non-prolonged death penalty	—	—	6	11

C. *Nature of major offense: qualified theft. First offenders*

Penalty	1651–1700		1701–1750	
	%	No.	%	No.
Exposure	3	5	—	—
Exposure and whipping indoors	1	1	—	—
Whipping	60	93	35	58
Branding	21	33	22	36
Burning sword	5	7	1	2
Non-prolonged death penalty	10	15	36	59
Breaking on the wheel	1	1	6	9

Table 11 (cont.)

D. Nature of major offense: as C. Recidivists

Penalty	1651–1700		1701–1750	
	%	No.	%	No.
Exposure	2	5	1	1
Exposure and whipping indoors	1	2	—	—
Whipping	38	100	17	20
Branding	34	90	30	36
Burning sword	1	2	—	—
Cheek cut	0	1	1	1
Non-prolonged death penalty	25	67	46	55
Breaking on the wheel	—	—	7	8

whipping indoors rises for the remaining petty larcenies. Domestic theft had been a typical non-public punishment crime before about 1710–15. It becomes scaffoldized afterwards, and branding is then used more often. In the eighth decade times became harder for prostitutes and procurers, who had always been mildly treated. Some of them were publicly punished now, but they remained a minority. Infraction of banishment returns to the scaffold. A number of offenders had been whipped in the early decades. After 1720 branding becomes prominent. The judges grew slightly milder towards qualified thefts after 1730. This coincided with a significant drop in the number of trials for these offenses. But simple thefts continued to evoke a high degree of severity, notably domestic thieves, who were often branded. Similarly, the other offenses mentioned did not undergo significant changes.

Cases of infraction of banishment which were not publicly punished form the exception to the development in the direction of severity. Whipping indoors has the highest percentage in the first period of the sample. This is the only example of a counter-movement. Swindling shows no clear pattern, although it is possible to argue that this offense too met with increasing severity. It can be observed among the scaffold cases in the eighteenth century. But the non-public majority remains characterized by a non-corporal punishment. Other offenses are too infrequent to permit conclusions.

The development towards severity takes place in spite of a decrease in both recidivism and the average number of offenses in a trial. If we include these factors in our analysis, the contrast between the seventeenth and eighteenth centuries becomes even more marked. This contrast, finally, can also be noted on the most general level of the percentual relation between scaffold cases and the total of punishments. Before 1700 no more than 7% of the offenders were punished publicly. It rises to 31% in the eighth decade and drops slightly afterwards.

2 THE IDENTITY OF THE DELINQUENTS

Before we start looking for an explanation for the trend just demonstrated, attention should be paid to the identity of the delinquents who mounted the scaffold. Besides showing their crimes, the quantitative analysis yields information on who they were. They were vagrants, immigrants or residents of the city, poor or with some means. There were men and women, young and old offenders. A few belonged to outsider groups. A brief look at the available data can make the analysis of repression more precise.

Vagabonds and patricians

The first question concerns the social status of the condemned. In this connection we may inquire whether they belonged to the settled population or not and to which stratum they belonged. It should be noted immediately that both problems cannot be solved to a satisfactory degree. The sources merely yield some suggestions. A treatment of the problem of residency is most fruitful when we place it in the context of a discussion of changes in the total number of prosecutions. This will be looked at first.

Table 1 at the beginning of the chapter showed a continuous decline in the number of trials – i.e. all trials, regardless of the penalty – after 1700. The drop cannot be explained by a decrease in population. We are well informed about Amsterdam's demographic situation through the work of S. Hart.[84] The city's population had reached the 200,000 mark about 1670. Thereafter it increased only slightly until about 1740. Thus the decline in trials is also a decline in prosecuted offenses relative to the population. It is not my intention to repeat the worn-out discussion around the dark number here. Nevertheless, attention should be paid to the possible factors that determined the decline.

There is no indication that the prosecution policy of the authorities was altered markedly. The number of all groups of offenses declined, though not quite in the same proportion. The efficiency of the police force cannot have decreased. The number of nightwatches had even been increased shortly before. The attitudes of the public may have changed a little. People remained negative towards property offenders, but it is possible that they were increasingly willing to protect offenders against authority. The increase in attacks on police functionaries lends some credibility to this presupposition. Moreover, the decline in the number of trials is most pronounced in the authority group. But we should not forget that warnings against resisting the almshouse-provosts when doing their job of picking up beggars were issued from 1650 onwards. This meant that there was at least some resentment against the prosecution of authority crimes in the seventeenth century. In any case a possible growth in this resentment alone cannot account for the decrease in the number of trials.

The promise of a reward might induce people to report crimes. But the court did so only on rare occasions of serious breaches of the law and the practice was known both before and after 1700. The *schout* also made use of paid informers from the thieves' milieu. But the few informers to which the sources refer belong to the eighteenth century. A rather efficient custom of the court was manipulation through terms of confinement. The prospect of a reduction led many prisoners to accuse others. This custom was as common in the seventeenth as it was in the eighteenth century. But it might still account for part of the decline in the number of trials by reinforcing an existing trend. If the number of arrested criminals decreases, fewer persons are available to accuse others, so that subsequently even less arrests are made. We should not overestimate this factor, however. A fair amount of the accusations by former comrades were levelled against persons who had already been caught for some other offense and would have been tried anyway. In those cases the accusations – if a confession followed – only served to raise the number of offenses in a trial. We saw that the average indeed declined in the eighteenth century.

It is hardly likely that the number of real crimes dropped after 1700. In a preindustrial context only two situations could have accomplished such a feat: rising prosperity or continuous warfare. The first did not prevail and the Republic was not at war between the Peace of Utrecht and its involvement in the War of the Austrian Succession. Thus, there is only one way out: to criticize the demographic data. They may not be representative for those groups among the population from which most delinquents were recruited. This may indeed be the case with Hart's figures. They are based on Amsterdam marriages. Matrimony is a good indicator when it comes to determining the general state of the population and the flow of immigration. But the presence of specific groups in a city is something else. Hart himself has to admit that some people never married at all.[85]

Now there were of course single people among the established classes. But the majority of the unmarried in the metropolis were simply people who did not care to go to the preacher or the town hall. They might live in concubinage, with or without a frequent change of partners. They lived a less-settled life and were hardly bound by community-controls. Most of them belonged to the marginal population or to wandering groups. Let us suppose then that the majority of the prosecuted offenders, those mounting the scaffold as well as those punished otherwise, belonged to this section of the population. The supposition may at least be valid for the prostitutes and the thieves. I noted the frequent references to concubinage in the sentences. Moreover, many thieves operated throughout the province and some confessed thefts in far-away places. They went from town to town, after being banished or just when the place became too hot. To a large extent this floating section of the population escaped demographic registration.

Now we may add a second supposition: the floating section decreased in size in Amsterdam after 1700. For some reason the marginal and wandering groups, gypsies excluded, increasingly avoided the city. The decrease in the percentage of recidivists among the offenders points in that direction. Here are two suppositions, both based on very scanty evidence. But if they are true, they explain the drop in the number of trials. And in that case one important question about the social identity of the delinquents has been answered. A large part, and probably to an even larger extent those punished on the scaffold, did not belong to the settled population. In that case the situation must have been as follows: infrajudicial conflict solving prevailed for the 'honorable' lower and lower-middle classes. The others were more liable to judicial prosecution.

But to a certain extent table 12 confuses the picture again. It compares the percentages of born Amsterdamers among the marrying population and among persons punished on the scaffold per decade. Both series of figures can be compared conveniently. The percentages of scaffolded persons are probably representative for all delinquents punished in the period. The distribution of places of birth among those subjected to a non-public penalty shows a remarkable similarity to that of those who mounted the scaffold. The average age of the S-group (twenty-nine years and four months), moreover, is only slightly higher than that of the M-group. In 1676–7 the latter was twenty-seven years and eight months for

Table 12. *Immigrants in Amsterdam and scaffolded
delinquents*

Decade	M	S		D
	%	%	No.	%
1651–1660	42.3	11.4	28	30.9
1661–1670	45.2	21.3	63	23.9
1671–1680	45.3	29.3	54	16.0
1681–1690	51.4	44.9	92	6.5
1691–1700	54.3	38.4	134	15.9
1701–1710	55.5	41.1	74	14.4
1711–1720	58.6	46.8	217	11.8
1721–1730	57.2	30.1	137	27.1
1731–1740	50.7	28.6	78	22.1
1741–1750	49.9	28.7	79	21.2

M: Percentage of persons born in Amsterdam among those having
the banns published for a first marriage (based on the figures in
Hart, 1976: pp. 137 and 139)
S: Percentage of persons born in Amsterdam among those
punished on the scaffold
D: Difference between M and S

the bridegrooms and twenty-six years and six months for the brides. In
1726–7 this was twenty-seven years and ten months and twenty-seven
years and two months, respectively.[86]

It seems reasonable to assume that the floating section contained a
larger proportion of persons born elsewhere than the settled population.
The table shows indeed that the scaffolded delinquents numbered a
smaller proportion of born Amsterdamers among their ranks than the
marrying population in each decade. This would confirm my supposition
that the first group largely belonged to the marginal sector. But the
supposition of a decrease in this sector is not entirely confirmed. In that
case we would expect to find that the percentage of born Amsterdamers
among the criminals would increasingly match the percentage of born
Amsterdamers among the settled population after 1700. This is not borne
out by the table. The difference between the two groups becomes
relatively large again in the last three decades, although it does not reach
the level of the first. Thus, the matter remains inconclusive.

Whatever the origin of the delinquents, when they were prosecuted it
could not help them. No significant differences can be traced in the

punishment of categories grouped according to place of birth. Social distance between the judges and the delinquents apparently remained the same. The former did not care whether the latter were born in Amsterdam or outside the city. They might have treated *poorters* (citizens) differently from the rest of the population. But the sentences usually do not mention whether the convict is a *poorter*. These could of course be immigrants as well as born Amsterdamers and they were few in number anyway.

The sentences contain yet another indicator for the prisoner's social status. Usually they mention an occupation. This information has to be handled carefully as well. For one thing, the sources seldom differentiate between employer and employee, master and journeyman. If a prisoner is mentioned as a baker or a butcher, it does not necessarily imply that he had his own shop. Therefore it is impossible to differentiate the population of convicts accordingly. Second, doubts are justified as to the value of the information. If an occupation is mentioned, it does not have to mean that the convict is actually working in that field. Some clerks formulate it as 'shoemaker is the prisoner's trade'. This merely signifies that he once learned to make shoes. In a few of such cases the sentence continues 'but he declares not to have worked for several years'. The same might be true in other cases, where it was not mentioned. The authorities usually depended on the prisoner's own information about his occupation. Records of examinations also lead us to be cautious. They sometimes reveal the prisoner's exact answer and suggest that any kind of incidental job in which he once engaged could enter a sentence as his occupation. One man said he had first worked in the city's *lijnbaan* (ropemakers), then with a printer and that he had lately sold oysters. Another stated he earned his living by tailoring, if he had work. Their sentences mentioned then as oyster-seller and tailor, respectively.[87]

Hence a comparison between occupational groups would be unreliable. One observation is relevant nevertheless. Nearly all trades mentioned can be listed as lower or – at the most – lower-middle class occupations. Higher-class occupations are very rare, which holds for those mounting the scaffold as well as for the others. There is even a slightly higher representation among the former group (Appendix B, no. 20). The occupations listed as higher are 'civil service' (usually involving holders of a minor office in the city), publisher, broker, surgeon, notary and clerk. An occasional student was also added. Merchant was kept apart because of the ambiguity of the category. Rich commercial capitalists as well as poor small traders could be called a merchant. Members of the latter group were more often denoted as pedlars or 'people going around the streets'.[88] These belong to the category of lower occupations, together with shopkeepers, artisans and other workers. Absence of information about a prisoner's occupation, finally, does not necessarily mean that he or she did not have one, although this can be the reason.

Thus, a conclusion can be drawn about the other end of the social scale. In as far as the settled population brought forth delinquents, these did usually not come from groups above the lower-middle class. It is of course hardly a surprising conclusion. White collar crime was almost absent from preindustrial court records. Persons from the upper-middle class were only arrested when they had committed relatively serious acts. That may explain why they are twice as numerous in the scaffold series.

The sight of a relatively well-born person on the scaffold was indeed considered uncommon. In 1678 the sentence of a man giving 'corrector' as his occupation explicitly expresses indignation at the fact that the convict 'is to be found in a company of various rascals and thieves, although he is a man of learning and able to support himself honestly in this way'. He had earlier been condemned to public whipping in The Hague, but then intercession by his father had caused this to be changed into whipping indoors.[89] In 1753 Bicker Raye mentions as remarkable that one of those whipped was a Swiss of a very good family.[90]

One person belonging to the ruling elite of Holland itself was publicly punished during the period investigated. Theodorus van de Perre, lord of the manor of der Aa and twenty-eight years of age, was beheaded on 18 January 1670. He was found guilty of large-scale fraud, making use of false bonds. The sentence stated that his father had already punished him, while the old man was still alive. Afterwards a member of the College of Admiralty in Amsterdam warned him to quit his illegal practices. It was to no avail. Van de Perre even put the money collected for the poor of his manor in his own pocket. This was enough for the *schout* to demand a death sentence, to which *schepenen* consented.[91] The case offers a parallel to the trial of 'wicked Lord Ferrers' discussed by Hay, whose case was taken as proof that justice in England was administered independent of rank.[92]

Adults and juveniles

The prisoner's age is a recurrent item in sentences and records of examinations. In the scaffold series only 3.2% of the ages are missing. The mean age is twenty-nine years and four months. The median lies at twenty-six and two months and the mode at twenty-two. The youngest person on the scaffold was a twelve year old boy who was exposed for burglary and whipped indoors afterwards, in the fifth decade. The scaffold series contains no offenders of thirteen, but the age of fourteen is represented 9 times: 8 boys and 1 girl. Then the number of offenders increases with each age up to eighteen years. Convicts in their twenties make up 45.6% of the total. Then the number decreases with each group of ten years; 2.1% are older than fifty-nine; 0.4% older than sixty-nine. The oldest publicly punished persons were 2 men of eighty-five. Moses Persmayer was exposed and banished for twenty-five years – i.e. until his 110th birthday – for cheating, among others, the rabbi, in 1652.[93] Frederik van Hargen was broken on the wheel for murder in 1742.[94]

In the three samples taken together, the mode is also at twenty-two years. But the mean age is twenty-eight and the median twenty-five and a half. The ages range from seven to eighty-two. In 5.2% of the sentences the age is missing. Juvenile delinquents escaped public punishment to a proportionately higher degree. In the samples 17.3% are under twenty, while this is 15.9 among those condemned to a scaffold punishment. If we consider only those under sixteen the percentages are 3.9 and 1.3 respectively. Convicts in their twenties make up almost half (48.3%) of the samples. Let us take a closer look at the distribution of age-groups in the three separate samples for the offenses of wounding, infraction of banishment and simple theft (Appendix B, no. 23). Persons under twenty were rarely prosecuted for wounding/attacking. The second period contains none at all. Most offenders are in their twenties or thirties, especially in the second and third period. The percentage of attackers older than thirty-nine continually decreases. The reverse happens with infraction of banishment. The percentage of convicts in their forties and older takes a big jump from the second to the third period. The percentage for the group between fourteen and nineteen remains almost constant.

Simple theft offers a quite different picture. It is plain that the population of thieves is younger than the rest of the offenders in the sample. Persons under twenty make up about two-fifths (40.9%) of the total in the first period and about one half (51.5 and 49.1%) in the second and third period. If these young offenders are subdivided, changes from one period to the other are different according to how the ages are grouped. Note that 17% of the thieves in the third period are under fourteen, the 'minimum age' for mounting the scaffold, save for the one twelve year old boy. The average ages in all three periods become somewhat lower if we include those condemned for domestic theft, theft from employer and undressing children. Percentages of persons under twenty are then 38.4, 50.1 and 46.1. The same figures for the same groups in the scaffold series are 17.1, 17.1 and 21.3 in the three periods. The distribution of ages of thieves in the scaffold series deviates only slightly from the total distribution of ages. We can conclude that the offender's age constituted an important determinant for the decision whether a simple theft was publicly punished or not. Young thieves were more often excused from the scaffold than their older colleagues.

Can we observe changes in the punishment of different age-groups? If we consider all simple thefts (including domestic, from employer and undressing children; Appendix B, no. 24), we may be able to say something about it. The general increase in severity on the scaffold towards these crimes mainly consisted of a more-frequent use of branding in the eighteenth century. Separate age-groups more or less follow this pattern. Among the thieves under twenty branding either did not occur or was incidental in all but the eighth decade. The latter period also contains the only case of hanging. Eleven out of thirteen penalties more severe than whipping belong to the eighteenth century. Exposure is also incidental. Most of the young thieves were apparently sent to the scaffold not so much to be humiliated before the crowd, but because the judges found that, despite the prisoner's age, they could not impose a milder penalty than public whipping. Branding and capital punishment remain more frequent in the eighteenth century for all the age-groups. Likewise simple exposure is more characteristic for the seventeenth century among all convicts except those under twenty. The conclusion must be that the increase in severity observed in the preceding section took place regardless of the offender's age. It affected young and old.

Considering the whole period of 100 years, thieves of different ages were punished discriminately. Percentages are given in table 13. Branding increases up to the group of thieves in their forties. Then it drops considerably, but rises again in the oldest group, which, however, contains a mere thirteen offenders. But mildness also increases with the age-group. The frequency of simple exposure rises continually from 2.8% of those under twenty to 23.1% of those over fifty-nine. Capital punishment figures among all thieves but those in their fifties. Among the thieves whipped indoors, all age groups more or less follow the same pattern (Appendix B, no. 25).

So much for the thieves. Regardless of the offense one corporal penalty was exclusively reserved for juvenile delinquents. It is whipping on the wooden horse, which was always executed indoors. I discussed this form of punishment in chapter three. It was imposed on delinquents up to sixteen years of age. This is apparently a common limit. The *Parlement* of Paris likewise imposed special penalties on prisoners under sixteen.

Table 13. Thieves of different age-groups

Offenses: all simple thefts. Punishments in the scaffold series over the entire period 1651–1750

Penalty	Under 20 %	Under 20 No.	20–29 %	20–29 No.	30–39 %	30–39 No.	40–49 %	40–49 No.	50–59 %	50–59 No.	Over 59 %	Over 59 No.
Exposure	3	5	5	22	10	19	10	9	18	7	23	3
Exposure and whipping indoors	2	4	1	2	4	7	1	1	—	—	—	—
Whipping	88	159	78	332	67	134	59	55	72	28	54	7
Branding	7	12	15	63	19	38	27	25	10	4	15	2
Non-prolonged death penalty	1	1	1	5	2	3	3	3	—	—	8	1

Interestingly, the French knew whipping indoors as such as a juvenile penalty.[95]

The judgment of 'given to parents', the implication of which was that a corporal correction should take place at home, can be regarded as a special penalty for young persons too. It was imposed on two of the nine prisoners under eleven who entered the samples. Four of them received another minor punishment. Three boys of ten received an even heavier penalty. Jan Claasse was denied access to the city for two years in 1656, but he was living in Haarlem.[96] Baltus Hendriks was confined in the workhouse for three years in 1680. He had been a prisoner twice before.[97] In 1717 Jan Martin Voguens was whipped on the wooden horse.[98] He was the youngest corporally punished person in the samples, but at least one nine year old boy was also whipped. This took place in 1656.[99] After the age of ten, almost every type of non-public punishment was possible.

A number of sentences, finally, explicitly mentioned that the prisoner received a milder penalty because of his or her youth. The official formulation usually involved a condemnation to some corporal penalty followed by the announcement that it was remitted because of the convict's youth. As a rule the latter had to undergo symbolic exposure instead. For example, in 1651 a girl of seventeen had undressed one child. The condemnation was public whipping, but because of her youth she was exposed with rods hanging from her shoulder.[100] The same symbolic penalty was imposed on a boy of sixteen the next year. He had committed six burglaries. The sentence merely mentioned that he actually deserved a more severe punishment.[101] Two juvenile delinquents simultaneously mounted the scaffold on 23 September 1662. Pieter Jeroense was fifteen years old and had already been tried three times before. In 1660 he was whipped on the wooden horse and confined in the workhouse for a year. Now he had stabbed someone to death. The victim had died two weeks after the incident, but the doctors declared that the inflicted wound was the cause of death. The condemnation included sword over head and public whipping. Because he was so young and small, he was not whipped publicly but indoors on the wooden horse. Twelve years in the rasphouse and a banishment from the city for ever made up for the remittal.[102] The sword also waved over the head of Jan Hendriksen, sixteen years old. This case closely paralleled the preceding one. A condemnation to whipping on the scaffold was likewise altered to one on the wooden horse. Jan Hendriksen had also been a prisoner three times before. He had dangerously wounded someone, but the victim had not died. His term in the rasphouse was six years and a banishment from Holland for ever completed the sentence.[103]

The next case of remittal because of youth took place in 1687 and involved a boy of fifteen. He was a recidivist and had committed six qualified and fifteen non-qualified thefts. A penalty of branding was remitted and exposure, without specification, took its place. He was confined in the rasphouse for four years, to be sent to the colony of Surinam for ten years afterwards.[104] A burglar of fifteen and one of sixteen received the same original penalty the following year. They were both exposed with the rope around their necks and also sent to Surinam.[105] Another case involves the boy of twelve, mentioned above. He received a milder punishment because of his youth.[106] In the same year (1691) a burglar's sentence to public whipping was remitted because of his 'smallness'. He was seventeen. The rope was likewise laid around his neck for a while.[107]

These nine cases in the seventeenth century are matched by just one recorded remittal in the eighteenth: a sentence of branding was changed to exposure with the rope for a boy of sixteen in January 1709.[108] A boy of fourteen was even hanged in the eighth decade. He had committed rape and other acts of violence, which made him the youngest capitally punished person during the period investigated. Public whipping was the most severe penalty among the other fourteen year old prisoners. Two of the nine representatives of this age-group appear in the seventeenth century and they were burglars. Among the others, thieves are also present.

Sixteen out of twenty-eight offenders of the age of fifteen belong to the eighteenth century. Half of these twenty-eight fall into the period 1711–30. Four convicts of this age were branded and these cases also belonged to the same two decades. The sixteen year old group offers a comparable picture. About two-thirds of the offenders belong to the eighteenth century and nearly a half to the period 1711–30. The latter period again contains the three death penalties. They involved a robber and a burglar. The third had committed murder and became the youngest person broken on the wheel. The youngest capitally punished prisoners in the seventeenth century were seventeen. A burglar was hanged in the first decade and a participant in the Undertakers' Rebellion in the fifth. Six more representatives of this age-group received a death penalty in the eighteenth century. Among the trials of the Paris *Parlement* in the eighteenth century a few even more extreme cases occurred. Two twelve year old boys were branded for stealing cattle. Two others, fifteen and condemned for murder, were broken on the wheel. A girl of seventeen was burned alive.[109] But in Amsterdam too the age of seventeen was not really considered young and marked the 'transition to normal'. In the milder period two seventeen year olds were given remittals and two the death penalty. Prisoners of eighteen and older were treated more or less as adults. They knew it and sometimes gave a younger age to the judges. Jan Bosmijer did not get away with it in 1719. He said he was seventeen, but the court did not believe him. He had been educated in the Catholic orphanage and people from the institute declared that he was nineteen. He was hanged for robbery.[110]

Thus, it is no wonder that Bontemantel was unsuccessful when he tried to convince his colleagues that a twenty-two year old prisoner should be treated as a minor. The latter had killed a prostitute in 1659 and was beheaded for it. Bontemantel was the only one of the *schepenen* to oppose capital punishment. To be sure, the argument that the convict was a minor was just one out of three. It was complemented by the consideration that he 'had never been master of his senses' and that the victim of the crime was an infamous woman.[111]

Remittals were also granted for old age and/or infirmity. The two categories are not clearly differentiated, so I will discuss them together. The age of Anna Jans, alias 'Shit in the Kettle', was not mentioned in January 1654. She was exposed with rods instead of being whipped, because of her bad health.[112] A curious case, two months later, did not actually constitute a remittal, but is worth mentioning. A man had stabbed to death his opponent in a fight. Before he was slain the victim dangerously wounded his attacker. The latter was beheaded eight days later, sitting on and tied to a chair on the scaffold.[113] Sentences of whipping were further changed into exposure with rods for a seventy-two year old receiver and a sixty year old swindler in October 1654[114] and for a woman of sixty-one, surnamed 'The Rich Beggar', convicted of cheating in 1655.[115] Two beggars, who tried to escape from the workhouse, were granted the same remittal the next year. The reasons were 'indisposition' for the first (fifty) and old age for the second (seventy-two).[116] Indisposition had also befallen a female burglar (twenty) in 1660,[117] while a male receiver (thirty-two) in 1664 was 'weak and sickly'.[118] Old age was the excuse for a woman (seventy-one) and another (fifty) three years later; both had harbored thieves in their houses.[119] In all these cases exposure with rods took the place of public whipping.

Even the symbolic scaffold penalty could be remitted. A woman of thirty was fined for keeping a brothel in 1722. The sentence originally included exposure with rods as well, but this was remitted because she was ill.[120] The judges could also refrain from having whipping indoors executed because of sickness of the prisoner, as was recorded in 1686.[121] A person caught for infraction of banishment in 1678, was only ordered to leave the city again. He escaped a more severe punishment thanks to a tumor in his throat.[122]

These remittals also concentrate in the early years of the period investigated. Throughout this period persons of sixty and older occasionally received a corporal penalty as well. An exceptional thing happened in 1771. A sentence of branding for a seventy year old swindler, who was no longer able to stand, was executed nevertheless. He was whipped sitting on a bench beneath the gallows.[123] But of course this case falls outside the period investigated.

Men and women

Although the sentences do not explicitly mention the prisoner's sex, it can easily be ascertained in all cases. In the first sample women outnumber men, but their percentage decreases in the second period and still more in the third (see table 14). In the scaffold series the percentage of men is higher than that of the third sample in seven decades. It is only lower in the first, second and tenth. While the percentage of non-publicly punished women steadily decreases, that of women on the scaffold increases again after 1720. Part of this development is due to the prosecution of servant girls for domestic theft. Men were always more likely to mount the scaffold, except perhaps between 1741 and 1750. The fact that prostitution and procurership were seldom publicly punished explains a good deal of the difference. No men were tried for prostitution and keepers of brothels were mainly women too.

In the scaffold series, on the other hand, four offenses were commited only by males. They are homicide, rape, sodomy and stealing cattle. Infanticide and secretly having a stillborn child only involved women. In the remaining murder cases men prevail. Wounding/attacking was mainly a crime committed by men (Appendix B, no. 26), and only four out of 159 persons publicly punished for the offense were women. With smuggling this is twenty out of 111. Robbery and burglary are also a predominantly male business, with only some 12% of those mounting the scaffold for it being women. The 2 : 1 ratio is only reached in the category participation in robbery. The percentage of men condemned for theft in the samples is higher than that among the total of offenders. The increase over the three periods follows the general pattern. In the scaffold series male thieves are about twice as frequent as female. But in the category of participation in theft women slightly outnumber men.

We can conclude that women played a less active role in the companies of thieves. This is also confirmed by the fact that infraction of banishment

Table 14. *Distribution of the sexes*

A. *Scaffold series. Percentages of male and female convicts*

Period	Male	Female
1651–1660	54.7	45.3
1661–1670	61.0	39.0
1671–1680	67.0	33.0
1681–1690	76.4	23.6
1691–1700	80.3	19.7
1701–1710	76.1	23.9
1711–1720	80.1	19.9
1721–1730	65.7	34.3
1731–1740	66.4	33.6
1741–1750	52.1	47.9
TOTAL	68.6	31.4

B. *Sample. Percentages of male and female convicts*

Period	Male	Female
1651–1683	45.9	54.1
1684–1716	52.7	47.3
1717–1749	61.9	38.1

is a predominantly female offense. Prisoners condemned for it were often picked up as members of such companies. If no other offense could be proved against them and they had been banished before, they were punished for infraction. The proportion of women tried for infraction of banishment in the samples is constantly higher than their total proportion. In the scaffold series 107 women were punished for the offense and seventy-nine men. Among the remaining thefts, which were usually committed alone, women outnumber men on the scaffold. They make up 83% of those punished for domestic theft and 97% of child undressers. With theft from employer they figure in 16% of the cases. Swindling is a predominantly male offense in both sample and scaffold series. With receiving, finally, the 2 : 1 ratio is reversed in favor of the women.

There were no specific penalties for the two sexes, as there were for the age-groups. But no women were actually beheaded or had a thumb cut off. What remains is to inquire into differences in severity towards men and women. The comparison is only relevant for offenses where the absolute number of both sexes is high enough. This is the case with infraction of banishment in the scaffold series. Over the whole period of 100 years men received slightly more severe punishments for the offense. But this is due to the fact that their numbers are proportionately higher in the eighteenth century. The judges were undoubtedly milder towards female swindlers. For this offense in the scaffold series 43% of the women and 28% of the men were only exposed. Penalties more severe than whipping amount to 6% and 22% for the two sexes respectively. Again the proportion belonging to the seventeenth century is greater among the female than among the male swindlers. But after 1700 both sexes came to be more harshly treated. Exactly one-third of the men received a penalty more severe than whipping and about 14% of the women.

A good possibility for comparison is again provided by taking all non-qualified thefts together (Appendix B, no. 27). In the scaffold series exposure remains an important penalty for both sexes until 1710. It almost disappears afterwards, but more for the men than for the women. In those first six decades the sexes alternate in having the highest percentage for the penalty. The figures for those exposed and whipped indoors are always higher for the men. If we consider all cases of exposure together, fluctuations remain about the same as with those to which whipping indoors was not added. Thus both sexes equally take part in the development towards severity, as far as the decrease in exposure is concerned. With branding it is different. Male thieves were more frequently branded after 1710, but only the eighth and tenth decades stand out in that respect. Percentages in the seventh and ninth decades are only slightly higher than in the first two. Among the female thieves branding clearly increases after 1700 and especially after 1720. Between 1730 and 1750 a greater proportion of women than men were branded. Thus, women particularly take part in the development towards severity, as far as the increase in branding is concerned. The frequent use of the penalty for domestic theft at the end of the period accounts for this development. Men, however, predominate in the cases of capital punishment; only one out of fourteen involved a female thief.

In the samples women were always treated more mildly than men for a non-qualified theft. Less women were whipped indoors. But the jump from the second to the third period is more pronounced for women. The percentage of corporal penalties for male thieves is about twice as high as that for female in the first and second periods. In the third it is somewhat less than one and a half times as high. If we consider the three categories of corporal punishment separately, the percentage for the women is sometimes slightly higher. This is so with 'corporal only' in the first and 'corporal/confinement' in the second and third periods. Banishment largely makes up for the lower percentage of corporal penalties for women. The difference is marked in the category of 'banishment only' in the first and third periods and of 'confinement/banishment' in the second.

Women had one more possibility of receiving milder treatment. Some of the sentences explicitly mention remittals which parallel those granted to juvenile and infirm offenders. Women were spared a corporal penalty if they were pregnant or had – as the sentences express it – a sucking child. This legal practice was common enough. According to Von Hentig, 'primitive as well as civilized peoples' have always refrained from (capitally) executing pregnant women. Witchcraft trials form the exception: there could be no mercy for a child conceived of the devil.[124] I will not discuss the Amsterdam cases in detail, because there is little variation in them. The scaffold series contains twenty-two such remittals. All but one belong to the period 1652–77. The remaining case was in 1697. The ages of the women involved range from twenty to thirty-seven (one was missing). The original corporal penalty was whipping. Exposure with rods was the actual punishment in all but two cases, where the prisoner stood on the scaffold with only a letter attached to her. Two of the women involved received the remittal because of a 'sucking child'. The others were – or pretended to be – pregnant. The offenses included burglary, theft, undressing children, swindling, receiving, infraction of banishment, resistance to authority and spending counterfeit money. Two cases involved the same woman, convicted in two successive months.

What happened to pregnant women in the eighteenth century can be inferred from the sources. The sentence-books usually give the day when the sentence was pronounced as well as the one on which it was executed. A relatively large period occasionally lies between the two. Sometimes the sentence is pronounced prior to the justice day preceding the one on which the prisoner concerned mounted the scaffold. These cases all involve women condemned to a corporal penalty. Only once do the sources give the reason why. Etje Harmens was condemned to be whipped for domestic theft on 9 October 1721. Her name was written on the list of persons who had to undergo public punishment on 31 January of the next year. It was erased again and the secretary added in the margin: 'has to give birth'. The sentence was executed on 4 July.[125] Thus, in the eighteenth century, or maybe even after 1677 – the date of the last but one remittal – pregnant women were simply 'preserved' long enough to receive the corporal penalty anyway.

Annoyance because of pretended pregnancies in an age unfamiliar with biochemical tests may have been an important reason for this increase in severity. In some of the cases of remittal in the first three decades the judges or the secretary explicitly expressed their doubts as to whether the prisoner was really pregnant. And Abigail Jans was not believed at all. She was to be branded for burglary on 19 November 1667 but on the day before she declared she was pregnant. The judges consented to have her merely exposed, but stipulated that the original sentence would be executed the next time, if it turned out that she had lied. This was indeed done on 27 January of the next year.[126] It is the only instance of a sentence 'executed twice'.

Whipping indoors was remittable in the seventeenth as well as in the eighteenth century. It was recorded twice in 1673 in cases of pregnant women infringing upon their banishment. Their terms were merely prolonged.[127] It was recorded once in 1740. When a woman who was pregnant was convicted for a petty larceny, she was only denied access to the city.[128]

Avoiding danger for the innocent unborn child seems the most plausible reason for refraining from imposing a corporal penalty on the guilty mother. The procedure in witchcraft trials confirms this. The danger was apparently still thought to be present when the child was not carried in her body but merely dependent on her breasts for food. This gives us one more idea of the possible harm done by a whipping on the convict's back.

Jews and gypsies

Place of birth, occupation, age and sex of the offenders are recurrent items in the sentences. Other clues to their social identity are incidental. Two designations, which both stigmatize the condemned as belonging to a minority-group, occur often enough to permit a few comments. The first marks the delinquent as Jewish; the second as *heiden* or Egyptian, meaning gypsy.

Sephardic Jews and *Marranos* from Spain and Portugal had first established themselves in Amsterdam at the end of the sixteenth century. Most of them were or became relatively wealthy. The restrictions inherent in the guild-system were no barriers to them. This was less so for the Ashkenazic Jews. The latter had arrived a little later and held their first separate meeting in 1639. The Sephardic community always remained small in number, but immigration of German and Polish Jews continuously increased from about 1725 onwards. According to Hart's estimates, the two Jewish communities made up 3% of the city's population in the first half of the eighteenth century and 6 or 7% in the second half.[129] The Ashkenazic Jews did not really live in a ghetto but were concentrated in a few neighborhoods. They could be employed in industries without guilds. A fair number were tobacco-spinners and, as elsewhere, many became small traders, pedlars, dealers in second-hand goods or owners of pawn-shops. 'And they sold the stolen goods to the Jews', is a recurrent phrase in thieves' sentences.

The Jews' opponents included the guilds and the Reformed consistory. A complaint common to both referred to Sunday trading. In addition, the guilds often observed infringements of their monopoly from Monday to Friday as well. Their actions were sometimes accompanied by open expressions of anti-semitic feelings. Additional grievances of the consistory concerned Jews having sexual intercourse with Christians, trying to convert them to Judaism or insulting the Christian religion. Its attacks, however, were few compared to the numerous complaints about Papists.[130]

Christians usually referred to Sephardics and Ashkenazics as Portuguese and High-German Jews. Both groups constituted semi-autonomous communities within the city. Small misdemeanors were judged by their own leaders, the *parnassims*. More serious offenses were referred to the court. Although the Jews had acquired the factual right to exercise their religion, they were still an outsider group, as the information above makes clear. The existence of a specific crime of sexual intercourse between Jews and Christians illustrates the limits of tolerance. To be sure, it was punishable for both. Two of the four persons who mounted the scaffold for it were Christians. When a public penalty was imposed, there were always aggravating circumstances. Salomon Levi, born of Jewish parents in Ferrara and still practicing the religion, had falsely stated himself to be a Christian in 1671, in order to be married to a Christian Stockholm-born woman.[131] In 1724 a woman let her daughter be used as a prostitute by a Jew.[132] Two partners were whipped in 1730. Philip Bles and a formerly Catholic woman named Antonia had been living together for ten years. She was married to another but separated from him. Philip converted her to Judaism and gave her the name of Rebecca. Philip and Rebecca had three children who received a Jewish education.[133] Incidentally, we can conclude that it made no difference if the 'Christian' partner was not a Protestant.[134]

The increasing immigration of Ashkenazic Jews is reflected in the trials. They are hardly present in the first and second samples (1 and 2%), but they make up 8.4% of the third. Since the Ashkenazic community comprised about 4% of the general population in the latter period, it means that they were overrepresented.[135] This was also the case in the scaffold series in the last two decades. Then Ashkenazic Jews made up 7.3% of the condemned. The overrepresentation can be due to two factors. The Ashkenazic community may have had a larger proportion of delinquents among its ranks. Its relative marginality and the low standard of living could be an explanation. But it is equally possible that servants of justice were more attentive when confronted with Jews.

A total of ninety-nine Jews mounted the scaffold during the century investigated. Interestingly, nineteen were condemned for swindling, which offense represents 7.6% of the crimes in the total scaffold series. The difference could be due to the fact that many Jews were small traders, who had a relatively good opportunity for it. But again it could also mean that the court was especially ready to listen to complaints about Jewish swindlers. The rest of the Jewish prisoners were condemned for almost all the crimes also committed by gentiles. The absolute number of Jewish trials per crime does not permit statistically significant conclusions. Therefore it is not possible to establish whether they were treated differently from other offenders.

Tensions between the Jewish community and the Christian world around it were reflected in *keuren* and sentences about violence between the two groups. Fights between Jewish and Christian youths frequently occurred in the first half of the eighteenth century. On 19 October 1716 a *keur* was promulgated against it: 'The Gentlemen of the court have heard that many boys, Christians as well as *smousen*[136] often meet each other to fight, especially on St Anthonisbreestraat, Jodenbreestraat and Ossemarkt. Many times they have severely wounded each other or injured passers-by. Horses sometimes run away, which brings the danger of accidents. The court already prohibited fighting in 1627. Anyone engaging in it will be punished without distinction by banishment, whipping or otherwise as the matter requires.'[137]

The first persons to be publicly punished for it were Jews. A fourteen year old boy was exposed and whipped indoors in 1718. He had engaged in such a fight and fled to a wine-ship when the policemen came to end it. The sentence mentioned the possibility of accidents, the trouble for people living close by and the fact that a city-*keur* prohibited it, as motivation for the penalty.[138] The *keur* was promulgated anew in 1720, when an orphan boy had been killed in a Jewish–Christian fight. The court also threatened a stay in the house of correction this time.[139] Abraham Symensz, whose religion was not mentioned, indeed received a sentence of ten years in the rasphouse after being whipped on the scaffold in 1724. He had 'joined in one of the fights in which Jews and Christians so often engage'.[140] Another Ashkenazic Jew had taken part in such a fight a couple of times with a knife in his hand. He was also condemned for robbery and theft and, finally, for contempt of the Christian religion. He had pulled down his pants and knocked on his behind in front of a church. He was branded and exposed with the rope around his neck and a knife above his head in 1728.[141] In the next two years, two Christian fighters mounted the scaffold. Jan Cornelisz Dingeman, alias 'Johnny from Zeeland', was actually condemned for five thefts. One of these involved stealing from a woman who had taken him in out of pity, when he had been stabbed when retiring from a fight in which the Christians had to yield because of the superior numbers of their opponents.[142] The other was just condemned for engaging in a Jewish–Christian fight with a knife in his hand. He was whipped and it was mentioned that he had been banished for the same offense.[143] The implication is that a non-public punishment could also be imposed, but no condemnations for fights between the two groups entered the sample.

These few sentences do not permit a conclusion about the punishment of Jews and Christians. In any case, members of both groups were in fact tried. The series of scaffold punishments actually represented an unsuccessful attempt by the authorities to stop the fights. They did not stop after 1730. Braatbard referred to them in 1744; during that summer Jews and gentiles were fighting almost every Sunday. But he did not hear of any unpleasant incidents.[144] Apparently Braatbard did not consider the fights as such unpleasant incidents. Incidentally, he suggests that non-observance of the Lord's day was used as an excuse. It would imply that the initiative lay with the Christians. Yet a major incident took place on a Sabbath. In 1748 a regiment of provincial soldiers attacked the Ashkenazic community, shouting 'Christ-betrayers' at them. The *schout* stood by powerless, but burgomasters reacted with pressure on the captains. The latter consequently proclaimed that any soldier who further molested a Jew would be hanged. When the Tax Farmers Rebellion broke out a few months later, Jews prevented the plunderers from entering their neighborhood.[145]

Apart from Jewish–Christian fights, a few more trials stemmed from the tensions between the Ashkenazic community and its surroundings. Elias Polak was whipped on the scaffold for resistance to authority in 1716. He had committed violence against a nightwatch 'together with twenty-five other *smousen*'. His sentence did not say why.[146] In 1735 Samson Moses Cohen was charged with being the leader of a group of Ashkenazic Jews trying to prevent servants of the *schout* from apprehending a member of their community. The latter sold glasses illegally. Dung and sticks were thrown at the policemen. The prisoner confessed to having thrown sticks, after being threatened with torture. He was whipped indoors and banished.[147]

On the whole, the Amsterdam magistrates were far from encouraging or even acquiescing in violence towards Jewish people. They were primarily interested in law and order, which meant that their representatives were allowed to go about their business unhindered and the degree of private violence was kept as low as possible.

Portuguese Jews hardly figure in the court records. The Sephardic community did not provide an exception to the rule that few wealthy persons were criminally punished. Two of them entered the sample, one in the first and one in the third period. The same number was represented ·n the scaffold series, one in the first and one in the eighth decade. When another Portuguese Jew was publicly whipped in 1756, the spectators realized this was an exceptional occurrence. People told each other that no Portuguese Jew had mounted the scaffold for thirty years. The rumor went that 20,000 guilders had been offered for his release.[148]

There can be no doubt that gypsies were generally worse off than Jews. The former were not even allowed to be residents of the city. If they appeared in the jurisdiction of Amsterdam, they were usually apprehended. Therefore the numbers of prosecuted gypsies reflect their general presence in and near Amsterdam. They did not enter the first sample, although a few were arrested during the period. Three men and seven women were found on Kuiperspad in 1667 and were denied access to the city for ever.[149] Gypsies make up 0.8% of the second sample and the first in the scaffold series appears in the fourth decade. The third sample contains 0.6% gypsies. Most members of the group were publicly punished, at least after about 1715. It testifies to the severity towards gypsies. The total scaffold series contains sixty-nine of them, concentrated in the seventh and eighth decades.

The increasing presence of gypsies in the province of Holland led the Estates to issue a new placard in 1695.[150] Gypsies as such were banished from the entire province. If they disobeyed the placard and were discovered, they were to be publicly whipped. When caught again, the penalty was branding and capital punishment would await them the third time. The death penalty was also prescribed for those making trouble or committing violence.[151] In 1725 this was extended to those carrying firearms or a sword and those forming part of a 'troup' of six or more men above the age of sixteen. Confinement in a house of correction, for as long as the judges thought fit, was added to the punishments after apprehension for the first and second time.[152]

The gypsies tried in Amsterdam were treated relatively severely, but not as severely as the placard prescribed. The fact that they were banished as such, meant that they could be charged with infraction of banishment without being a recidivist.[153] In the scaffold series 59% were condemned for infraction of banishment, vagabondage or begging. It means that more than half were punished merely for being a gypsy. But only four received a death penalty: three for burglary and one for infraction of banishment. The latter was not usually a capital offense, save for those who had been condemned earlier by default. The sentence stated there was no other way: Maurits Hendriks, born in Antwerp, a *heiden* aged thirty years, had been punished five times before, three times in Amsterdam and twice in Amstelland. Burglary and resistance to authority figured in these former trials. On the last occasion he had been explicitly banished on penalty of the gallows, so he knew what awaited him.[154]

Persons born among gypsies as well as those who joined them were designated as *heidens*. The judges were generally aware of the fact that other wandering people used to join groups of gypsies. A prisoner in 1699 is called a 'former soldier, now *heiden*'.[155] Two women and a man in the eighth decade were charged with having lived among gypsies for years since their youth. The latter assumed the name of Antremony instead of the one he originally possessed.[156] A gypsy name had also been given to Margriet Hendriks, whipped in 1742, which she stated as her real name to the court. This cost her an additional charge of lying to the judges.[157] All these persons were still called gypsies. But another woman was first designated as *heidin*, which word was erased in a new sentence six months later. Likewise the offense was now simply vagabondage, 'as a gypsy' being deleted.[158]

Gypsies were recognizable at the time. A nineteen year old boy confessed to have gone out to steal with two others, of whom one 'looked like a gypsy'.[159] A woman was interrogated in 1747. The first question was whether she had not been 'black as a gypsy', when she was brought into jail, which she denied. Two servants of justice came as witnesses: when they apprehended her, 'she had a much browner skin than now'.[160] Gypsies were apparently recognizable by a relatively dark complexion. Those who joined them sometimes darkened their skin artificially.[161]

The argument that gypsies were vagabonds, stealing from and cheating innocent people, especially in the countryside, often sustained restrictive and oppressive measures against them. But since they were banished as a group, they were unwelcome even if they did not roam around. In December 1718 the *schout*'s servants raided a house in which gypsies were lodged. One of them, a boy of fifteen, was whipped for resistance. He was also charged with living in the city and working on the construction of buildings all summer long.[162]

Gypsies were prosecuted no matter if they were vagabonds or sedentary. They were considered a criminal category as such. Ashkenazic Jews were not treated in this way. They were a little overrepresented among the trials. They did not possess all the rights of other citizens, but they were not considered a criminal category as such. They were allowed to establish themselves in the city, whereas gypsies were chased from the area. Both groups were outsiders, but the latter to a much higher degree.

Jews and gypsies were present almost exclusively in the eighteenth century. Therefore it is impossible to establish to what degree the trend towards severity affected them. Two other categories certainly were affected: juvenile delinquents and pregnant women. Up until 1709 young offenders were sometimes excused from the corporal penalty which the judges thought they deserved. Two boys of fifteen and sixteen, having killed somebody, escaped capital punishment. A boy of fourteen and three boys of sixteen received the death penalty after 1709. Pregnant women and those having a 'sucking child' were never corporally punished. They were exposed with rods instead in the seventeenth century. In the eighteenth a different method was pursued. The judges postponed the sentence's execution until after pregnancy.

3   TOWARD A MODEL FOR THE EXPLANATION OF FLUCTUATIONS IN THE INTENSITY OF REPRESSION

As stated at the beginning of this chapter, the quantitative analysis of delinquents and their penalties of necessity had to be a case-study. Hence the preceding pages, though concerned with a period of 100 years, dealt to a lesser extent with the macro-level than chapters one, two, three and four. The focus was on punishment in a more concrete sense. Percentages of branding and whipping are obviously something other than semi-articulated feelings of acceptance or rejection with regard to public repression, although the two are equally obviously related to each other. Similarly, a case-study of terms of imprisonment would be more concerned with the micro-level than an investigation of long-term changes in prison regime. The intensification of scaffold punishment in Amsterdam between 1650 and 1750 is a more or less distinct process of intermediate length and, therefore, needs a separate explanation, which does not have to be in the same terms as the one for the long-term trend. The latter proceeded roughly through the stages of disappearance of serious mutilation – stabilization of the system of public punishment – critique of the system – abolition of public executions. This was certainly not a unilinear development. In Amsterdam the period 1650–1750 corresponded to the second of these phases: the last century in pre-industrial times when the system of public repression was largely unquestioned. It turned out that within this period the intensity of repression, in terms of the relative quantity of those scaffold punishments which were still in use, increased. In this book I attempt to explain the long-term trend primarily with reference to processes of state formation in Europe. The middle-range trend in Amsterdam should be explained in a different way, if only because, as I will discuss below, no spectacular changes in the Dutch state occurred during those years. We have to inquire which other factors, besides state formation, influenced the degree of severity of punishment. Then we can draw a sketch of a model for the explanation of fluctuations in the intensity of repression.

By calling the intensification of punishment in Amsterdam between 1650 and 1750 a middle-term trend, I also want to distinguish it from mere short-term changes. An isolated shift in the court's treatment of a specific category of offenders would constitute such a minor change. It could best be explained in terms of the crime itself. The offense may have increased in frequency or it may have been committed in a more professional way. Thus, it could be argued that the operations of robber bands around Amsterdam between 1710 and 1730 caused the court's severity towards property offenses. Even though some of the robbers had killed their victims and were consequently charged with murder or homicide as the major offense, their actions might have affected the court's treatment of the others. But this is an unsatisfactory explanation for two reasons. First, the trend towards severity in dealing with robbers and burglars had set in earlier. The robber bands can only explain an incidental peak in it. Second, and more important, the trend affected almost all crimes, not property offenses alone. Notably smuggling, an authority offense so clearly different in the minds of the people and probably committed by persons from a different social stratum, was also included in the trend. Thus, we have to look for an explanation in wider terms than those of the vicissitudes of particular crimes. Marc Bloch already stated this principle about half a century ago. He criticized the habit of historians trying to explain the rise of Estates in each European territory by relating it to just as many local circumstances. If parallel developments take place everywhere more or less simultaneously, these should be explained together in general terms.[163] Similarly, the rise in severity towards nearly every major offense in Amsterdam should be treated as a single process.

One possible 'internal' explanation should still be considered: the decline in the absolute number of trials might have caused the rise in severity, in which case the court would merely have kept to the usual number of scaffolded delinquents. But this is not a very probable explanation either. First, during the peak in severity in the 1710s and 1720s absolute numbers of scaffold cases rose to unprecedented heights. Second, the trend towards severity had already set in before 1700, when the drop in trials began. Third, the trend mainly consisted of a use of the more serious penalties *within* the scaffold series.

It would be futile to look for an explanation put forward by contemporaries. They were simply unaware of what was going on. At the beginning of the period Bontemantel stated that 'the judges of this country are more inclined towards mitigation of punishment or absolution than towards heavy condemnation'.[164] He was aware that the practice of punishment was mild compared to a certain standard, which was probably set by existing criminal legislation. We saw that Van Hogendorp expressed a similar opinion, at least with regard to property crimes, at the end of the period. He still perceived the court's standards as relatively mild. It is understandable that those living in the middle of the eighteenth century failed to recognize that these standards had actually changed. The more serious penalties imposed for certain offenses in the later period had usually also been executed for those crimes before; they just came to be imposed more often. Contrasts in severity were relative contrasts. No eighteenth-century lawyer did the kind of quantitative investigation performed by the twentieth-century researcher. Contemporaries were unconscious of the increase in the court's severity between 1650 and 1750. Hence we cannot infer explanations for this process from their direct and concrete comments on it. We have to look elsewhere for plausible explanations.

I will briefly review the middle-range processes in Amsterdam and the Republic as a whole which would possibly explain the trend in punishment.[165] Let me start with those which, I think, cannot explain it and end with the one that can.

A process hardly investigated is the stabilization of the Republican state. A Dutch state, however particularistic, gradually developed out of the earlier resistance against the Habsburgs' efforts at centralization. A ruling group stabilized its control and several local patriciates in Holland even intermarried to an increasing degree. But there is little knowledge about other aspects. Information is lacking in matters such as integration of different regions and professionalization of the administration. At the moment we have to assume that integration and centralization hardly progressed. In any case the Republic lagged behind the monarchies in this respect. Amsterdam's bureaucracy expanded somewhat, but it was all rather unspectacular. On the other hand, there were no serious breakdowns of authority during the period. The Estates of Holland and the magistrates of Amsterdam continued their rule uninterrupted between 1650 and 1750. A direct relation between the stabilization of authority in Holland and the trend in punishment in Amsterdam is not demonstrable.

One aspect of relations of authority in the Republic claims our attention: the alterations of periods with and without a *stadholder*. It is conceivable that the dependence or relative independence of Amsterdam's magistracy was reflected in the decisions of *schepenen*. Considering the data, however, we must conclude that this was not the case. The century investigated comprises both *stadholder*less periods with the rule of William III in between. The first of these periods witnessed the greatest mildness. Increases in severity took place during the *stadholder*ship of William III. After that time it jumped to a still higher level. So no relation exists between the two variables.

A point could also be made of the 'juridicization' of Amsterdam's college of *schepenen*. In the eighteenth century more of them bore the title of master of law than in the seventeenth. It is conceivable that professional lawyers favored more severe punishments. In the case of property offenses, for instance, they may have wished to stick closer to the prescriptions of the 1614 placard. But then again I should warn against overestimating the professionalization of the early eighteenth century or underestimating the legal knowledge in the later seventeenth. Moreover, legislation and actual practice continued on their separate ways after 1700. And there was no tendency towards juridicization among the *schouten*. So we do not observe a definite professionalization of the court, which, in its own right, could have been sufficient to explain the increases in the frequency of serious penalties.

Developments in the area of commerce and industry – economic fluctuations – easily come to mind when one is looking for explanations of changes in the standards of the court. The judges might have reacted to widening or narrowing employment opportunities or otherwise unconsciously adapted their standards to shifts in wealth and poverty in the city. But if we accept this possibility, some problems remain. The period 1650–1750 was – certainly for Amsterdam – one of continuous wealth. Holland's rapid economic expansion took place before the period and decline only set in after it. Relative decline occurred, but was not noticed by contemporaries. It was only after the period investigated that we hear complaints about economic regression. The relative continuity in prosperity in Amsterdam between 1650 and 1750 cannot have produced the observed trend. Short-term economic fluctuations likewise had no demonstrable influence on the severity of the court. The early years of the eighth decade witnessed the first of three eighteenth-century crises. Yet the eighth decade was about as severe as the seventh. Finally, I should point out the fact that the judges do not seem to have reacted to fluctuations in grain prices and resulting shifts in the standard of living of the poorer classes. A relation between rye prices and punishments cannot be established. The first went up and down without a particular pattern, while the second showed an increase in seriousness.

A more plausible explanatory possibility lies in demographic developments. The earliest shifts in the direction of greater severity of the court were visible after 1680, just when the enormous demographic expansion of Amsterdam had come to a halt. Thereafter only slight fluctuations occurred in the number of inhabitants. Here is a remarkable coincidence, but a causal relationship between the two phenomena still seems odd. We would have to suppose then that the judges were mild when the population increased and became increasingly more severe when it stayed at the same level. Moreover, the city continued to have a large proportion of immigrants, always well over 40%. It is likely that the awareness of having to keep a metropolis in line entered the judges' considerations. But it is doubtful whether the court actually perceived the fluctuations between, say, 45 and 60% of immigrants. And even if it did, it is more likely that severity would increase during a rise than during a decline in immigration. The fact that the standards of punishment for natives and immigrants did not demonstrably differ, finally, does not lend credibility to a demographic explanation.

Only one middle-range process remains, which went on continuously during the period investigated and can indeed explain the trend in punishment. It is the process of aristocratization.[166] This constitutes a combination of two interconnected developments: the urban patriciate acquired a greater hegemony over the other social strata and simultaneously it was transformed from a class of burghers into a semi-aristocracy with regard to mentality and modes of behavior. In the course of the seventeenth century the Dutch patriciate, notably in Holland, gradually became more of a ruling class. It asserted its dominance over the other strata and reached a *modus vivendi* with several of their representatives. The necessity of careful manoeuvering gradually diminished, although it never reached a zero-point. The increasing control of the patriciate over the strata they ruled brought a growing social distance with it. The patricians wished to be a kind of aristocrat and differentiated themselves also from the upper-middle class. They started to adopt French models of behavior. Aristocratization was first visible in The Hague in the first half of the seventeenth century. Amsterdam lagged behind but drew closer in the second half. The earliest complaints about a growing social distance between the patricians and the 'commonalty' were expressed by the Amsterdam lawyer Valkenier in the 1670s. Especially for Amsterdam the years 1650–1750 were a century of continuous aristocratization. At the end the ruling classes of Holland had caught up with the elites in the surrounding countries. Their standards of behavior, their manners, their views of civility were similar. With a certain retardation, they partook of the general European trend towards refinement in manners.

Of course there had always been social distance between the patrician judges and the delinquents they tried. But it must have increased as a concomitant of the process of aristocratization. Simultaneously the general stabilization of control caused the court to feel more secure and conscious of its position as an agent of repression. The judges of the *ancien régime* were always more severe towards outsiders: people with whom they had no close contact. Now the Amsterdam patricians increasingly felt themselves superior to and aloof from the classes they ruled. They cared less about the latter's fates and became harsher towards the law-breakers among them. Thus, probably without being conscious of it, they began to impose the serious kinds of scaffold punishment more quickly.

The repression of crimes forms a small but important part of the activity of ruling. The patricians were in a position to choose between more or less serious forms of repression. They were faced almost invariably by members of inferior strata, ranging from marginal vagrant groups to the lower-middle class. It is only natural that changes in the nature and severity of punishment should reflect changes in the relations between social strata. On a short-term level we observed this in the case of riots. Then the authorities were always confronted by the question of whether to react compliantly or uncompromisingly. This chapter focused on the routine administration of criminal justice rather than on short-term emergencies. The increase in serious punishment was connected to gradual changes in the relations between the ruling patriciate and the strata below. These changes make up the process of aristocratization.

More clearly than in the case of property offenses, the mechanisms involved are reflected in the punishment for smuggling. Smuggling is the only crime of which the character changed a little during the period investigated. The delinquents who passed through the city-gates with flour in the eighteenth century were more fierce and determined than their beer-tapping predecessors. And they were more clearly popular heroes. The heightening tensions were expressed in the attacks on impostmasters' servants. The court reacted by having more smugglers whipped on the scaffold. Here we have one case in which the offense indeed became more serious in the eighteenth century. But it is so inextricably tied up with the tense relations between the magistrates and the lower strata – and hence with the process of aristocratization – that it actually reinforces my point. The attacks and the whippings culminated in the Tax Farmers Rebellion of 1748 and the hangings afterwards.

The Amsterdam evidence suggests that changes in the relations between social strata, especially between the elites and the remaining classes, bring about changes in the intensity of repression. Hardly any data from other areas are available to determine whether this is a common mechanism in preindustrial societies. Within the period investigated a few quantitative figures concern the punishment of theft. Both in Frankfurt from 1651 to 1690 and in New York in the first half of the eighteenth century whipping was a common penalty. In Frankfurt banishment ranked high as well.[167] These are merely scattered data from widely different contexts and they are not embedded in an analysis of public execution. No conclusions can be drawn from them.

A noteworthy parallel to the Amsterdam developments is to be found in eighteenth-century England. Most English historians argue that repression became harsher during that period. To be sure, this primarily concerns criminal legislation. Throughout the eighteenth century ever more capital offenses were created, although, according to Hay, absolute numbers of capital executions remained relatively steady.[168] The increase in capital statutes still testifies to Parliament's wish to show a tough face. Here it was the ruling elites on the national level who wished to set the standards of repression. And these very elites were also involved in a process of consolidation of their position from the Glorious Revolution onwards. It looks as though comparable developments in the relations between the elites and the other social strata produced comparable developments in the field of repression in England as well as in Amsterdam.

This is all, to emphasize it once more, a matter of middle-term trends which refer to the degree of intensity of repression. The longer-term developments encompass the gradual decline of the public character of repression and of the element of deliberate infliction of physical suffering. That is the main subject of the present study. The longer-term development forms part of changes in mentalities and is primarily related to processes of state formation. Fluctuations in the intensity of repression, on the other hand, may rather be related to tensions between social strata (which in their turn are of course related to state formation). Here we have the contours of a model for the middle-term trend: stabilization of control by the ruling elites and increasing social distance bring about a rise in the relative severity of punishment within the framework of the stage reached by the longer-term development. I do not want to argue that a rise in the intensity of repression can only be produced by the factors mentioned. I merely present a model of a relationship which, I think, occurs more frequently. Empirical evidence from other areas can test the value of the model.

Chapter six

THE DISAPPEARANCE OF PUBLIC EXECUTIONS

After the mid-eighteenth century confidence in public punishment began to crumble. In the Netherlands the earliest signs of a fundamental change of attitudes can be traced back to at least the 1770s, although the completion of the transformation of repression was a long way off. The actual abolition of public executions took another hundred years. A similar chronology characterized most European countries. The transformation of repression was a far from sudden transition, which began in the middle of the eighteenth century and ended towards the close of the nineteenth century. It comprised changes which took place both on the ideological and on the institutional level. At least three phases can be distinguished: first, there is the quest for legal and penal reform which began during the Enlightenment. It is relatively well known and has been analyzed in several studies of the period.[1] Second, there is imprisonment: not the 'birth of the prison', as is sometimes stated, but the rise of confinement to a more prominent position within the penal system and the emergence of the penitentiary. Several recent works document this phase.[2] Finally, and only after the rise of the penitentiary, there is the abolition of public punishment. This phase and the political struggle involved have only been made a subject of systematic research in the case of England.[3] None of these three phases forms the main subject of this chapter. What is of concern here is the change of mentality implicit in them. The aim is to present the following argument: first, the transformation of repression, before and after 1800, was not a matter of political and legal changes alone, but primarily a consequence of a fundamental change in sensibilities, and, second, this change in sensibilities preceded the actual abolition of public executions. This abolition constituted the 'political conclusion', only drawn at the end. The question of an explanation for the change in sensibilities is reserved for the book's conclusion.

The term 'sensibility' should not be misunderstood. It refers to verifiable expressions of anxiety or repugnance and the question of whether these reflect a genuine concern for the well-being of delinquents or for that matter of anyone at all is left aside. Traditional historiography attributed the Enlightenment's opposition to *ancien régime* justice or the early nineteenth-century advocacy of imprisonment simply to humanitarianism. This is actually no explanation at all. Words like 'humanitarian' are recurrent in the rhetoric of reformers in several countries, but the historian cannot use humanitarianism as a neutral, descriptive category, as he does 'industrialization' or 'nation-state'. Paradoxically, the criticism of this traditional approach by Foucault and others has confirmed humanitarianism in its status of historical category.[4] Instead of striving for a more adequate conceptualization of changes in mentality, Foucault essentially argues that the reformers were not humanitarian. He stresses that their motives were basically utilitarian and that their concern was with the prevention of crime. Control was the guiding principle, instead of a respect for the humanity of delinquents. This contrast, however, is a false contrast. An increased sensitivity toward executions is not at all incompatible with the wish to establish more control over lawbreakers. In fact, the desire to control was always there; also in the sixteenth century. But the ways sought to achieve this control change and these changes reflect an underlying shift in mentalities. As I will demonstrate in this chapter, the gradual transformation of attitudes leading to the privatization of repression set in earlier and took longer than the penal reforms of the late eighteenth and early nineteenth centuries. Therefore I think that the former was more fundamental.

Without elaborating on it, Foucault himself indicated the real nature of the shift in sensibilities. The suffering, he says, which the mitigation of punishment was supposed to prevent, was primarily that of the judges and the spectators. The convicts might still be seen as traitors or monsters.[5] Both remarks are crucial. The privatization of repression meant first and foremost the removal from public view of a spectacle that was becoming intolerable. The convict's fate within prison walls was of less concern. Second, the fact that the criminals were still seen as wicked underlines the change in sensibilities which is involved. It means that the spectacle of punishment, even though it was inflicted upon the guilty, was still becoming unbearable. By the end of the eighteenth century some of the audience could feel the pain of delinquents on the scaffold. The implication, paradoxically, is that inter-human identification had increased. The aspect of identification in connection with the execution of rioters was examined. The lower-class audience identified with these specific convicts and hence could feel their pain. This is a static analysis but it can be transformed into a dynamic one. Increasing inter-human identification is an element of the changes in mentality discussed in this book. The death and suffering of fellow human beings were increasingly experienced as painful, just because other people were increasingly perceived as fellow human beings.

This process of identification proceeds along two lines. More categories of persons are considered as 'just like me' and more ways of making people suffer are viewed as distasteful. The first element was illustrated by several examples already given in the preceding chapters. Even in the Middle Ages spectators sometimes experienced sadness at the sight of an execution. When the audience in Paris wept in the early fifteenth century, it was because the person on the scaffold was a nobleman and an Armagnac leader. Not many other people would have been the object of pity. When an intended execution in Seville around 1600 'provoked the compassion of all'[6] it was because the condemned was seventeen years old and believed to be innocent. Around the same time a few Amsterdam magistrates stated that the house of correction should serve to spare juvenile delinquents who were not real rogues a scaffold punishment. They identified with them enough to want to avoid a physical punishment. But it was only after the mid-eighteenth century that the pain of delinquents who had committed serious crimes and whose guilt was not in doubt, produced feelings of anxiety in some of the spectators. This implies that a new threshold was reached in the amount of mutual identification human beings were capable of.

The second element has also been noted before. The disappearance of most forms of mutilation in the early seventeenth century has been discussed. Commentators from the later eighteenth century already took their absence for granted and often considered it as a sign of the greater civilization of their own times. Writers who commented on the esoteric, physical punishments still in use on ships felt obliged to excuse themselves for confronting the reader with a tale of 'cruelty and inhumanity'.[7] Again it is only around 1800 that certain groups among the elites considered all forms of public, physical punishment as 'uncivilized'.

Thus, the process certainly covered many centuries. Around 1800, however, it accelerated. Before that date human identification was only extended to the few or, to put it differently, a large amount of suffering was considered acceptable. Yet another way of putting it is to say that the system of public repression met with no significant opposition. Rejection increased from the 1770s onwards. If delinquents were made to suffer, it should at least be done privately. Towards 1870 continued opposition indeed resulted in the privatization of repression.

In the Dutch Republic a few 'precocious' spurts towards sensitivity antedated the main transformation of repression: a shift from stone to wooden scaffolds and an early wave of opposition to torture. The first has not yet been clearly verified and can only be reconstructed tentatively. In chapter four it was noted that some members of the elites felt a little uneasiness about public executions in the late seventeenth century. It looks as though this feeling extended to the sight of the scaffold. They agreed that public punishment was necessary, but they disliked to be reminded of it every day. Hence the outward signs at the place of execution should not be there permanently. In the sixteenth century most Dutch towns had a permanent scaffold with a gallows on it. It was often made of stone. A characteristic shape of the execution place was that of a so-called *groen zoodje*: a square surrounded by a low fence and grass verges. In the middle the floor was elevated or a small scaffold built. These execution places seem to have disappeared in the course of the seventeenth century.

We saw that Amsterdam had a removable scaffold. According to Wagenaar, the wooden poles and planks were ready-made, so that the scaffold could be erected and dismantled 'in a very short time'.[8] The city had permanent places of execution in the sixteenth century. The shift must have occurred in the early seventeenth century. It occurred in other towns as well. The city of Leiden had been executing its delinquents on a *groen zoodje* for centuries. This was pulled down in 1671–2 and from then on a wooden scaffold was erected in front of the Papestraat before each execution.[9] In Maastricht the stone scaffold on the Vrijthof, which had stood there from about 1300, was removed in the middle of the seventeenth century.[10] In Haarlem, however, the reverse happened. As part of a project to rebuild the town hall in the 1630s the old wooden – but permanent – scaffold was replaced by one made of stone. This stone scaffold on the east wall remained there until 1855. Although this is clearly a counter-example, it should be noted that the new scaffold had the appearance of a classical balcony and that the equipment of justice was normally kept inside the building.[11]

The case of Haarlem calls for caution. Nevertheless, the shift from permanent to removable scaffolds must have been common in the seventeenth century. The Court of Holland made such a decision rather late, but in this case it can be clearly observed that the shift was an expression of changing sensibilities. Constantin Huygens had already lobbied for the destruction of the stone scaffold in the 1670s. It stood along the Vijverberg close to the meeting place of the Estates and in that part of The Hague where most patricians and foreign ambassadors lived. It was precisely in that area which fell under the immediate jurisdiction of the Court of Holland; the rest of the agglomeration was judged by the court of The Hague which had recently replaced its stone scaffold with one of painted wood. Huygens wished that the Court of Holland would follow this example. Incidentally, since 1672 the scaffold conjured up the memory of the grand pensionary John de Witt and his brother who had fallen victim to popular justice on that very spot. There is no indication, however, that Huygens was motivated by a desire to eradicate the memory of the event.

In 1674 he wrote to William III about the matter: his pleas to several magistrates had been to no avail, although they had at least decided not to do repairs. Huygens considered the Vijverberg as the most beautiful place in the world; the scaffold, on the other hand, was 'the most villainous of all possible constructions'.[12] The Vijverberg was 'a too noble and glorious place to be perpetually embarassed by the sight of wheels and gibbets, to the great chagrin of so many residents of quality'. Huygens proposed to replace the stone scaffold by a statue of *Justitia* with sword and balance. Beneath it a fountain should be constructed, against which a wooden scaffold could be erected when necessary.[13] Apparently the *stadholder* could not help him either. Seven years later he wrote a poem in which he regretted the failure of his efforts: 'A foreign gentleman saw this stinking thing in The Hague' . . . 'and wondered why Holland's rulers were so gross as to let it stand there'.[14] Huygens did not live to see its demolition. A wooden scaffold was finally introduced in 1720.[15]

Huygens' poem suggests that revulsion against the sight of the scaffold – which in any case is clearly different from the popular fear of touching it – was international. This would be in line with the remark about the unpleasantness of executions by the English gentleman visiting Holland in 1695 (see chapter four). An event in Danzig in 1708 also tunes in to it. Because the Queen of Poland was in the city and lived right opposite the regular place of execution, a decapitation was performed elsewhere.[16] In this case the reason might simply be that the queen did not wish to see a multitude of people gathered in front of her door. But on the whole the conclusion seems warranted that a slight increase in sensitivity toward executions was already visible among the elites in the later seventeenth century. They felt some uneasiness about public justice and did not want to be confronted with its physical apparatus all the time. But they did not oppose the prevailing system of repression. It was a mere prefiguration of the transformation which set in after the middle of the eighteenth century.

The second 'precocious' spurt was a prefiguration as well, but probably confined to the Netherlands. A few seventeenth-century writers pleaded for the abolition of torture. The movement became widespread and international in the second half of the eighteenth century. The actual abolition of torture was the first visible expression of the transformation of repression. Although we are not dealing with a public feature, torture is still typical of *ancien régime* repression because infliction of pain is the essence of it. Its abolition in some states was the only reform of criminal law which was carried through under the *ancien régime*.

Torture was practiced privately because secrecy during the trial itself was a guiding principle of criminal procedure. But the authorities were quite open about its existence as such. The sentences recited during an execution often began with the standard formula that the prisoner had confessed 'outside of pain and chains'.[17] Apart from this, they occasionally contained references to concrete acts of torture. Thus the sentence of a burglar in 1661 adds to the account of his crime: 'and the court did not take the other accusations into consideration, which he, prisoner, impertinently denied even during torture at the post'.[18] Similar passages, with only one erasure, slipped into other sentences, also in the early eighteenth century.[19]

Historians often assumed that the abolition of torture during the Enlightenment was a logical consequence of the rationalism of the age. This is simply not true. Throughout history authorities have been aware of the uncertainties inherent to the procedure and of the possibility of convicting an innocent person. The fabric of rules which had been woven around the practice of torture, was meant precisely to combat uncertainties. Still, various prominent persons, including Augustine, Pope Nicholas I and several humanists, condemned torture.[20] But, despite the uncertainties, the authorities thought it a necessary custom. In a recent study Langbein rejected the 'rationalist explanation': 'The eighteenth-century abolitionist literature is the produce of its age in tone, but not in substance. The works of Thomasius, Beccaria, Voltaire, and the others do little more than restate the arguments that have been advanced against torture for centuries.'[21] According to Langbein, abolition was an overdue reaction to the fact that the old law of proof lost its force from the seventeenth century onwards. I find his argument unconvincing, but it would be beyond the scope of this book to go into it. I think that the first of the two quoted sentences is more important than Langbein himself

seems to realize. The rationalist critique, which had never been successful before, could acquire a new effectiveness because of a change in
sensibilities.

This argument forms the reason why I called the opinion of a minority
in the Dutch Republic in the first half of the seventeenth century a
prefiguration of the abolition movement. Its representatives, besides
repeating the rationalist critique, also put forward emotional arguments.
Johannes Grevius, an exiled Remonstrant preacher, wrote the first book
devoted entirely to the abolition of torture.[22] It was written in Latin and
published in Hamburg in 1624. Hence its influence was restricted. A less-
radical view was espoused by Johan van Heemskerk, a member of the
High Council. He advocated a moderate use of the rack and expressed his
compassion for the delinquents subjected to it.[23] The most influential
work was published by Daniel Jonctijs in 1650. He was *schepen* in
Rotterdam. His is actually a Dutch adaptation of Grevius' book. Jonctijs
condemns the 'fieriness' of the judges who find torture necessary. They
have become immune to the 'sighs and moanings of the miserable'.[24]

This emotional appeal was not successful at the time, because the
majority of the elites did not harbor such feelings of repugnance toward
the physical treatment of suspected delinquents. In the seventeenth
century the common feeling was probably only a little uneasiness with
regard to torture, just as in the case of executions. This was also expressed
in France. During the preparation of the criminal ordinance of 1670 two
counselors, Lamoignon and Pussort, discussed the articles on torture.
The first proposed to prescribe a uniform method, because the practice
was 'too rude' in certain places. The other, however, argued that this was
simply impossible: it would necessitate a description of torture, 'which
would be indecent in an Ordonnance'.[25] This opinion prevailed. The
solemnity of an official legal document could not stand the blunt
description of physical suffering.

A major change in sensibilities occurred in the second half of the
eighteenth century. It is most clearly expressed in the fact that the
defenders of torture felt obliged to display feelings of repugnance as well.
Characteristically a writer would open with the announcement that he too
found it an unpleasant method. Thus the Amsterdam lawyer Calkoen
acknowledged a 'humanitarianism' towards delinquents but wished to
bestow his compassion in the first place on 'the body of respectable
citizens'. He advocated 'humanitarianism without cowardice and
severity without cruelty'.[26] The opening remarks of the Viennese pro-
fessor Josef von Sonnenfels' 'On the abolition of torture' are the exact

opposite of Calkoen's argument and therefore reflect the general sensitivity of the age just as well. 'Many people', he said, 'reproach the opponents of torture because they only appeal to their readers' feelings, while they fall short of convincing them rationally. Therefore I renounce all the advantages which such an appeal to emotion and pity for the suffering could provide me with. I am treating the topic with the cool indifference of the lawyer, who turns his face away from the twitchings of the tortured; who closes his ears to their cries and sees nothing but a scholarly debate before him.'[27] Thus Sonnenfels took feelings of repugnance for granted. He wished to attain a new detachment from these feelings, if not his opening represents a covert emotional appeal after all.

Torture was abolished in Prussia in 1754; in Saxony in 1770; in Austria and Bohemia in 1776; in France in 1780–8, in the Southern Netherlands in 1787–94; in the Dutch Republic in 1795–8.[28] The rise of sensitivity with regard to torture had prepared the way for other elements of the transformation of repression. The next step was the abolition of exposure of corpses.

The display of the dead bodies of capitally punished delinquents was discontinued in Western Europe around 1800. It antedated the abolition of public executions by at least half a century. There can be no doubt that increased sensitivity moved the authorities to act. Abandonment of the custom was usually motivated by calling it a relic of the 'barbarity of former times'.[29]

Before the second half of the eighteenth century people were occasionally bothered by the exposure of corpses. The reason was usually that the standing gallows was situated too close to inhabited areas. The growth of a city meant that the site of exposure, originally well outside the walls, came to be nearer and nearer the outskirts. When a storm had blown down Utrecht's standing gallows in 1674, the owners of the nearby sawmill and brick-fields took the opportunity to petition for a change of location. They noted that gallows fields were normally situated 'outside the common frequency of people'. Their arguments are a little ambiguous. The request calls the smell of the dead horrible, but also the sight. Another consideration may have been more important: the value of buildings and premises was lower when situated close to the gallows. Thus, to live and work permanently in the proximity of corpses was considered objectionable in the seventeenth century. Nevertheless, the magistrates in Utrecht turned down the request.[30]

In the second half of the eighteenth century exposure of corpses became objectionable *tout court*. For example, when the bodies of condemned mutineers were to be exposed in 1764, a protest was leveled. A court martial had sentenced, among others, ten persons to hanging and three to breaking on the wheel. They had led a mutiny the year before on a ship owned by the East India Company. Their bodies were to be exposed on a gallows erected on the first row of dunes along the sea close to the village of Huisduinen. The scene was to be a warning to all sailors on the company's ships, which left the coast of Holland from that very spot. The gallows could be observed from a distance of three hours at sea.[31] The court martial wished to secure permanence for the gallows for at least fifty years. The regional administrative council protested against this, though in vain. They argued, among other things, that the villagers and fishermen of Huisduinen disliked the idea. The council referred to the gallows as an 'offensive and horrible spectacle'; the more so since it was not meant for the inhabitants at all.[32]

Another indication comes from events in the town of Amersfoort in 1770. There the council decided indeed to move the standing gallows, which the magistrates of Utrecht had refused to do a century earlier. The old gallows was pulled down because of its bad state of repair and a provisional wooden one was erected some twenty meters to the north. The original site was situated quite close to the Utrecht road. The magistrates stated that the sight of the corpses 'cannot be but horrible for traveling persons'.[33] In this case there is no talk of people living close by. Traveling persons were precisely the ones for whom exposure of corpses had been instituted in an earlier age.

In many countries the abolition of exposure of delinquents' bodies coincided with the end of the *ancien régime*. In the Netherlands it was the only major alteration in the system of public punishment brought about by the Batavian Revolution. In Bavaria it took place at the beginning of the nineteenth century. The structures on the gallows mountains there were often made of excellent oak. Following an order by the royal administration, all gallows and *Rabensteine* were sold between 1805 and 1814 to the highest bidders.[34]

Why should exposure of capitally punished delinquents have disappeared earlier than public executions? There are two reasons for it. The first is that the change was not primarily related to a shift in attitudes towards the infliction of pain and suffering. It was rather related to changing attitudes toward death. Obviously, developments in both realms are interconnected in their turn. In the long run familiarity with death and with the infliction of pain decreased. In both cases actions directly related to the human body were hidden behind the scenes of social life; in both cases the encompassing process of privatization is the force behind it. But the realm of attitudes toward death is the one to which exposure of corpses is most directly related.

The historiography of death shows that a major transformation took place in the second half of the eighteenth century. Philippe Ariès speaks of a 'promiscuity between the living and the dead' in Western Europe from the end of the fifth century until about 1750.[35] It was especially visible in the cemeteries. Shops and market-stalls stood in or beside churchyards. Musicians and actors played during burials. Graves were opened and cadavers removed, some of which were not yet entirely decomposed. A remarkable feature of many cemeteries was the ossuary: a gallery in which skulls and limbs of the poor among the interred were displayed for ornamental purposes.[36]

This feature of death disappeared after 1750. More and more people wished to be buried in the new cemeteries outside the walls. Enlightened authors attacked the situation prevailing in the old churchyards: the overcrowding with bodies and the display of bones.[37] Finally, the authorities prohibited burials in churches, although this met with popular resistance. Hygienic arguments were important, but they were not at the top of the list in the Enlightened writers' attack. Luther had already posited the hygienic argument against burials in churches.[38] In the second half of the eighteenth century a new sensitivity towards death had arisen. The parallel between the disappearance of the artistic use of (parts of) dead bodies after 1750 and the discontinuation of the judicial use around 1800 is evident. It was only the – relatively recent – medical use that remained. But in that case too the transformation is evident. Public anatomical lessons became a thing of the past. The process of privatization is discernible just as much in this area.

A discussion of the second reason why exposure of corpses disappeared first, anticipates a theoretical explanation for the transformation of repression. Following the general thesis of the book, this will be attempted in terms of state formation processes. A change in the latter field was directly related to the end of exposure. I noted the existence of a dual system of exemplarity. Public executions were meant to impress the residents of a town or district, while the display of bodies was to discourage newcomers from undesirable acts. Especially the latter feature had a symbolic value: it signified that the place was a city of law. During the early modern period further pacification was reached around these cities. This did not make much difference for executions as such, which continued to express the personalistic rule of dynastic states and patrician republics. But it gradually eroded the primary function of exposure.

Cities and principalities long retained an emotional value for their inhabitants, as the main focus of the latter's allegiance. This changed in the course of the eighteenth century and the definitive breakthrough came in the Revolutionary period. With the early beginnings of the nation-state the image of a *city* of law had definitely lost its meaning, so it was easier to abolish the display of dead bodies. No political counterargument opposed the demands of increased sensitivity. This situation did not yet prevail in the case of executions.

Although the abolition of exposure of corpses can be explained in its own terms, it is evident that another major step had been taken on the road towards the privatization of repression. Expressions of repugnance against the sight of executions date back to a period before the disappearance of exposure. The oldest in Amsterdam is an anonymous pamphlet printed in 1773.[39] That year 6 November was a justice day on which, among others, no less than six delinquents were hanged and one broken on the wheel. The pamphlet proves that increased sensitivity implies stronger inter-human identification. The author had no particular relationship with the condemned, whom he knew to be guilty and to whom he refers as malefactors. But he still wonders if they deserve such a heavy penalty and if they had not come to their crimes because of a bad education or from poverty. He experiences an inner struggle between his sensibilities and the demands of public security. If such punishments, he says, really prevent crime, everybody should rejoice in justice. The author ends with a word of praise for the Amsterdam magistrates for punishing disturbers of the peace, so he does not oppose the penal system. Nevertheless, his sensitivity is clear:

Be quiet, I see the multitude pressing; they all fix their eyes simultaneously on the spot where the sufferers have to enter the scaffold. No wonder, one of the guilty is already presented there. But good heavens, what a frightening spectacle! Miserable man, I am indeed overwhelmed by pity for the state you are in. What a face, what a deadly complexion (. . .) This one having finished his breath, is followed by others numbering six, who have all been condemned to the rope because of their wicked acts. How full of fright was my soul! How affected was I inside, when I saw them climb the ladder one after the other! I was cold, I trembled at every step they took. I often turned away my face and distracted my eyes from the mortal spectacle to the endless number of spectators. I thought that I noticed in some of them the same horror at such a terrible spectacle, the same repugnance which I felt. This raised an inner joy in me: it gave me a positive view of my fellow-creatures again.[40]

This pamphlet sets the tone for later ones. The spectator, belonging to the middle class or higher, is shivering inside. He notices with satisfaction that some of those around him felt the same; but he denounces the lower-class multitude who still watched for the sensation. The authorities, who arrange for all this, are not yet denounced.

A comparable attitude was expressed shortly after the Batavian Revolution. A preacher described the last days of a condemned entrusted to his care and hanged on 26 November 1796.[41] He hardly pays attention to the execution itself but focuses on an inner struggle in the minds of the judges. They have to impose public, physical punishment once in a while, but they do not really want to. They are torn between 'human compassion' and their 'legal duty springing from the interests of society'.[42] Van Hall, the attorney, has a 'sense of his obligations' as well as 'the highest degree of love of humanity and compassion'.[43] Because these magistrates impose scaffold punishments against their will as it were, they are worthy of praise again: 'People of Amsterdam! What a delightful acclamation to you that you handed over the sword of justice into such hands.'[44]

Expressions of repugnance against scaffold punishments at the end of the eighteenth century are not confined to the Dutch Republic. In the Southern Netherlands, for instance, sensitivity had increased too. When, at a beheading in Brussels in 1774, the executioner missed a couple of times, there is no talk of the traditional popular hostility, but magistrates who were present referred to it as a 'horrible spectacle' from which all spectators turned their eyes. The court should ensure that it never happened again, 'because it is in the interest of humanity to prevent such cruelty'.[45] In Germany Goethe expressed his aversion to the appeal of executions. A passage in *Wilhelm Meisters Lehrjahre*, written around 1780, describes it as an irresistable fascination. The spectators 'abhor' the execution, but yet are inevitably drawn to the 'terrible spectacle'.[46] Even the Prussian authorities adopted a similar terminology. They referred to a breaking on the wheel in 1798 as a 'sad spectacle'.[47]

In France during that period a number of voices were raised against what many persons had come to perceive as the 'cruelty of justice'. A piece of literary criticism is to be found in Restif-de-la-Bretonne's *Les Nuits de Paris* (1788). His account is dramatized, as always, but expresses his sensibilities all the more clearly:

We were proceeding toward the Place de Grève. It was late and we thought the execution over. But the gaping mob proclaimed the contrary (. . .)

The man was broken on the wheel, as were his two companions. I could not endure the sight of that execution; I moved away; but Du Hameauneuf watched it all stoically. I turned to look at something else. While the victims suffered, I studied the spectators. They chattered and laughed as if they were watching a farce. But what revolted me most was a very pretty young girl I saw with what

194

appeared to be her lover. She uttered peals of laughter, she jested about the miserable men's expressions and screams. I could not believe it! I looked at her five or six times. Finally, without thinking of the consequences, I said to her 'Mademoiselle, you must have the heart of a monster, and to judge by what I see of you today, I believe you capable of any crime. If I had the misfortune to be your lover, I would shun you forever.'

As she was no fishwife, she stood mute! I expected some unpleasant retort from her lover – he said not a word . . . Then, a few steps away, I saw another young girl, drenched in tears. She came to me, leaned upon my arm, hiding her face, and she said, 'This is an *honnête homme*, who feels pity for those in anguish!'

Who was that compassionate girl? . . . . A poor woman who had abandoned herself to the procurers on the Quai de la Ferraille! I looked at her; she was tall and attractive. I led her to the Marquise's refuge without waiting for Du Hameauneuf.[48]

Despite the abolition of penalties such as breaking on the wheel, sensitivity toward public executions became more outspoken and widespread in the first half of the nineteenth century. Although examples are restricted to a few expressions from the Netherlands, no doubt comparable fragments can be found in writings from all over Western Europe.[49] Characteristic of the Dutch writings is that a number of authors mix their sentiments with pride. They express their gladness at the disappearance of the more agonizing forms of punishment and of torture and incidentally launch the opinion that the practice of these penalties was less frequent in their own country. Thus, J. van Leeuwen, in a speech in 1827, says that the old forms of punishment were not due to persons then living but to 'the lower standard of civilization and enlightenment of that age'.[50] Being a judge himself, he apparently agrees with the scaffold punishments which were still executed. Nevertheless, he assumes that his listeners harbor feelings of repugnance: 'While I excuse myself for the unpretty accounts which cannot be but painful for the heart of the sensitive reader, I beg you to pay attention only to the importance of the matter.'[51]

Van Leeuwen published his speech in *Love and Hope*, the journal of the Society for the Moral Improvement of Prisoners. Other members of this philanthropic society were more radical and in favor of the abolition of scaffold punishments. In a petition to the king (1827) they state that the 'most civilized and enlightened part of the nation' feels 'a certain shrinking' from and a 'repugnance' of all corporal penalties. Executions were only attended by the 'lower, less civilized and less enlightened popular classes'.[52] Yet even the broadsheets, written primarily for these very popular classes, change in tone. A pamphlet announcing an Amsterdam execution in 1838, begins in this way:

Alas what a sad alteration is exhibited before our eyes. A few days ago this place was a place of joy, where people played and danced at the fair and pretty stalls winked at them. But alas! this has been changed into sadness. There the *stage of sorrow* stands again. O God! how many shall mount it this time, to carry their shame and repentance with them. Spectators, see there exposed before your eyes a few criminals who deserve your contempt; but aye, look at them also with eyes full of compassion: once they were as innocent as you are.[53]

This tone of sorrow and the exhortation to feel pity are absent from eighteenth-century execution broadsheets. They illustrate the author's inner struggle between his sensibilities and the wish, retained from an earlier age, to moralize the lower-class audience. At the execution in question a few delinquents were branded, some more whipped, one exposed with the rope around his neck and one had the sword waved over his head.

In the middle of the nineteenth century sensitivity towards executions is taken so much for granted that, just as with torture three generations earlier, the defenders feel obliged to show their revulsion too. Thus, in 1847 a Utrecht physician takes care to explain that he also dislikes them. Nevertheless, he argues, whipping cannot be abolished yet because of the low standard of civilization and moral development of the lower classes. A year earlier a lawyer from the same town had pleaded for the abolition of physical punishment. According to him, the appearance of recidivists on the scaffold proved that public executions only made people more obdurate in their ways. He found the spectacle a 'barbaric' one and wished to see it disappear in the name of 'civilization' and 'enlightenment'.[54]

This sensitivity was largely confined to the upper and middle classes. They comprised polite society of the time, who formed public opinion and whose members expressed themselves in writing. The lower classes continued to be attracted to the event until the end. The elites had frowned upon their fascination from the middle of the seventeenth century onwards. Two hundred years later some people still thought that control depended on a display of toughness. Many others, whose forefathers had fully approved of the spectacle, now considered the eagerness of the lower classes to watch it as a sign that they were not yet as civilized as themselves.

To conclude, the actual abolition is examined briefly. It has been documented most fully in England. In that country the privatization of repression set in relatively early and originally for reasons of public order. It was noted earlier that executions in eighteenth-century London were more problematic from the public order point of view than in any other preindustrial city. The procession from Newgate to Tyburn in particular was often seen by the authorities as a march of undue triumph for the convict. He was acclaimed by the public rather than regarded as a warning. As this occurred frequently, it is understandable that the authorities concluded that the spectacle of punishment no longer served the purpose which, to their minds, it had always done in the past. This conclusion was drawn by Henry Fielding, police magistrate for Westminster. He wished executions to be performed a little off-stage as it were. Being private to a certain degree, they would appear 'more shocking and terrible to that crowd'.[55] In 1755, together with his brother John, he proposed to move them to Newgate.[56]

At that time the opposition was still too strong. The idea received a new impulse around 1780. In 1779 branding was abolished,[57] which left whipping and hanging as the major tools of public justice. Two years later the Corporation of London wrote to the Secretary of State about the ineffectiveness of high numbers of capital executions. These would rather 'encourage crime by accustoming the populace to acts of brutality and by cheapening the value placed on human life'.[58] In 1783 Fielding's proposal was realized, with the arguments already put forward by him. Capital executions were removed to a place just outside the walls of Newgate. Linebaugh concludes: 'Hangings were still public, but in the abolition of the procession to the gallows, a step had been taken towards privately inflicted punishment and a major source of disorder at hangings had been removed.'[59]

The second part of Linebaugh's statement refers to the immediate context of the decision. Late eighteenth-century London was the biggest metropolis that preindustrial Europe had ever seen. At executions it faced problems of a magnitude that did not occur elsewhere. No other European city, except Paris, grew that big before public justice was abolished. Hence the events of 1783 were peculiar to London. The Corporation's request does exhibit the first signs of a sensitivity with regard to physical punishment. Just as in other countries, however, it was still a long way from private executions.

This road has been ably charted by David D. Cooper and it is unnecessary to repeat his analysis here. Besides hanging, whipping came to be executed in private too. Flogging continued to be practiced well into the twentieth century and its use was even extended in 1863.[60] But it was no longer public. A description around 1870 says: 'Few or none are present except the officials of the gaol or visiting justices; spectators are not admitted within the prison walls to see a fellow human being beaten when they have no better motive than mere curiosity.'[61] In the meantime hanging had also ceased to be public. The last public capital execution in Britain took place at Newgate on 26 May 1868. Three days later the Capital Punishment within Prisons Bill received royal approval. On 13 August the first private hanging followed in Maidstone.[62]

The other Western European countries witnessed a similar development. The last public execution in Vienna also took place in 1868. From the early 1850s onwards most German states transferred capital punishment to within prison walls. In one case we hear that the new privateness was circumvented. An execution in Darmstadt in 1853 was to be performed in the prison's courtyard. An enterprising citizen had a stand built outside the wall and charged a fee to mount it.[63] In a few other countries, such as Spain, the abolition of public executions occurred somewhat later than 1870, but it is only in France that the transformation of repression extends far beyond the chronology 1770–1870. It began around the same time as elsewhere in Western Europe but was completed much later.

A major step was taken in the early years of the July Monarchy. Just as in London a half century earlier, capital executions were moved from the center of Paris. In 1830 the name of the Place de Grève had been changed into Place de l'Hôtel-de-Ville. Two years later a square on the outskirts of the *faubourg* St Jacques was chosen as the location and henceforth the execution was scheduled at 8.0 a.m. instead of 4.0 p.m. According to Victor Hugo, fear of the multitude in the center of the city had induced the transfer. Reasons of traffic control were also given.[64] In the same year branding and exposure were abolished.[65] Corporal punishment came to be executed exclusively within prisons.

In the middle of the century the location of capital executions was again changed. They were now done next to the prison walls on the Place de la Roquette. This meant that the condemned did not have to be transported through the streets. Still the crowds kept on assembling. In January 1870 the notorious murderer Troppmann was guillotined. Although the event had been brought forward to 7.0 a.m., numerous spectators watched it, among them Turgenev. In June of that year the deputy Crémieux proposed a law that would transfer capital executions to within prison walls. It never came to a vote because of the approaching war.[66] The Third Republic apparently did not wish to change the situation. We hear of large crowds assembling at the decapitation of murderers in Béthune and Carpentras in 1909.[67] The last public execution in France took place in 1939.[68]

In the Netherlands a conscious transfer of punishment to indoors never took place. Public executions simply ceased to exist because all public penalties were abolished. Amsterdam witnessed a partial parallel to the geographic marginalization of executions which occurred in London and Paris. The last justice day on Dam Square was 12 December 1807. Louis Napoleon wished to use Amsterdam's town hall as a royal palace. The court evacuated the building in February 1808 and on 21 May the scaffold was erected in front of the St Anthony weigh-house at the Nieuwmarkt.[69] The Nieuwmarkt was still very much within the city, but not as central as Dam Square. In 1812 the spectators were able to admire the guillotine there.[70] The new Dutch regime did not adopt this instrument, but the location of executions in the city remained the same.

In 1839 the Second Chamber sanctioned the removal of branding from the penal code, but the First Chamber voted against it the next year. The disappearance of public, corporal punishment took another fourteen years. Exposure, whipping and branding were abolished by a law of 1854.[71] Only the spectacle of death remained. The hanging which took place in Maastricht on 31 October 1860 was the last public execution in the Netherlands. No death sentences were executed from then until the abolition of capital punishment ten years later. In 1870 it was discovered that due to an 'oversight' a few forms of public, corporal punishment had been officially valid since 1854. These were simultaneously abolished.[72]

At the time most countries did not follow the Netherlands in the total abolition of the death penalty. In England only the Radicals favored this. They opposed the Capital Punishment within Prisons Bill for that very reason, arguing that it would consolidate the position of the death penalty. Other opponents were, according to Cooper, reactionaries who wished to show a tough face and denounced 'philanthropic weakness'.[73] An analysis of the political affiliations of those arguing for and against the privatization of repression in various countries is still lacking. I do not think it would be very important. The argument of public security gradually lost ground before the rising tide of sensitivity toward the open infliction of physical suffering and death. It may be correct to designate those who tenaciously held on to the public security view as conservatives or reactionaries, but this is largely tautological. At one time the spectacle of punishment had been self-evident for all. We have to explain the emergence of 'philanthropic weakness' and to inquire into the pre-conditions for its ultimate victory. What was the changed social context in which this was in fact no weakness at all?

STATE FORMATION AND MODES
OF REPRESSION

At the beginning of this book I emphasized the differences between two areas of societal development: the development of mentalities and changes in human organization. Although the two areas can be clearly distinguished, any sociological–historical theory should make a pronouncement about the way they are related. In doing so, I will attempt to explain the fate of executions.

Modes of repression belong to the history of mentalities. They reflect the elites' willingness to deal in one way or another with persons exhibiting undesirable behavior. The sort of repression which is advocated or tolerated in a particular society is an indication of the psychic make-up of its members. Publicity and the infliction of physical suffering were the two main elements of the penal system of the *ancien régime*. They should be understood as part of the mental atmosphere prevailing in preindustrial Western Europe. Many events in social life, from childbirth to dying, had a more open character, while with regard to physical suffering in general, a greater lack of concern prevailed than is current today. This mentality was never static; it began to crumble from the seventeenth century onwards. Simultaneously, repression was changed too.

In this study the routine character of seventeenth- and eighteenth-century executions has been demonstrated. From about 1600 the seeds of the later transformation of repression were manifest. The two elements, publicity and suffering, slowly retreated. The disappearance of most forms of mutilation of non-capital convicts constituted the clearest example. An equally important expression of the retreat was the spread of houses of correction; a theme which could not be discussed here.[1] A slight uneasiness about executions among the elites in the second half of the seventeenth century has also been shown. These developments all anticipated the more fundamental change in sensibilities which set in after the middle of the eighteenth century: an acceleration which led to the privatization of repression. The acceleration after the middle of the eighteenth century had a parallel in other areas of the history of mentalities. Processes of privatization are notably reflected in the rise of the domesticated nuclear family.

I am explaining the evolution of modes of repression with reference to processes of state formation. The latter do not of course belong to the history of mentalities; we enter the field of human organization. State formation and such events as the rise and fall of social strata comprise a separate area of societal development. As noted in the preface, Norbert Elias offered a model for the interdependence of developments in the two fields.[2] I indicated the revisions to be made in the model: notably the shift in emphasis from single states to the rise of a European network of states. In early modern Europe this network extended its influence to areas, such as the Dutch Republic, which lagged behind in centralization. There too a relative pacification produced domesticated elites. On the other hand, the stability of the early modern states remained vulnerable, and this holds true for both patrician republics and absolute monarchies. Ultimately, however, the early modern state was transformed almost everywhere into the nation-state; in Britain, France and the Netherlands among others. These developments provide the key for understanding the evolution of repression in Europe.

This study has continually emphasized the functions which public executions had for the authorities. The theme was not restricted to chapter three, but recurred in others. The observations they contain are, I think, enough to argue that late medieval and early modern executions served especially to underline the power of the state. They were meant to be an exemplary manifestation of this power, precisely because it was not yet entirely taken for granted. This explains the two basic elements of the preindustrial penal system. Publicity was needed because the magistrates' power to punish had to be made concretely visible: hence the ceremony, the display of corpses and the refusal to refrain from executions in the tense situation after riots. That public penalties usually involved the infliction of physical suffering is in tune with their function as a manifestation of the power of the magistrates. Physical punishment achieved a very direct sort of exemplarity. The authorities held a monopoly of violence and showed this by actually using it. The spectators, who lived in a relatively pacified state but did not yet harbor a modern attitude towards the practice of violence, understood this. Public executions represented *par excellence* that function of punishment which later came to be called 'general prevention'.

So far the relationship has been demonstrated largely in a static context. It can be further clarified if we consider the dynamics. In the first chapter I explained that the beginnings of criminal justice were intertwined with the beginnings of state formation and, to a lesser extent, with urbanization. Gradually urban and territorial authorities conquered the vendetta and limited private reconciliation. They started to protect their servant, the executioner, and attempted – though unsuccessfully – to raise his status. The magistrates became the agents who exercised justice.

Public executions first served to seal the transfer of vengeance from private persons to the state. The justice which the authorities displayed served to bolster up their precarious position. They were preoccupied with the maintenance of a highly unstable and geographically limited monopoly of violence well into the sixteenth century. When these monopolies became slightly more stable and crystallized into dynastic states or oligarchic republics uniting a larger area, new considerations came to the fore. Control of the monopoly had to be defended against real or imagined incursions. Bandits and armed vagabonds were still omnipresent. Maintaining the dominance over lower strata and marginal groups was another pressing concern.

Thus, the display of physical punishment as a manifestation of authority was still considered indispensable in the early modern period, because the existing states were still relatively unstable in comparison to later times. In other words, the spectacle of suffering was to survive until a certain degree of stability had been reached. The spectacle was part of the *raison d'état*. I noted this in connection with the penalty of sword over head for semi-homicide in the Netherlands. The peace of the community stood more centrally in dealing with crime than today. Hence the existence of a category such as 'half guilty', which would be inconceivable in modern criminal law. Similar considerations applied to torture. In the second half of the eighteenth century, when opinions *pro* and *contra* were both expressed, this becomes eminently clear. The reformers, placing an individual person at the center of their considerations, argued that he could be either guilty or innocent. It made torture unnecessary since innocent persons should not be hurt and those found guilty should simply receive their punishment. The defenders of torture argued from a different point of view. They stuck to an intermediate category of serious suspicion. The heavily suspect were dangerous to the community, so that it was lawful to subject them to torture.[3] This argument is based on the *raison d'état*, where the security of the community takes precedence.

The relative instability was not the sole characteristic of early modern states that explains the nature of repression. A second one, also inherited from the later Middle Ages, was equally important. It is the personal element in wielding authority. I discussed this at the end of chapter three. In the later Middle Ages the preservation of authority was often directly dependent on the person of the ruler. This was illustrated by urban ordinances which put a higher penalty on acts of violence if committed when the lord was in town. In the early modern period this personal element was not as outspoken as it had been before, but it continued to make its mark on the character of the state. A crime was a breach of the king's peace. Public executions constituted the revenge of the offended sovereign.

The personal element should not be viewed as referring exclusively to the king or sovereign. If that were the case, the fact that public executions in countries ruled by patrician elites – such as the Dutch Republic and eighteenth-century England – did not differ significantly from those in France and in German principalities, would be inexplicable. In France the state meant the king and his representatives; judges in the royal courts, for instance. In the Netherlands the state meant the gentlemen assembled in The Hague, the Prince of Orange or the burgomasters of Amsterdam. Foucault's image of physical punishment as the king's branding-mark is relatively well known.[4] But the marks usually represented the jurisdiction. The symbol was equally forceful in a patrician republic. The reaction to the removal of a body from Amsterdam's gallows field, noted in chapter four, is revealing. The magistrates considered such a body as the property of the city and saw the removal as a theft. The inhabitants of urban and rural communities, also in dynastic states, must have associated authority – perhaps even in the first place – with local magistrates. The conspicuous presence of these magistrates at executions sealed the relationship.[5]

These observations, finally, bring a solution to the problem of the disappearance of public executions. They suggest that a transformation of the state constitutes the explanatory factor. Indeed other transformations are less likely candidates. It would be futile, for instance, to relate the change to industrialization. In many countries the privatization of repression preceded the breakthrough of an industrial society. This chronology is evident in the case of the Netherlands. In England, on the other hand, public executions were still a common spectacle when industrialism was already fully developed. The situation produced hybrid combinations of modern transport and traditional punishment, especially in the larger cities. For a hanging in Liverpool the railway company advertized special trains ('parties of pleasure'), departing from the manufacturing towns.[6] The chronology of industrialization varied from country to country, while the retreat of public executions took place almost everywhere between about 1770 and about 1870. Similarly, the transition from the early modern to the nation-state also occurred in most Western European countries in this period.[7]

Thus, the closing of the curtains can be explained with reference to state formation processes as well. We may schematically divide the inherent transformation of sensibilities into two phases. The first comprised the emergence of an aversion to the sight of physical punishment and a consequent criticism of the penal system among certain groups from the aristocracy and the bourgeoisie. This aversion became manifest in the late eighteenth century and was a result of processes of conscience formation. The relative pacification reached in the early modern states cleared the way for the appearance of domesticated elites. The psychic changes which they underwent first found an expression in a refinement of manners and restraints in social intercourse. But the slight sensitivity to public justice that was already manifest before 1700 prefigured later developments. Originally, psychic controls were largely confined to a context of one's own group. Emotions and aggressive impulses were hardly restrained with regard to inferior classes. This situation altered gradually. In the course of the early modern period mutual dependence between social groups increased. Consequently, the context of psychic controls widened. Once more I should note the importance of the identification aspect: an increase in mutual identification between social groups took place. This increase certainly had its setbacks. We saw that the Amsterdam magistrates became – within the confines of the general standard of the period – slightly harsher towards delinquents between 1650 and 1750 due to their increasing social distance from the classes they ruled. This can also be understood as a temporary decrease in identification of rulers with the ruled. But in the long run this identification grew stronger. By the end of the eighteenth century an unknown number of individuals among the elites had reached a new stage and identified to a certain degree with convicts on the scaffold. These delicate persons disliked the sight of physical suffering: even that of the guilty. The first phase of the transformation of sensibilities had set in.

This first phase, so it appeared, resulted from developments that took place within the context of the early modern state. It did not immediately produce a major reform of the penal system. Two ancient features of repression disappeared though: torture and exposure of corpses. Abolition of the latter custom was often part of revolutionary measures. The gallows field symbolized a monopoly of justice particularly within an urban or regional context. The image of the individual city or county as a relatively independent entity had eroded during the seventeenth and eighteenth centuries. The final blow was long overdue. It came everywhere as a direct consequence of the downfall of the *ancien régime*.

The early modern state, however, did not disappear overnight in the Revolutionary period. The final establishment of the nation-state in Western Europe took most of the nineteenth century.[8] The second phase of the transformation of sensibilities set in parallel to it. Repugnance to the sight of physical punishment spread and intensified. In the end the 'political conclusion' was drawn and public executions were abolished. The privatization of repression had been completed.

It could be completed because the nation-state lacked the two essential elements of which public executions had been a function. The nation-state, because of closer integration of geographic areas and wider participation of social groups, was much more stable than the early modern state. And the liberal/bourgeois regimes, with their increasingly bureaucratized agencies, had a much more impersonal character. Hence the later nineteenth century witnessed more impersonal and less visible modes of repression. Public executions were not only felt to be distasteful; they were no longer necessary. In its internal affairs the nation-state could largely do without the *raison d'état*. Beccaria had anticipated the transformation a century earlier. His often-quoted saying that effective prevention of crime depends on the certainty of being caught rather than on the severity of punishment was actually a plea for a stronger state, and in particular for a police force. This was realized in the nation-state. Consequently the authorities could afford to show a milder and more liberal face.[9]

Once more it should be emphasized that absolutes do not exist. Even the privatized repression which emerged in the course of the nineteenth century needed a minimum of exemplarity. We find it expressed, for instance, in the location of prisons on a conspicuous spot where a road or railway entered a town.[10] In an indirect way punishment remained public. L. O. Pike, writing in 1876, reminded his readers that a second-hand impression of a whipping indoors was occasionally brought home to the public by the press.[11] Indirect knowledge of the death penalty, executed within prison walls, remained alive.

National variations in the chronology of the disappearance of public executions must be related to national singularities. The relative importance of the two elements, stability and impersonal rule, may also have varied. In England, for instance, the first half of the nineteenth century was the period of the great public order panic. Thereafter only occasional outbursts of fear occurred and a relative orderliness prevailed.[12] No doubt this situation made the completion of the privatization of repression easier. The kingdom of the Netherlands, on the other hand, was relatively peaceful. The old patrician elites, however, largely dominated the scene until the middle of the nineteenth century. Shortly thereafter the abolition of public executions was a fact. Around the same time the system of public order maintenance was also depersonalized and acquired a more bureaucratic character.[13] These remarks about the specifics of the transformation are of a hypothetical nature and call for detailed research. The continuation of public guillotining in France until 1939 likewise needs a separate explanation.

The fact that the completion of the privatization of repression took about two-thirds of the nineteenth century in most Western European countries adds up to a critique of Foucault's views. He pictures early nineteenth-century imprisonment as suddenly and almost totally replacing a penal system directed at the display of the human body. The new penal system, and especially solitary confinement, was also directed at the mind. It is true that a widespread enthusiasm for 'moral treatment' prevailed in the first half of the nineteenth century. But the penitentiary cannot be considered as the successor to public executions. The observations of the present study make the conclusion inescapable: classical nineteenth-century imprisonment represented an experimental phase contemporary to the last days of public executions. Several authors emphasize that the middle of the nineteenth century was the heyday of the penitentiary and solitary confinement, after which the enthusiasm declined.[14] Of course executions were less frequent at the time, but this is not relevant to the argument. From a quantitative viewpoint they had always been in the minority, though they were the pearl in the crown of repression. In the course of the nineteenth century public physical punishment was increasingly questioned. This coincided with experiments in new penal methods such as solitary confinement. The experiments were discontinued and public executions disappeared. Routine imprisonment succeeded – with capital punishment indoors for a few heinous offenses – to the top of the penal system.

Modern imprisonment would need another story. The penal system of today, however, bears the mark of the developments that gave rise to it. On the one hand, it has retained its ancient characteristics to a certain degree. Everyone still has to realize that punishment exists, and this is the essence of the notion of general prevention. And a penalty still involves, in one way or another, the infliction of injury. Feelings of sensitivity, on the other hand, did not vanish after their appearance in the late eighteenth century. Time and again those concerned with the condemned have looked inside prisons and told the public the painful story. The result is a permanent tension. Every modern Western society witnesses the conflict between a perceived necessity of punishment and an uneasiness at its practice. Perhaps this remains inevitable, unless we find a way to do without repression entirely.

SOURCES AND METHOD FOR THE QUANTITATIVE STUDY IN CHAPTER FIVE

Serial records concerned with criminal trials in the Amsterdam judicial archive number six. They are the *schoutsrol, schapenboeken, confessieboeken* ('confession-books'), *secrete confessieboeken, justitieboeken* ('justice-books') and *sententieboeken* ('sentence-books'). The first, second and fourth series were not included in the investigation. The *schoutsrol* is almost exclusively concerned with minor transgressions of all kinds of regulations, leading to a fine in most cases. In the *schapenboeken* a particular kind of misdemeanor was registered: insolvently gambling at an auction. Those involved in this act (called *schapen*) were directly imprisoned in the rasphouse for a few months and were only subjected to an official trial when caught for the third time for the offense. Just one *schapenboek* has been preserved. The *secrete confessieboeken* bring us into the criminal area. They contain the interrogations of those charged with particular 'political' or morals offenses, the penalty being mostly imprisonment. Cases are very few in the period 1651–1750 and I did not include the series in the investigation. To be sure, the few persons who received a public punishment had their sentence normally recorded in the sentence-book, so that these end up among the figures.

The interrogations of the prisoners are reproduced in the confession-books. These also give some personal information and add the judgment in the margin. Use of torture during an examination was registered likewise. In cases leading to a public punishment an official sentence was written down. In the other cases a short note was made containing personal information on the prisoner, a summary of the offenses he or she had confessed and the judgment by *schepenen*. This was written down in the justice-books. Public sentences were registered in a separate series: the sentence-books. This series starts in 1696. The scaffold sentences prior to that year were registered in the justice-books, in which they were inserted by clusters per execution. They stand out from the short notes of the non-public cases by their length and, especially, by the fact that they begin with the word 'because' instead of with the prisoner's name.

Thus, it is easy to select the scaffold punishments from the sources throughout the period 1651–1750. They amount to 2,991 sentences in ninety-seven years. Information is missing for the three years between January 1706 and January 1709. Besides that, the sources are complete. The lists of those publicly executed (GA, RA 638–640), starting in 1713, give no cases for which I did not find a sentence. A control was provided by the sample from the non-public punishments: multiplication of the number of times I encountered a scaffold sentence in the confession-books with that of the intervals used, gave the number of 3,107 for the years 1651–1749. The gap in the sentence-books largely accounts for this small difference.

The sentences of the delinquents who received a public punishment, registered in the justice-books before 1696 and in the sentence-books after that date, formed the basis of the investigation. They contain all relevant information. To contrast this with the cases involving a non-public penalty, a sample of these was taken. The confession-books provided the source. I divided the century into three periods of thirty-three years, leaving aside 1750. A number of 500 cases from each period was chosen for consideration. The method of equal intervals was used. A complete aselect sample would have brought time-consuming practical consequences, while not significantly enhancing reliability. The indexes of the confession-books formed the bases for the intervals. Each book contained an alphabetical index, grouping the prisoners according to their first name. The order of the prisoners in the books was just chronological, according to when they were brought in. It follows that the order of the prisoners in the indexes was not selective with regard to any variable figuring as relevant in the investigation. The confession-books contain the cases leading to a scaffold punishment too. Of course they were not included when one turned up. The number of times this occurred also provides a control on the reliability of the sample. The result was mentioned above. I likewise excluded trials leading to a judgment which meant a simple release (without even a rebuke or the obligation to pay the costs of the trial) rather than a penalty. Thus the sample is truly one from the non-public *punishments* only and can conveniently be compared with the scaffold series.

The names in the indexes were counted by Oldewelt (1964). This made it possible to determine the intervals beforehand. But his figures need correction. One and the same trial occasionally slipped into the indexes twice. The number of times such a mistake was discovered and the number of times a judgment of release in the various periods was discovered provided indicators for the percentual distribution of these two categories in the indexes. In this way tentative figures for the absolute number of trials ending in punishment were arrived at. The absolute numbers of the scaffold cases among them were already known. The percentual relation of the three samples to the approximate total number of non-public punishments in the respective periods varies somewhat, because of the variation in the totals:

Period	Approximate total of non-public punishments	Percentage of sample
1651–1683	14,400	3.5
1684–1716	11,600	4.3
1717–1749	3,500	14.3

Keeping the percentage constant, instead of the absolute number, would have led to complications. Either the total amount of trials to be considered would have become unreasonably high, or the absolute number in the third period unacceptably low. Therefore the procedure of three times 500 was used. This means of course that reliability is greatest in the third sample.

Percentual relations between the trials in the scaffold series and the approximate total are given in chapter five, table 2. Because of the gap in the sentence-books the percentage for the sixth decade was calculated from a supposed number of 269 scaffold cases (i.e. three-sevenths of 188 added). In a few cases between 1650 and 1670 the records speak of 'public banishments'. These were not included in the series of public sentences, which, for the sake of convenience, are referred to as 'scaffold series', although it includes sentences executed on the pillory. It should be noted that convicts who were branded were always whipped as well. The designation 'branding' in the tables is meant to include the flogging which preceded.

Non-public sentences were rather variegated and often consisted of a combination of different types. To be able to handle them I grouped them into eight categories. The different types were basically five: corporal penalty, confinement, banishment, fine and a residual category of other types. Eight combinations figure in the tables, each time composed in such a way that some types are included in the combination (+), other types are not (−) and still other types are included or not (±):

	Corporal penalty	Confinement	Banishment	Fine	Other types
Corporal/confinement	+	+	±	±	±
Corporal/banishment	+	−	+	±	±
Corporal only	+	−	−	±	±
Confinement/ banishment	−	+	+	±	±
Confinement only	−	+	−	±	±
Banishment only	−	−	+	±	±
Fine only	−	−	−	+	±
Minor punishment	−	−	−	−	+

Other sources were used for the overview of official legislation. Criminal legislation in the Dutch Republic is a complicated matter. No official law code existed. Legislation on crimes was largely incidental and often hardly influenced the judges' decisions. The Estates General and the Estates of Holland issued placards. The Amsterdam court could make its own laws: the *keuren*. These were registered in the *keurboeken*, which also contained notifications of the court and all kinds of regulations pertaining to life in the city. Their contents vary from promises of rewards for information about a murder to directions for the size of cookies. Those *keuren* which were still considered in vigor, were published – together with the ancient privileges – as the *Handvesten* of the city in 1748. The following laws were taken into consideration: 1. those placards to which one or more sentences actually referred, 2. the contents of the *keurboeken* between 1650 and 1750 (labelled M–T; *keurboek* N, 1656–62, is missing), 3. *keuren* prior to 1650 included in the *Handvesten*.

Appendix B

THE SCAFFOLD AND
PUNISHMENT IN AMSTERDAM

I. INCIDENCE OF 'ROPE AROUND THE NECK' IN COMBINATION WITH
OTHER PENALTIES

With	%	No.
Simple exposure	1.1	5
Whipping indoors	0.2	1
Public whipping	34.9	155
Branding	55.4	246
Burning sword	6.5	29
Cheek cut	0.7	3
Thumb off	1.1	5
TOTAL		444

2. INCIDENCE OF EXPOSURE WITH AN OBJECT IN COMBINATION WITH
OTHER PENALTIES

With	%	No.
Simple exposure	41.1	321
Whipping indoors	5.1	40
Public whipping	49.2	384
Branding	4.4	34
Burning sword	0.1	1
Cheek cut	0.1	1
TOTAL		781

3. CHARGES BY THE PROVINCIAL EXECUTIONER IN THE EIGHTEENTH CENTURY

A. *Actual punishments*

	Guilders
Breaking on wheel: per blow	3
for strangling or cutting off head afterwards	6
Drowning in barrel	12
for lifting body out of barrel	3
Hanging	6
Garrotting	6
Beheading	6
Piercing tongue	3
for the awl	3
Cutting off thumb	6
Burning sword on back	6
Cutting cheek (or elsewhere)	3
Hitting head with hammer or stone	3
Waving sword over head	6
Exposure with rope around neck under gallows	6
Exposure with rods hanging from shoulders	6
Exposure with letter or object at railing of scaffold	6
Exposure with rope and letter/object	9
Branding	3
Whipping	3

B. *Acts performed on dead bodies*

Cutting off head	6
Cutting off other part of body	6
Scorching face	3
Placing head on stake on scaffold	3
Removal of corpse from gallows, cross or garrotte	3
Removal of head from stake	3
Removal and putting in a sack of other part of body	4
Bringing corpse into town hall	3
Coffining	3
Dragging corpse to Volewijk	3
Placing corpse on wheel or hanging it from gallows on Volewijk	6
Placing head on stake on Volewijk	3
Placing other severed part of body on its trunk on Volewijk	3
Dragging corpse to Y or sea and throwing into water	6
for tying weight to body	3

C. *Acts with objects*

Hanging weapon above convict's head (also on Volewijk)	3
Hanging object symbolizing stolen property above convict's head (also on Volewijk	3
Burning *corpus delicti*	3

3. (cont.)

D. Costs of material

For ropes and cords	12
For sword (with beheading as well as sword over head)	3
For cloth (with same)	3
For knife (with cut in cheek)	3

E. Miscellanea

Day-money[1]	12
Mile-money[1]	12
For assistance	12
Rent of carriage[2]	7
Wagon-freight[2]	10

1 From 10 November 1742 until the end of 1746 Frans Diepenbroek, then living in Utrecht, received twenty-four guilders for day- and mile-money.
2 Only mentioned at the end of the eighteenth century.

4. DISTRIBUTION OF PENALTIES IN THE SCAFFOLD SERIES, 1651–1750

Penalty	%	No.	Penalty	%	No.
Simple exposure	13.9	417	Beheading	2.4	71
Exposure & whipping			Hanging	8.4	252
indoors	1.6	49	Garrotting	0.8	24
Whipping	54.8	1638	Drowning	0.1	2
Branding	14.3	427	Breaking on the wheel	1.3	40
Burning sword	1.6	49	Burning	0.0	1
Cheek cut	0.5	16	TOTAL	100.0	2991
Thumb off	0.2	5			

5. SUBDIVISION OF THE CATEGORY OF MINOR PUNISHMENT
(DISTRIBUTION IN THE THREE SAMPLES)

	1651–1683		1684–1716		1717–1749	
	%	No.	%	No.	%	No.
Minor restriction	36.6	49	46.5	66	42.5	48
Minor order	21.6	29	7.7	11	4.4	5
Minor threat	0.7	1	1.4	2	—	—
Rebuke (*cum capitulo*)	33.6	45	31.7	45	42.5	48
Trial costs only	3.0	4	4.2	6	7.1	8
Given to parents	1.5	2	1.4	2	1.8	2
Miscellanea	3.0	4	7.0	10	1.8	2
TOTAL		134		142		113

6. PENALTIES IMPOSED FOR HOMICIDE, 1651–1750

	%	No.
Sword over head	5.9	4
Sword over head & whipping indoors	1.5	1
Beheading	72.1	49
Hanging	14.7	10
Garrotting	1.5	1
Breaking on the wheel	4.4	3
TOTAL	100.0	68

A. *Scaffold series. Absolute numbers of punishments*

	1651–1660	1661–1670	1671–1680	1681–1690	1691–1700	1701–1710	1711–1720	1721–1730	1731–1740	1741–1750
Exposure/sword over head	5	3	2	—	—	—	—	—	—	—
Exposure/sword over head and whipping indoors	—	2	—	—	—	—	1	—	—	—
Whipping	5	6	5	6	8	7	22	15	9	3
Branding	—	—	—	—	—	—	2	2	2	—
Burning sword	—	2	1	1	2	4	9	5	7	1
Cheek cut	—	—	1	3	4	—	2	1	3	—
Capital punishment	—	1	1	—	2	1	3	—	—	—

B. *Sample. Numbers of observed punishments*

Period	Corporal/ confinement	Corporal/ banishment	Corporal only	Confinement/ banishment	Confinement only	Banishment only	Fine only	Minor punishment
1651–1683	—	—	—	—	6	2	16	8
1684–1716	—	—	—	—	4	6	13	1
1717–1749	1	5	1	1	2	7	10	6

8. THREATENING AND DAMAGING

A. *Threatening in the sample. Numbers of observed punishments*

Period	Corporal/banishment	Confinement/banishment	Confinement only	Banishment only	Fine only	Minor punishment
1651–1683	—	—	8	1	9	3
1684–1716	—	—	7	—	5	3
1717–1749	1	1	2	2	—	3

B. *Damaging in the sample. Numbers of observed punishments*

Period	Corporal/confinement	Confinement/banishment	Confinement only	Banishment only	Fine only	Minor punishment
1651–1683	1	1	7	1	3	9
1684–1716	—	—	2	1	—	3
1717–1749	—	—	1	—	—	1

A. *Scaffold series. Penalties for prostitution and procurership in absolute numbers*

Period	Prostitutes		Procurers	
	Exposed	Whipped	Exposed	Whipped
Before 1720	1	—	—	—
1721–1730	6	6	17	6
1731–1740	1	1	24	2
1741–1750	—	—	32	1

B. *Prostitution in the samples. Numbers of observed punishments*

Period	Corporal/banishment	Confinement/banishment	Confinement only	Banishment only	Minor punishment
1651–1683	1	3	5	28	49
1684–1716	—	—	14	23	67
1717–1749	—	8	20	14	45

C. *Procurership in the samples. Numbers of observed punishments*

Period	Confinement/banishment	Confinement only	Banishment only	Fine only	Minor punishment
1651–1683	—	—	10	1	14
1684–1716	1	2	7	—	16
1717–1749	3	6	5	3	6

10. ADULTERY AND OTHER FORMS OF EXTRAMARITAL INTERCOURSE

A. *Adultery in the sample. Numbers of observed punishments*

Period	Confinement/ banishment	Confinement only	Banishment only	Fine only	Minor punishment
1651–1683	—	1	1	—	3
1684–1716	—	—	3	2	—
1717–1749	2	2	6	4	—

B. *Other morals offenses in the sample. Numbers of observed punishments*

Period	Confinement only	Banishment only	Fine only	Minor punishment
1651–1683	2	2	—	3
1684–1716	1	1	2	3
1717–1749	3	1	—	3

II. BEGGING AND VAGABONDAGE

A. Beggars in the sample. Numbers of observed punishments

Period	Corporal only	Confinement/banishment	Banishment only	Minor punishment
1651–1683	—	1	3	2
1684–1716	—	—	4	1
1717–1749	1	2	16	3

B. Vagabonds in the sample. Numbers of observed punishments

Period	Confinement only	Banishment only	Minor punishment
1651–1683	—	4	4
1684–1716	2	3	—
1717–1749	—	3	2

C. Beggars in the scaffold series. Distribution of punishments in absolute numbers

Penalty	1651–1660	1661–1670	1701–1710	1711–1720	1721–1730	1731–1740
Exposure	—	—	8	1	—	1
Exposure and whipping indoors	2	—	2	—	—	—
Whipping	—	1	3	6	4	2

12. VARIOUS OFFENSES AGAINST AUTHORITY

A. *Scaffold series. Punishments, 1651–1750, in absolute numbers*

Penalty	Resistance to authority	Abandonment of children	Escape from prison	Bigamy	Labor conflict	Miscellanea
Exposure	7	15	3	17	—	14
Exposure and whipping indoors	2	4	—	2	—	2
Whipping	21	5	9	1	4	31
Branding	2	—	5	—	—	5
Burning sword	3	—	—	—	—	—
Thumb off	1	—	—	—	—	—
Hanging	1	—	3	—	—	1
Garrotting	—	—	—	—	—	1
Breaking on the wheel	—	—	—	—	—	—
TOTAL	37	24	20	20	4	54

Miscellanea are: treason, desertion, illegally crossing a border, perjury, deceiving the court, being a *schaap* for the third time, keeping vagabonds, printing/singing illegal texts

B. *Sample (three periods together). Numbers of observed punishments, 1651–1749*

Penalty	Resistance to authority	Abandonment of children	Escape from prison	Labor conflict	Miscellanea
Corporal/confinement	—	—	1	—	1
Corporal/banishment	3	—	—	—	—
Corporal only	1	—	2	—	—
Confinement/banishment	—	—	1	1	2
Confinement only	3	1	3	3	5
Banishment only	3	2	—	1	5
Fine only	3	—	—	1	9
Minor punishment	1	1	—	2	14

13. ALL PROPERTY OFFENSES

Scaffold series. Absolute numbers and percentages of punishments

Decade	Exposure		Exposure and whipping indoors		Whipping		Branding		Burning sword		Cheek cut/ thumb off		Non-prolonged death penalty		The wheel	
	%	No.	%	No.	%	No.	%	No.	%	No.	%	No.	%	No.	%	No.
1651–1660	14.0	25	0.6	1	61.2	109	16.3	29	—	—	1.1	2	6.7	12	—	—
1661–1670	14.3	36	0.4	1	64.5	162	17.1	43	0.4	1	—	—	3.2	8	—	—
1671–1680	20.7	28	4.4	6	60.0	81	10.4	14	0.7	1	0.7	1	2.9	4	—	—
1681–1690	17.1	28	4.3	7	48.2	79	14.6	24	1.8	3	—	—	14.0	23	—	—
1691–1700	16.5	44	3.7	10	46.1	123	17.2	46	1.5	4	—	—	15.0	40	—	—
1701–1710	22.1	30	2.9	4	41.9	57	9.6	13	0.7	1	0.7	1	21.3	29	0.7	1
1711–1720	1.6	5	—	—	59.6	192	19.3	62	0.3	1	—	—	15.5	50	3.7	12
1721–1730	1.6	4	—	—	56.4	141	25.2	63	—	—	—	—	15.6	39	1.2	3
1731–1740	0.6	1	—	—	68.5	111	24.7	40	—	—	0.6	1	4.9	8	0.6	1
1741–1750	0.6	1	—	—	68.5	113	26.7	44	—	—	0.6	1	3.6	6	—	—

14. ROBBERY

Scaffold series. Punishments for robbery including participation in and attempted robbery

Decade	Exposure		Whipping		Branding		Burning sword		Cheek cut		Non-prolonged death penalty		The wheel	
	%	No.	%	No.	%	No.	%	No.	%	No.	%	No.	%	No.
1651–1660	—	—	60	3	20	1	—	—	—	—	20	1	—	—
1661–1670	—	—	65	17	31	8	4	1	—	—	—	—	—	—
1671–1680	—	—	79	11	7	1	7	1	—	—	7	1	—	—
1681–1690	—	—	52	12	17	4	13	3	—	—	17	4	—	—
1691–1700	—	—	36	8	14	3	14	3	—	—	36	8	—	—
1701–1710	7	1	27	4	—	—	7	1	7	1	47	7	7	1
1711–1720	—	—	22	11	20	10	2	1	—	—	37	19	20	10
1721–1730	—	—	19	6	31	10	—	—	—	—	41	13	9	3
1731–1740	—	—	46	5	18	2	—	—	—	—	27	3	9	1
1741–1750	—	—	—	—	33	1	—	—	—	—	67	2	—	—

15. BURGLARY

Scaffold series. Punishments for burglary including participation in and attempted burglary

Decade	Exposure		Exposure and whipping indoors		Whipping		Branding		Burning sword/cheek cut		Non-prolonged death penalty		The wheel	
	%	No.	%	No.	%	No.	%	No.	%	No.	%	No.	%	No.
1651–1660	6	3	—	—	39	21	37	20	—	—	19	10	—	—
1661–1670	2	1	—	—	43	21	41	20	—	—	14	7	—	—
1671–1680	—	—	—	—	52	14	37	10	4	1	7	2	—	—
1681–1690	5	4	—	—	48	38	23	18	—	—	24	19	—	—
1691–1700	2	2	3	3	39	47	30	36	1	1	25	30	1	1
1701–1710	—	—	—	—	22	8	25	9	—	—	53	19	—	—
1711–1720	—	—	—	—	28	20	33	24	—	—	36	26	3	2
1721–1730	—	—	—	—	35	14	20	8	—	—	45	18	—	—
1731–1740	—	—	—	—	67	6	33	3	—	—	—	—	—	—
1741–1750	—	—	—	—	31	4	39	5	—	—	31	4	—	—

Scaffold series. Punishments for simple theft including participation in and attempted simple theft and theft from employer and undressing children

Decade	Exposure		Exposure and whipping indoors		Whipping		Branding		Capital punishment	
	%	No.	%	No.	%	No.	%	No.	%	No.
1651–1660	11	9	1	1	81	69	7	6	—	—
1661–1670	11	12	1	1	77	82	10	11	—	—
1671–1680	22	13	5	3	70	42	3	2	—	—
1681–1690	15	5	12	4	70	23	3	1	—	—
1691–1700	22	14	6	4	64	41	8	5	—	—
1701–1710	18	8	—	—	71	32	9	4	2	1
1711–1720	2	3	—	—	79	104	17	22	2	3
1721–1730	2	2	—	—	65	75	29	34	4	5
1731–1740	—	—	—	—	70	59	24	20	6	5
1741–1750	1	1	—	—	78	63	21	17	—	—

17. THEFT

Sample. Punishments for simple theft including participation in and attempted simple theft and being found in the company of thieves

Penalty	1651–1683		1684–1716		1717–1749	
	%	No.	%	No.	%	No.
Corporal/confinement	7	5	1	1	17	9
Corporal/banishment	12	8	7	5	28	15
Corporal only	—	—	1	1	11	6
Confinement/banishment	4	3	10	7	2	1
Confinement only	28	19	25	17	6	3
Banishment only	32	22	32	22	21	11
Fine only	2	1	—	—	—	—
Minor punishment	15	10	23	16	15	8

18. SWINDLING

Scaffold series. Absolute numbers of punishments

Penalty	1651–1660	1661–1670	1671–1680	1681–1690	1691–1700	1701–1710	1711–1720	1721–1730	1731–1740	1741–1750
Exposure	10	10	11	12	22	4	2	2	—	—
Exposure and whipping indoors	—	—	2	3	1	1	—	—	—	—
Whipping	5	14	8	3	16	5	16	16	11	14
Branding	1	2	—	—	1	—	2	4	10	7
Thumb off	2	—	—	—	—	—	—	—	1	1
Beheading	—	1	1	—	1	—	1	—	—	—
Hanging	1	—	—	—	—	2	—	1	—	—

19. CHEATING THE EAST INDIA COMPANY

A. Scaffold series. Absolute numbers of punishments

Penalty	1661–1670	1671–1680	1681–1690	1691–1700	1701–1710	1711–1720	1721–1730	1731–1740	1741–1750
Exposure	10	3	5	6	17	—	—	1	—
Exposure and whipping indoors	—	1	—	1	3	—	—	—	—
Whipping	—	—	—	—	—	1	2	1	4
Branding	—	—	—	—	—	1	1	—	—

B. Sample. Numbers of observed punishments

Period	Corporal only	Confinement only	Banishment only	Fine only	Minor punishment
1651–1683	—	—	—	15	—
1684–1716	—	2	1	22	3
1717–1749	11	1	—	39	1

20. NON-CONFESSED THEFTS

Sample. Numbers of observed punishments of non-confessed qualified and non-qualified property offenses

Period	Corporal/ banishment	Confinement/ banishment	Confinement only	Banishment only	Fine only	Minor punishment
1651–1683	—	1	6	19	—	11
1684–1716	1	7	3	22	1	7
1717–1749	1	12	4	42	—	10

A. *Distribution of recidivists in the scaffold series*

Decade	First offenders		One–three times prisoner before		Four or more times prisoner before	
	%	No.	%	No.	%	No.
1651–1660	41.7	106	37.0	94	21.2	54
1661–1670	45.7	137	31.0	93	23.3	70
1671–1680	42.6	80	26.6	50	30.8	58
1681–1690	40.6	84	44.9	93	14.4	30
1691–1700	59.2	212	27.4	98	13.4	48
1701–1710	60.6	114	29.8	56	9.6	18
1711–1720	61.1	286	33.3	156	5.5	26
1721–1730	59.4	277	32.7	152	8.0	37
1731–1740	73.9	207	23.6	66	2.5	7
1741–1750	68.2	191	31.4	88	0.4	1

B. *Average number of offenses in a sentence per decade (scaffold series)*

	1651–1660	1661–1670	1671–1680	1681–1690	1691–1700	1701–1710	1711–1720	1721–1730	1731–1740	1741–1750
In all cases	5.4	4.5	2.9	6.2	5.5	3.7	3.2	2.3	2.2	2.4
All property offenses	7.2	4.9	3.5	7.2	6.5	4.0	3.6	2.7	2.2	2.9
Qualified thefts only	12.9	6.6	5.2	9.0	8.6	6.1	4.7	4.0	2.3	3.6
Other property offenses	3.9	4.0	2.6	3.6	3.6	2.7	2.9	2.2	2.2	2.8

Two categories were not included in the averages of part B: sentences in which no definite number, but just "some" or "a lot", etc. was indicated and those involving difficult to quantify offenses like begging or prostitution. These categories amount to 8.4% of the total. Among the qualified thefts they only represent 0.1%, while making up 4% of the other property crimes.

229

22. TYPES OF OCCUPATION AMONG THE CONDEMNED, 1651–1750

Types	Frequency in scaffold series		Frequency in sample	
	Relative	Adjusted	Relative	Adjusted
Lower	67.5	96.2	66.8	98.5
Merchant	0.5	0.7	0.1	0.2
Higher	1.8	2.6	0.9	1.3
Unidentifiable	0.3	0.5	—	—
Not mentioned	29.9	missing	32.3	missing

A. *For wounding/attacking*

Period	11–13		14–16		17–19		20–29		30–39		40–49		50–59	
	%	No.	%	No.	%	No.	%	No.	%	No.	%	No.	%	No.
1651–1683	—	—	3	1	7	2	39	12	32	10	13	4	7	2
1684–1716	—	—	—	—	—	—	46	10	41	9	9	2	5	1
1717–1749	6	2	—	—	3	1	61	20	24	8	—	—	6	2

B. *For infraction of banishment*

Period	14–16		17–19		20–29		30–39		40–49		50–59		over 59	
	%	No.	%	No.	%	No.	%	No.	%	No.	%	No.	%	No.
1651–1683	2	1	9	5	55	31	29	16	2	1	4	2	—	—
1684–1716	2	1	8	4	65	34	19	10	4	2	2	1	—	—
1717–1749	3	1	6	2	46	15	18	6	21	7	3	1	3	1

C. *For simple theft (including participation, attempt and company)*

Period	Under 11		11–13		14–16		17–19		20–29		30–39		40–49		50–59		over 59	
	%	No.	%	No.	%	No.	%	No.	%	No.	%	No.	%	No.	%	No.	%	No.
1651–1683	5	3	8	5	12	8	17	11	38	25	9	6	5	3	5	3	3	2
1684–1716	2	1	4	3	19	13	27	18	27	18	10	7	6	4	4	3	2	1
1717–1749	4	2	13	7	21	11	11	6	32	17	9	5	2	1	6	3	2	1

24. THIEVES UNDER TWENTY

Scaffold series. Offenses: simple theft (including participation, attempt and company), domestic theft, theft from employer and undressing children. Absolute numbers of punishments

Penalty	1651–1660	1661–1670	1671–1680	1681–1690	1691–1700	1701–1710	1711–1720	1721–1730	1731–1740	1741–1750
Exposure	1	—	—	—	1	2	—	1	—	—
Exposure and whipping indoors	—	—	1	2	1	—	—	—	—	—
Whipping	18	18	5	4	5	6	39	24	21	19
Branding	1	1	—	—	—	—	1	7	—	2
Hanging	—	—	—	—	—	—	—	1	—	—

25. THIEVES WHIPPED INDOORS IN DIFFERENT AGE-GROUPS

Sample. Offenses: as in table 24. The table gives, for each age-group, the percentages of those whipped indoors (all thieves of the age-group = 100%)

Period	Under 14	14–16	17–19	20–29	30–39	All ages
1651–1683	25	22	31	24	—	21
1684–1716	—	15	16	19	14	14
1717–1749	56	90	78	52	38	57

233

26. DISTRIBUTION OF THE SEXES FOR THREE OFFENSES

Sample. Absolute numbers

Period	For wounding/attacking		For infraction of banishment		For simple theft (inc. participation etc.)	
	Male	Female	Male	Female	Male	Female
1651–1683	28	4	21	51	37	31
1684–1716	20	4	25	27	47	22
1717–1749	31	2	19	14	41	12

A. *Scaffold series. Absolute numbers of punishments for both sexes (offenses as in tables 24 and 25)*

Penalty		1651–1660	1661–1670	1671–1680	1681–1690	1691–1700	1701–1710	1711–1720	1721–1730	1731–1740	1741–1750
Exposure:	M	2	5	10	4	3	5	1	—	—	—
	F	7	7	3	3	11	3	2	2	—	1
Exposure and whipping indoors:	M	1	1	2	3	4	—	—	—	—	—
	F	—	—	1	1	1	—	—	—	—	—
Whipping	M	32	52	26	11	28	19	88	62	50	46
	F	42	45	22	13	20	17	53	40	38	43
Branding:	M	6	9	1	1	4	2	16	24	11	12
	F	—	2	1	1	1	2	8	15	13	17
Non-prolonged death penalty:	M	—	—	—	—	—	1	3	5	4	17
	F	—	—	—	—	—	—	—	—	1	—

B. *Sample. Numbers of observed punishments for both sexes (offenses as in A.)*

Penalty	1651–1683		1684–1716		1717–1749	
	Male	Female	Male	Female	Male	Female
Corporal/confinement	5	—	1	1	6	3
Corporal/banishment	7	5	5	1	16	5
Corporal only	—	1	2	—	6	—
Confinement/banishment	1	2	3	4	—	1
Confinement only	12	8	12	5	2	1
Banishment only	7	21	15	8	8	5
Fine only	1	—	—	—	—	—
Minor punishment	7	3	11	5	7	3

28. INFRACTION OF BANISHMENT (GYPSIES INCLUDED)

Scaffold series. Absolute numbers of punishments

Penalty	1651–1660	1661–1670	1671–1680	1711–1720	1721–1730	1731–1740	1741–1750
Exposure	6	1	1	—	—	—	1
Exposure and whipping indoors	—	—	1	—	—	—	—
Whipping	27	4	16	5	47	13	39
Branding	—	—	—	—	14	5	3
Capital punishment	—	3	—	—	1	—	—

Appendix C

ARCHIVAL SERIES USED FOR THE QUANTITATIVE INVESTIGATION OF CHAPTER FIVE

A. *Gemeente-archief Amsterdam* (Municipal Archive of Amsterdam)
Oud-Rechterlijk archief (Judicial Archive)

RA	1–44	*Missiven-boeken van de Hoofdofficier* (letters)	1656–1811
RA	45–134	*Rekeningen van de Hoofdofficier* (accounts)	1732–1811
RA	308–409	*Confessieboeken* (Confession books)	1650–1750
RA	571–604	*Justitieboeken* (Justice-books)	1616–1709
RA	605–14	*Sententien van die publicq moeten geexecuteert* (Sentence-books)	1696–1750
RA	638–40	*Lijsten van geexecuteerden*	1713–1811

B. *Keurboeken* M, O, P, Q, R, S, T   1650–1750

C. Jacob Bicker Raye, *Notietie van het merkwaardigste meijn bekent* (in the notes: Raye ms.)   1732–1772

NOTES

Titles of books and articles are always given in abbreviated form. The bibliography contains the full references. Abbreviations of archival references are:

ARA   Algemeen Rijksarchief, The Hague
GA   Gemeente-archief (municipal archive), followed by the name of the municipality concerned. Unless otherwise mentioned, this is Amsterdam
RANH   Rijksarchief in de provincie Noord Holland, Haarlem

PREFACE

1 V. S. Naipaul, 'Among the Believers: An Islamic Journey'. From a pre-publication of two fragments in *New York Review of Books*, 8 October 1981, 26 and *Vrij Nederland*, 19 September 1981.
2 Especially Bée, 1975.
3 Foucault, 1975.
4 A few other recent studies on public executions exist, which will be referred to in the following chapters. They are: Cooper, 1974; Linebaugh, 1975; Bée, 1975; Spierenburg, 1978; Lofland, 1977; Blok, 1977.
5 Rusche and Kirchheimer, 1939. For another critique of this work see Steinert and Treiber, 1978.
6 Elias, 1969.
7 For a discussion of this problem, see Spierenburg, 1983.
8 Sjoerd Faber, 'Strafrechtspleging en Criminaliteit in Amsterdam, 1680–1811', *De Nieuwe Menslievendheid*, 1983.

I. THE EMERGENCE OF CRIMINAL JUSTICE

1 For a model and detailed analysis of state formation in Western Europe from the tenth to the seventeenth centuries: Elias, 1969: vol. II; Tilly, 1975; Bloch, 1965.
2 Immink, 1973. Immink elaborated on a thesis first put forward by Radbruch (cf. Radbruch, 1950: 1 *et seq.*) and severely criticized another thesis by Achter (1951). Inspired by Radbruch, Sellin (1976) also elaborated on the theme. Sellin, however, does not appear to have known the books by Achter and Immink.

3 Immink, 1973:11.
4 Ibid.: 209.
5 Immink (p. 242) interprets this as collective vengeance by the tribe and thus not as punishment. We may just as well argue that in this case the tribe constitutes an authority which is on a higher level than the individual members and hence administers an embryonic form of punishment.
6 Sellin, 1976: 33; Immink, 1973: 210–11.
7 Cf. Achter, 1951.
8 Immink, 1973: 243.
9 Immink expressly confined his analysis to Continental Europe, but similar developments took place in England. There the allods disappeared after 1066 because William the Conqueror managed to establish the principle that all the land belonged to the king. The transformation of the concept of felony to refer to serious crime set in under Henry II.
10 Immink, 1973: 212.
11 Achter, 1951: 65.
12 Immink, 1973: 227 and 238.
13 'The Middle Ages, from beginning to end, and particularly the feudal era, lived under the sign of private vengeance': Bloch, 1965: 125.
14 Immink, 1973: 226–40.
15 Elias (1969: II, 139) does so.
16 Achter, 1951: 12–25.
17 Immink, 1973: 19.
18 Especially Amira, 1922. Inspired by Von Amira, other legal historians extended his notions about the sacrificial character of Germanic death penalties to public executions in preindustrial Europe. Notably authors on the executioner did so. This will be further discussed in chapter two. See also Erikson, 1966: 185–95, who presents a variant of this notion.
19 Bloch, 1965: 365.
20 Vries, Klaas de, 1955: 29–43; Herwaarden, 1978: 8–10.
21 Frederiks, 1918: 275–8.
22 Ibid.: 279–310.
23 Velius, 1617: 12–13.
24 Herwaarden, 1978: 25–8.
25 For a summary of the two procedures and their implications, see Cohn, 1975: 22–4 and 160–3.
26 Sellin, 1976: 36–7; Heijnsbergen, 1925: 32–4; Esmein, 1969: 93–100.
27 Cohn, 1975: 89–90.
28 Esmein, 1969: 78–92 and 100–58.
29 Vries, Klaas de, 1955: *passim*; Maes, 1947: 100–4.
30 Vrugt, 1978: 133–4. The Revolt did not seriously affect the development of criminal law. The ordinance of 1570 remained largely valid, in theory and practice, throughout the history of the Dutch Republic. Cf. ibid.: 169–73.
31 Vries, Klaas de, 1955: 102 and 236. For Malines: Maes, 1947: 102.
32 Esmein, 1969: 88–9 and 98.
33 Bellamy, 1973:105.
34 Ibid.: 9–10 and 18–21.
35 Stone, 1965: 199–250.
36 His, 1920: 370.

37 Becker, 1976: 288.
38 Vries, Klaas de, 1955: 92–5.
39 These subjects are discussed most extensively in Castan, N., 1980.
40 To take a person in the *maling* in modern Dutch means making a fool of him. The specific sense which the word had around 1700 does not appear in dictionaries, nor is the custom in question discussed anywhere in historical literature. For a more extensive discussion, see my unpublished Ph.D. thesis: 'Judicial Violence in the Dutch Republic. Corporal punishment, executions and torture in Amsterdam 1650–1750': pp. 39–40.
41 GA, RA 608: no. 421.
42 Castan, Y., 1974: 79.
43 Hanawalt, 1976: 311. See also Hanawalt, 1979: 269–73 and Given, 1977: 33–40.
44 Quoted in Cohn, 1975: 26.

2. THE ACTORS: EXECUTIONERS AND THEIR STATUS

1 Schuhmann, 1964: 205–7. Compare the case of Anton Hofmann, executioner of the city of Frankfurt. He pleaded with the town-council to let his son, Johann Heinrich, who was hangman in Gross-Gerau, execute a beheading in 1771. As the reason he gave the fact that Johann Heinrich had not yet had the opportunity to present his 'masterpiece'. Cf. Meinhardt, 1957: 44–5.
2 Gonnet, 1917: 8–11.
3 Huberts, 1937: 82, 198.
4 Ibid.: 82, 198.
5 Ibid.: 198.
6 Cf. Maes, 1947: 61.
7 Schuhmann, 1964: 223.
8 Cf. Oppelt, 1976: 266.
9 Meinhardt, 1957: 43–4. On a few other occasions it has been reported as well that executioners were fired in such cases. Cf. Beneke, 1863: 151; Schuhmann, 1964: 59–60.
10 Oppelt, 1976: 266–7.
11 Keller, 1921: 163–4.
12 Danckert, 1963: 30; Oppelt, 1976: 263–4.
13 Fehr, 1923: no. 123. Another such plate represents the unhandy beheading of the Duke of Monmouth: Cf. Bosch, 1698: III, 2: opposite p. 77.
14 Lebrun, 1971: 421.
15 Castan, N., 1976: 347.
16 Laurence, 1960: 195–8.
17 Other examples are: Vienna (1485), Strehl, Silesia (1530), Zellerfeld (1607), Breslau (1628), Nürnberg (1665), Brussels (1515) and Gaesbeek (1538) in: Oppelt, 1976: 261, 266, 267, 268, 270, 265, 265; Vienna (1501) in: Danckert, 1963: 29; Nördlingen (1514) in Schuhmann, 1964: 58; Nürnberg (1498) in: Keller, 1921: 163; Hamburg (1639) in: Beneke, 1863: 150; Würzburg (1739) in: Hentig, 1954: II, 135; Breslau (1811) in: unpublished paper presented to the First International Conference on the History of Crime and Criminal

Justice by Richard J. Evans: 48; Utrecht (1525), Dijon (1739) and Lyon (1754) in: Huberts, 1937: 121, 122, 122.

18 Danckert, 1963: 23.
19 Keller, 1921: 109.
20 Quoted by Oppelt, 1976: 1.
21 Danckert, 1963.
22 Cf. Pieter Spierenburg, 'The sociogenesis and development of houses of correction in Europe'. Paper presented at the First International Conference on the History of Crime and Criminal Justice, University of Maryland, 4–7 September 1980.
23 Cf. Castan, Y., 1974.
24 *Buurspraecboeck*: 84–107.
25 Huberts, 1937: 194; Molhuijsen, 1861: 76; compare Feith, 1865.
26 Molhuijsen, 1861: 75.
27 Maes, 1947: 60.
28 Oppelt, 1976: 260.
29 Angstmann, 1928: 29.
30 Oppelt, 1976: 460–1. The hangmen of New France were harassed well into the eighteenth century. Cf. Lachance, 1966: 97–8. Of course we are dealing with a different type of society in this case.
31 Angstmann, 1928: 82.
32 Huberts, 1937: 194; Oppelt, 1976: 370–1.
33 Molhuijsen, 1861: 74.
34 Lachance, 1966: 97.
35 Oppelt, 1976: 396–404.
36 Ibid.: 404–19.
37 Meinhardt, 1957: 49–50; Angstmann, 1928: 83–4.
38 Oppelt, 1976: 419–32.
39 Ibid.: 432–57; Schuhmann, 1964: 165–7.
40 Quoted in, among others, Angstmann, 1928: 85.
41 Oppelt, 1976: 479–90; Huberts, 1937: 194–6.
42 Lachance, 1966: 95.
43 Amira, 1922: 229.
44 Ibid.: 198–235.
45 Angstmann, 1928: 74–9; Schuhmann, 1964: 161–2.
46 Danckert, 1963: 9–20.
47 Oppelt, 1976: 263–5.
48 His, 1920: 589; Hentig, 1954: II, 134.
49 Gernhuber, 1957.
50 Ibid.: 163–77.
51 Oppelt, 1976: 342–3.
52 Ibid.: 12–13; 51–3.
53 Ibid.: 33.
54 Ibid.: 11; 348–9; 353.
55 Ibid.: 52; 9.
56 Ibid.: 46.
57 Huberts, 1937: 12–13.
58 Ibid.: 14.

59 His, 1920: 505–8, 525; Huberts, 1937: 19; Angstmann, 1928: 87. Execution by the plaintiff was likewise a possibility in late medieval England (cf. Bellamy, 1973: 187). As is well known, the inquisitorial procedure never fully developed there.

60 Oppelt, 1976: 64.

61 His, 1920: 507.

62 Ibid.: 525; Huberts, 1937: 19–21, 111; Oppelt, 1976: 58–62; Bellamy, 1973: 186; Laurence, 1960: 38–9.

63 Molhuijsen, 1861: 71–2; Unger, 1923: 436.

64 Molhuijsen, 1861: 71.

65 The case appears everywhere in the literature on the hangman. All versions, however, go back to a chronicle of Breslau by Samuel Benjamin Klose, paraphrased in Stenzel, 1847: 59–64. The year 1478 is actually the year in which Hans Rintfleisch is known to be dead.

66 Huberts, 1937: 25–6.

67 Hentig, 1962: 164–5; Maes, 1947: 60.

68 Lachance, 1966: 65.

69 Maes, 1947: 57.

70 Quoted by Huberts, 1937: 193.

71 Meinhardt, 1957: 38–40.

72 Castan, Y., 1974: 80 and personal information from Yves Castan.

73 Angstmann, 1928: 91.

74 Only one case of healing is a little, though not disturbingly early: Trier, 1494. Cf. p. 90, note 2.

75 Angstmann, 1928: 90–113. Cf. also Oppelt, 1976: 629–63.

76 Angstmann, 1928: 107. Cf. also Schuhmann, 1964: 126; Beneke, 1863: 148. The historical event to which the story refers, took place around 1488. It involved Klaus Störtebecker as pirate chief and Claus Flügge as executioner.

77 Quoted in Gonnet, 1917: 36–7.

78 Ibid.: 37.

79 Andel, 1925; Gonnet, 1917: 35–40; Huberts, 1937: 172–7.

80 Mattelaer, 1973: 145; Oppelt, 1976: 376–8; Huberts, 1937: 176.

81 Oppelt, 1976: 29.

82 Quoted in Andel, 1925: 2103.

83 Sanson, 1862: II, 270.

84 Huberts, 1937: 192.

85 Quoted in Meinhardt, 1957: 41.

86 Herwaarden, 1978: 191–4.

87 Quoted by Radbruch, 1950: 146.

88 Ibid.: 141–8; Hentig, 1962: 53; Angstmann, 1928: 77.

89 Oppelt, 1976: 416.

90 Maes, 1947: 61.

91 Quoted in Gonnet, 1917: 9–10.

92 Danckert, 1963: 30.

93 Meinhardt, 1957: 42; Cf. also: His, 1920: 509.

94 Oppelt, 1976: 330, note 2.

95 Coornhert, 1942: 424–9.

96 Quoted in Andel, 1925: 2102. My emphasis.

97 Huygens, 1644: 131.

98 Huberts, 1937: 43; Meinhardt, 1957: 40; Schuhmann, 1964: 158–9.
99 Angstmann, 1928.
100 Quoted in Huberts, 1937: 195.
101 Quanter, 1901: 96, 101–2.
102 Huberts, 1937: 46; Molhuijsen, 1861: 72.
103 Meinhardt, 1957: 51; Beneke, 1863: 171.
104 Lachance, 1966: 99–103.
105 Maes, 1947: 57.
106 Mountague, 1696: 177–8.
107 Eeghen, 1954: 122–4.
108 GA, RA 10: fo. 37 vs.
109 Eeghen, 1954: 120–4.
110 Meinhardt, 1957: 42–7; Oppelt, 1976: 5.
111 Schuhmann, 1964: 209; Oppelt, 1976: 2–3.
112 Huberts, 1937: 201.
113 Bontemantel, 1897: I, 68.
114 GA, RA 10, fo. 49 vs.
115 GA, Raye ms.: 30 January 1762; 22 August 1767; 20 January 1770; 23 March 1771.
116 GA, Bibliotheek, dossier no. J 1.086. The amounts of money are correctly given (save in one version); the hangman's name and the date of the execution are not.
117 Huberts, 1937: 198.
118 Quoted by Meinhardt, 1957: 54.
119 Jong, 1810: 82.
120 Eeghen, 1955: 100.
121 Lonsain, 1909; Huberts, 1937: 30–1; Maes, 1947: 57; Schuhmann, 1964: 211–12.
122 Vries, W. de, 1959.
123 See Spierenburg, 1981a.

3. THE STAGERS: THE AUTHORITIES AND THE DRAMATIZATION OF EXECUTIONS

1 Huizinga, 1976: 11.
2 Ibid.
3 Huberts, 1937:126.
4 Quoted by Gonnet, 1917: 23–4.
5 His, 1920: 508.
6 Koning, 1828: 58–61.
7 Puga, 1971: 259–60.
8 Herwaarden, 1978: 290. In Frankfurt this penalty was imposed even in the middle of the seventeenth century. Cf. Meinhardt, 1957: 144.
9 GA, Raye ms.: 11 January 1766.
10 Chaunu, 1978: 347–9.
11 Bontemantel does not describe the blood-sashes, but the Amsterdam Historical Museum has a few of them.
12 Bontemantel, 1897: I, 58–68.
13 GA, Bibliotheek, no. H32.

14 GA, Bibliotheek, no. H46.
15 GA, Bibliotheek, no. H31.
16 The presence of soldiers at executions is discussed in chapter four.
17 Wagenaar, 1760: XII, 160–72.
18 GA, RA 653: fo. 24.
19 GA, RA 600: fo. 21–6 vs.
20 GA, RA 638: 25 January 1721.
21 Unger, 1923: 434–5.
22 Racer, 1787: 12–13. Such a role for the executioner had been a more widespread custom before: Article 218 of the Carolina abolished it. Cf. Molhuijsen, 1861: 78.
23 Evers, 1869: 132.
24 Lonsain, 1917.
25 Wiersum, 1941: 101–4.
26 Fruin, 1880: 561–9.
27 GA Delft, no. 39 A 30, pp. 22–7.
28 'Een beulsexamen in de zeventiende eeuw' in: *Weekblad van het Recht*, 5631 (1888), 4.
29 Puga, 1971: 255–85.
30 Renger, 1913: 8–21.
31 Oppelt, 1976: 130–5.
32 Linebaugh, 1975: 67.
33 Sanson, 1862: II, 209–13, 353, *passim*.
34 Lebrun, 1971: 420; Cf. also Bée, 1975: 96.
35 Herwaarden, 1978: 16–17.
36 RANH, RA 6099 and 6100.
37 Lebrun, 1971: 417.
38 ARA, Archief Heinsius, no. 751/15. I owe this reference to Antonio Porta.
39 GA, RA 606: no. 61.
40 GA, RA 609: no. 145; RA 638: 14 November 1722.
41 Secretary, 1700: 230; Wagenaar, 1760: XII, 171.
42 GA, RA 638–40; RA 660: fo. 26 vs.
43 Cf. Molhuijsen, 1861: 223.
44 GA, RA 583: fo. 27 vs.
45 GA, RA 639: June 1787; Raye ms.: *passim*.
46 Lebrun, 1971: 422.
47 Hentig, 1954: I, 206–18; Jelgersma, 1978: *passim*.
48 Andrews, 1902: 54–5; Cf. also Gough, 1981: 54.
49 Keller, 1921: 95; Lachance, 1966: 41–3.
50 His, 1920: 374, 508.
51 Huberts, 1937: 53.
52 Hentig, 1954: I, 206 *et seq*. In New York the gallows was cut down by unknown persons in 1702. Cf. Greenberg, 1976: 181.
53 Brucker, 1889: 21.
54 Ibid.: 21–2.
55 Graaf, 1952: 154.
56 Jelgersma, 1978: 67–8.
57 Hermesdorf, 1964: 175.
58 Lois, 1746: 150.

59 Schuhmann, 1964: 69.
60 Wagenaar, 1760: x, 281–7.
61 Cf., among others: Bée, 1975: 101–6; Linebaugh, 1977.
62 GA, Bibliotheek, dossiers J 1. 079 and J 1. 080.
63 *Naamlijst*.
64 GA, RA 606: no. 63.
65 *Berigt* Grittinga: 5, 12–13.
66 Spierenburg, 1980: 140–1.
67 GA, RA 584: fo. 217 vs – 221.
68 GA, RA 583: fo. 172.
69 GA, RA 379: fo. 51 vs/52.
70 GA, Raye ms.: 14 March 1761.
71 Ibid.: 22 August 1767.
72 Ibid.: 16 June 1736, 22 September 1742, 3 September 1746, 11 January 1766.
73 Ibid.: 11 January 1766.
74 Mountague, 1696: 188–9.
75 Bée, 1975: 106–7.
76 Hodne, 1973: 105.
77 See, for example, Bée, 1975: 99–100; Unger, 1923: 435.
78 Brunner, 1932: 69.
79 Braatbard, 1960: 11.
80 Swedish Royal Resolution of 22 October 1725. I am indebted to Jan Sundin for this information.
81 Bellamy, 1973: 189.
82 Schuhmann, 1964: 75. For France: personal communication from Nicole Castan.
83 Spierenburg, 1980: 139.
84 Ms. by Balthasar Bekker, Koninklijke Bibliotheek, The Hague, *Handschriften* no. 131 G 29: 46.
85 GA, Raye ms.: 23 January 1734, 14 March 1761. See also Spierenburg, 1980: 141.
86 Linebaugh, 1977: 257.
87 Foucault, 1975: 64.
88 GA, RA 581: fo. 228.
89 GA, RA 606: nos. 41 and 50.
90 GA, RA 608: no. 423.
91 Erikson, 1966: 193.
92 Houten, 1803: 216–24; GA, RA 640: 22 January 1803.
93 GA, RA 614: no. 52; GA, Raye ms.: 17 December 1746; *Rechtspleeging*, 1746. The library of the Amsterdam municipal archive has a second and a fourth edition of the latter booklet.
94 *Rechtspleeging*, 1746: 27.
95 Andrews, 1902; Cate, 1975; Quanter, 1901; Rossa, 1966; Scott, 1938.
96 In exceptional cases persons have been put to death indoors: as a special favor (Huberts, 1937: 136–7), or, supposedly, when the offense was sodomy.
97 Bontemantel, 1897: I, 274–5.
98 See chapter five.
99 RANH, RA 6099: 24 November 1676 (listing of an earlier conviction in Kennemerland in a sentence by the Nieuwburgen court).

100 GA, Raye ms.: 26 August 1757.
101 GA, RA 590: fo. 64 vs.
102 GA, RA 586: fo. 21; 611: no. 152.
103 See chapter four.
104 Mountague, 1696: 178–9.
105 Cf. *Historie*, 1612: appendix.
106 GA, Raye ms.: *passim*.
107 Ibid.: 8 July 1767.
108 Quanter, 1901: 229–230; Scott, 1938: 34–5; Hentig, 1954: I, 381.
109 Bridenbaugh, 1955: 73.
110 GA, RA 613: no. 40.
111 Koning, 1828: 65; GA, RA 582: fo. 180.
112 Cate, 1975: 61–6 and *passim*; Herwaarden, 1978: 133, 208–9.
113 Maes, 1947: 424.
114 GA, RA 390: fo. 47. In eighteenth-century Languedoc surgeons performed the task. Cf. Castan, Y., 1974: 92.
115 GA, RA 1: 18 July 1658.
116 GA, RA 586: fo. 109 vs.: '*uithuyden*'.
117 GA, RA 380: fo. 46 vs.
118 GA, Raye ms.: 22 January 1763.
119 GA, RA 583: fo. 156.
120 GA, RA 596: fo. 180; RA 606, no. 106.
121 Huberts, 1937: 73.
122 GA, Bibliotheek: dossier J 1. 079.
123 GA, RA 600: fo. 18.
124 Hentig, 1954: I, 296–320.
125 Abbiateci, 1971: 13–32; Lecuir, 1974.
126 Huberts, 1937: 113; Quanter, 1901: 122–7; Quanter mentions various uses of the wheel by the Romans, but these are not primarily concerned with breaking bones.
127 Maes, 1947: 405–6. Meinhardt, 1957: 130–2; Fehr, 1923: no. 95 (plate).
128 Cf. Bosch, 1698: vol. II, book 2, opposite p. 225. The plate represents an historic event to which the name breaking on the wheel is not applied, but this penalty is clearly the model; Cf. also Fehr, 1923: no. 94.
129 Schuhmann, 1964: 77; Meye, 1935: 41.
130 GA, RA 641 and 638: 6 August 1718.
131 By strangling, according to the Amsterdamse Secretary. Cf. *Secretary*, 1700: 225–6.
132 GA, RA 614: no. 41; RA 406: fo. 211 vs.
133 Sanson, 1862: II, 201–51; Lebrun, 1971: 420; Lachance, 1966: 45; Nicole Castan, 'Violence et répression en Languedoc 1650–1778' (paper presented to the third IAHCCJ Colloquium at the Maison des Sciences de l'Homme, Paris, January 1979).
134 Vanhemelrijck, 1964: 189–90. In Prussia secret strangling was prescribed in 1811. Cf. Rossa, 1966: 143–4.
135 GA, RA 581: fo. 119 vs.
136 GA, RA 583: fo. 194.
137 GA, RA 584: fo. 4 vs.
138 GA, RA 585: fo. 28. Her dead body was etched by Rembrandt.

139 GA, RA 586: fo. 134 vs.

140 GA, RA 588: fo. 86 vs.

141 GA, RA 605 (not numbered).

142 GA, RA 609: no. 39.

143 GA, RA 611: nos. 163, 164.

144 GA, RA 614: no. 52.

145 *Placaetboek*, 1658: II, 1, 507. Cutting off an ear does not figure among the selection of early seventeenth-century sentences presented by Hallema (1952) but this may merely be accidental. Hallema does not give the criterion for his selection.

146 GA, RA 571: fo. 87.

147 Koning, 1828: 77. He mentions the case but inaccurately fixes the date at 1617.

148 GA, RA 581: fo. 56 vs. Cf. also Koning, 1828: 76.

149 GA, RA 5: 119 calls the knife a razor.

150 Bontemantel, 1897: I, 56.

151 Koning, 1828: 81; GA, RA 426: 2 *et seq.*; Raye ms.: 31 October 1766.

152 GA, RA 357: fo. 225 vs *et seq.*; RA 358: fo. 7 vs.

153 Wagenaar, 1760: XII, 159–60.

154 Bellamy, 1973: 181–5.

155 Alfred Soman, 'Judicial repression in ancien-régime France: punishment and torture in the sixteenth and seventeenth centuries' (paper presented to the third IAHCCJ-Colloquium at the Maison des Sciences de l'Homme, Paris, January 1979).

156 Mattelaer, 1973: 139.

157 Meinhardt, 1957: 141.

158 Cf. Castan, N., 1980.

159 Amira, 1891: 545–59; Wind, 1827: 36–9. Von Amira cites two late English cases, but adds himself that the evidence cannot be trusted.

160 His, 1920: 401–2.

161 Lachance, 1966: 46.

162 GA, RA 588: fo. 231 vs forms a related case, in which the degree of the offender's guilt remained uncertain because he was more or less entitled to self-defense.

4. THE WATCHERS: SPECTATORS AT THE SCAFFOLD

1 Sources: 1651–90: *justitieboeken*; 1711–50: *sententieboeken* and RA 638–40; 1751–1810: RA 638–40.

2 GA, RA 7: fo. 33 vs. Haarlem lay close by. On a few occasions the court used the services of Utrecht's executioner. Then the servant was sent two days before.

3 Bontemantel, 1897: I, 58.

4 GA, RA 11: fo. 56; my emphasis. The execution was not postponed, although it did indeed not include a death penalty. Cf. RA 610 and 638. Postponement of an execution could also be ordered for other reasons: In Nijmegen in 1551 an execution was postponed 'because of the bad weather'. Cf. Huberts, 1937: 131.

5 Spierenburg, 1980: 148 and *passim*.

6 Cf. section 3.
7 Unger, 1923: 435–6.
8 Helbing, 1926: 254.
9 Buchner, 1911: III, 87.
10 Cf. Vries, Jan de, 1977: 200, who confirms the severity of this winter.
11 RANH, RA 6100: fos. 65 vs–71 vs.
12 Meye, 1935: 45.
13 Quoted by Bellamy, 1973: 185.
14 Beneke, 1863: 185–9.
15 GA, Raye ms.: 23 March 1740; 17 December 1755.
16 The case remains unclear. Bontemantel says that four French soldiers were whipped and branded on the cheek. The latter, if true, would have been a major exception for the period. The case is also interesting because of the intervention of burgomasters. Cf. Bontemantel, 1897: I, 230–1.
17 GA, Raye ms.: 26 October 1744; 9 June 1754; 14 September 1767.
18 Mountague, 1696: 136–7.
19 Oppelt, 1976: 550–1; Schuhmann, 1964: 70–2; Danckert, 1963: 14, 18, 44–5; Hentig, 1962: 133–48; Huberts, 1937: 54.
20 Quoted by Oppelt, 1976: 569.
21 Ibid.: 569–70.
22 Martin, 1927: 171–4.
23 Hermesdorf, 1964: 174.
24 GA, *Handschriften*: no. 184. The ms. has also been published: in the *Nederlandse Jaarboeken voor Regtsgeleerdheid en Wetgeving* (1850): 426–9. There it is ascribed to burgomaster Nicolaas Witsen.
25 GA, *Schoutsrekeningen*: 1781 and following years.
26 Graaf, 1952: 167.
27 Laurence, 1960: 64.
28 Cf. Spaan, 1752; Puga, 1971.
29 Cf. Linebaugh, 1975.
30 Spierenburg, 1980: 143.
31 GA, *Keurboek* Q: fo. 179 vs.
32 Cf. Ariès, 1974 and 1977; Vovelle, 1973; Chaunu, 1978; Lottin, 1978.
33 In the twelfth and thirteenth centuries princes and nobles slain abroad were even boiled, so that their bones could be sent home. Cf. Huizinga, 1976: 139.
34 GA, Raye ms.: 21 December 1746. Hence the body was transported four days after its execution. It remains unknown whether this was exceptional or not. It is also possible that Raye made a mistake.
35 Ibid.
36 *Maandblad Amstelodamum* 25 (1938): 62. The fact that the youngest in rank did the transporting can be inferred from GA, *Ambtenboek*.
37 Wagenaar, 1760: X, 281–7.
38 Backer, 1903: 1–4. The site is presently occupied by the Central Station.
39 In the early seventeenth century members of all classes are represented, while at the end of the eighteenth the skaters are clearly pictured as lower and lower-middle class. This does probably not reflect a changed attitude to the gallows on the part of the elites but rather their withdrawal from popular pastimes. Le Francq van Berkhey notes that 'nowadays our people of merit usually regard skating as a mean pastime of the common man'. Fifty years

earlier the young nobleman would skate with a peasant girl. Cf. Berkhey, 1776: book 3, I, 371–2.

40 Linebaugh, 1975: plate 10; 1977: 246.
41 Linebaugh, 1975: plate 11.
42 Buchner, 1911: III, 91.
43 Cf. Bosch, 1698: II, opposite p. 61 and *passim*.
44 GA, Raye ms.: 27 August 1743, 2 May 1747.
45 Mountague, 1696: 179. Original italics.
46 GA, Raye ms.: 25 January 1749.
47 See, among others, Rudé, 1970.
48 Cf. Ignatieff, 1978: 23. See also chapter six.
49 Puga, 1971: 269–71.
50 Ibid.: 284–5.
51 GA, RA 589: fo. 68. He originally used this as a proof of his innocence: RA 322: fo. 186 vs. The decapitation of the other counterfeiter had taken place in April 1675. In the sentence, read at the execution, the procedure for making the coins had been described in detail: RA 589: fo. 5.
52 The book was published anew in 1752, which edition I consulted. Van Spaan lived from 1651 until 1711.
53 Spaan, 1752: 201, 222, 270. See also the broadsheet hangman's bill, discussed in chapter two.
54 Cf. the quotation in Oppelt, 1976: 157–9.
55 Avé-Lallemant, 1858; Linebaugh, 1975: 66.
56 Ibid.
57 Cf. Chapman, 1980.
58 Cf. Beneke, 1863: 172.
59 Cf. Bercé, 1976; Burke, 1978; Muchembled, 1978.
60 Burke, 1978: 197–9.
61 Angstmann, 1928: 103–4.
62 Muchembled has a section on 'the punished bodies' (1978: pp. 247–55), but it is a missed chance: not really containing more than re-digested Foucault.
63 Ibid.; Burke, 1978. Cf. also Beik, 1980.
64 Linebaugh, 1977: 259.
65 Linebaugh, 1975: plate 15.
66 GA, Bibliotheek: dossier no. J I. 079.
67 GA, RA 352: fo. 106 vs. The source gives no information about the content of the song. The printer was interrogated briefly on the *schoutsrol*, but he gives no further clue.
68 Buijnsters, 1980: 11.
69 GA, RA 581: fo. 214.
70 GA, RA 309: fo. 184.
71 GA, RA 316: fo. 232 vs.
72 Ibid.: fo. 246 and RA 585: fo. 119 vs.
73 Cf. Oppelt, 1976: 113.
74 Walker, 1968: 74–83.
75 GA, RA 209: fo. 184.
76 Especially: Ariès, 1960; Shorter, 1975; Stone, 1977; Flandrin, 1979.
77 See also Elias, 1969: I, 238 *et seq.*
78 Berkhey, 1776: book 2, 1238.

79 Cf. Cate, 1975: 114–15.
80 Cf. Wirth, 1925: 113.
81 Ibid.: 114.
82 Ibid.: 116.
83 Huberts, 1937: 131; Oppelt, 1976: 138.
84 Oppelt, 1976: 138–40.
85 Cats, 1655: XVI, 30 (quoted from *Alle de Wercken*).
86 Huygens, 1644: 131.
87 Bosch, 1698: preface and *passim*.
88 Zetzner, 1913: 22–3. He wrote it down thirty years later and is not accurate about specific penalties.
89 Droste, 1879: 13.
90 Cf. chapter three.
91 From the original ms., preserved in the *Bibliotheca Rosenthaliana* of the Amsterdam University Library. I am grateful to Mr Hoogewoud for providing this information.
92 *Secretary*, 1700: 223.
93 *Dekker*, 1982: 119.
94 Hay, 1975: 50. On the Gordon Riots: Rudé, 1970: 268–93. For a similar judicial policy after a riot in Maldon in 1629: Walter, 1980: 76–9.
95 Bercé, 1974: 595.
96 Ibid.: 445.
97 Dekker, 1979: 22–3.
98 Hay, 1975: 49.
99 Dekker, 1982: 120.
100 Dekker, 1979: 22–3.
101 ARA, Hof van Holland, no. 5457 (3). I owe this reference to Rudolf Dekker.
102 Bercé, 1974: 314–15.
103 Ibid.: 444.
104 Lachance, 1966: 78.
105 Poršnev, 1954: 399.
106 Hay, 1975: 50. For similar sorts of opposition to hanging in chains see Malcolmson, 1980: 92–3 and Styles, 1980: 209, 239.
107 Dekker, 1982: 113–16. The special tribunal was constituted by one of the colleges of *Gecommitteerde Raden*, which were normally administrative bodies, but acted as a court in such cases.
108 Dekker, 1977: 322.
109 Linebaugh, 1975: 89–102.
110 GA, *Keurboek* M: fo. 165 vs.
111 Ibid.: 116 vs.; RA 581: fos. 159 and 160 vs.
112 GA, RA 599: fo. 155.
113 Ibid.
114 Cf. Dekker, 1979: 95.
115 GA, RA 599: fos. 157 *et seq*. Hanging a rebel from his feet was a more widespread custom. It was also done in Haarlem in 1750. Cf. Dekker, 1979: 149.
116 GA, RA 599: fos. 200, 201, 202, 207. In addition three sailors who had organized a procession, the purpose of which remains unknown, were punished: fos. 204, 205, 206. Cf. also Dekker, 1979: 101–7.

117 GA, RA 605 (not numbered). Execution on 14 December 1697.
118 Ibid.
119 GA, RA 613: no. 105; Raye ms.: 23 January 1740.
120 GA, *Keurboek* S: fos. 239 vs, 250 vs, 270. The second (2 December 1739) has the strange addition 'Kept secret'. The sailor's sentence spoke of warnings in general.
121 GA, Raye ms.: 27 January 1748.
122 GA, RA 408: fo. 12 vs/13; 638: 28 June 1748; *Schoutsrekeningen* for 1748.
123 Braatbard, 1960: 58–61; Meiners, 1966: 230–1.
124 GA, Raye ms.: 26 January 1754.
125 GA, RA 639: 2 June 1787; *Schoutsrekeningen* for 1787.
126 GA, RA 639: 17 May 1788.
127 Manen, 1980: 12.
128 GA, Raye ms.: 23 October 1732; RA 611: no. 242. The girl was not tortured but examined four times between 9 July and 17 July. Cf. RA 390: fo. 65 vs.
129 Foucault, 1975: 63–8.

5. THE VICTIMS: DELINQUENTS AND THEIR PENALTIES IN REPUBLICAN AMSTERDAM

1 Cf. especially: Cobb, 1975; Hufton, 1974.
2 Cf. Porta, 1975.
3 GA, RA 589: fo. 110 vs.
4 The correlation is between the degrees of non-capital scaffold punishments from exposure to thumb off and terms of confinement coded in categories from 'less than a year' to '25 years and more'. This relatively loose division in categories necessitated the use of a Kendall correlation coefficient.
5 GA, RA 613: no. 61. It does not become clear what exactly these precautions are.
6 Dated 29 January. Cf. *Handvesten*, 1748: 1049.
7 Dated 4 April Cf. ibid., p. 575. The previous law was amplified in 1625: men and women were not allowed to beat each other, on penalty of one and a half guilders, which was raised to six in 1644.
8 *Handvesten*, 1748: 1079. This *keur* was renewed in 1716, because of fights between Jews and Christians.
9 GA, *Keurboek* Q: fo. 86 vs. A new *keur* was promulgated in 1693, almost identical, with only the name 'laberlotten' omitted. Cf. ibid.: fo. 239 vs. In the Dutch–French lexicon by Marin of 1730 laberlot has become a noun. The author explains it by referring to the 'stories about the awful deeds of the Amsterdam laberlots of the year 1681'. They were supposed to have named themselves after the captain La Berlotte, who fought on the Spanish side against the Dutch around 1600. Cf. P. Marin, *Groot Nederduitsch en Fransch woordenboek*, 2nd edn, Dordrecht, 1730: 506.
10 GA, *Keurboek* S: fos. 20 vs, 25 and 100.
11 See for instance GA, RA 607: no. 90.
12 GA, RA 610: no. 259.
13 Cf. Abbiateci, 1971.
14 GA, RA 584: fo. 96; GA, RA 591: fo. 215 vs.
15 GA, RA 582: fo. 93.

16 GA, RA 581: fo. 148 vs.

17 GA, RA 613: no. 235.

18 GA, RA 612: no. 15.

19 The cases of sword over head as (additional) penalty mentioned so far number twenty-two. It was imposed in only five more cases. Then the major offenses were: robbery (two occurrences), swindling, rape and spending counterfeit money.

20 Sellin, 1944: 87–101. See also Slobbe, 1937; *Hoerdom Amsterdamsch*, 1681; Volmuller, 1966.

21 With regard to the early seventeenth century, we should probably read deputy-*schout* instead of *schout*. One of the deputy-*schouten* was apparently entrusted with the prosecution of morals offenses then. Cf. Hallema, 1961: 334 and *passim*. This article should be read with care. Hallema is a master in jumping to conclusions that are hardly warranted by his data.

22 Bontemantel, 1897: I, 31. The amount of 630 guilders was an excessively high sum at the time. Yet even higher sums have been recorded elsewhere. Cf. Hovy, 1980: 428.

23 Hovy, 1980: 429.

24 Carpzovius, 1752: I, 395–6.

25 GA, RA 589: fo. 154. The case was in March; the above-mentioned resolution against *compositie* was issued in September.

26 GA, RA 312: fo. 101 vs.

27 GA, RA 308: last folios.

28 Hovy, 1980: 428.

29 Women engaging in it were called *nachtloopsters* in the seventeenth and *kruishoeren* in the eighteenth century.

30 Cf., for instance, GA, RA 399: fo. 87 vs.

31 *Handvesten*, 1748: 572.

32 He was seventeen and a sailor. His 29 year old comrade seduced him under heavy threats; at least he made the judges believe that. Only his youth, however, was explicitly mentioned as the reason for passing by capital punishment. Cf. GA, RA 614: no. 36.

33 Carpzovius, 1752: I, 641–2.

34 Spierenburg, 1980: 131–3. See also Boon, 1976. Boon is in the process of completing a dissertation on the persecution of 1730–1.

35 GA, Bibliotheek: dossier J 1. 079. Cf. RA 611: nos. 168 and 167.

36 Ibid.

37 Or a violence offense. Compare, for instance, the trial of a man in 1693. His entire interrogation is about a case of wounding, which he persistently denies. At the end there is simply recorded: 'The prisoner is fined 100 guilders for concubinage.' Cf. GA, RA 339: fo. 16 vs.

38 Hufton, 1974: 284–305; Winslow, 1975.

39 The tax in question is the *convooien en licenten*. Its evasion was often secretly allowed. Cf. Dirksen, 1966: 241.

40 Apart from Republican and provincial taxes there were several municipal ones. Amsterdam had a few. In the beginning of the eighteenth century, for instance, some 10–13% had to be paid extra above the provincial tax on grains. Cf. Sickenga, 1864: 474. In 1678 and 1680 the court promulgated

keuren against evasion of the provincial and municipal wine-tax. Cf. GA, *Keurboek* P, fos. 195 vs and 232. In 1686 it was the turn of the evasion of the liquor-tax. Cf. GA, *Keurboek* Q: fo. 120 vs.

41 Sickenga, 1864: 300–1.
42 Muinck, 1965: 345.
43 Sickenga, 1864: 322–3, 327, 314–15.
44 Dekker, 1977: 307.
45 Oldewelt, 1958: 129–41; Dekker, 1977: 307.
46 Sickenga, 1864: 295.
47 *Placaetboek*, 1658: III, 785–1004; Oldewelt, 1958: 128.
48 *Placaetboek*, 1658: I, 1761.
49 Bontemantel, 1897: I, 31–5.
50 *Placaetboek*, 1658: III, 898.
51 Ibid.: V, 1086.
52 GA, *Keurboeken* Q: fo. 12 vs; R: fos. 36 vs and 274.
53 GA, *Keurboek* R: fo. 218 vs.
54 *Placaetboek*, 1658: V, 1067.
55 GA, Raye ms.: 9 February 1742. The sentence was pronounced on 15 February and executed on 7 July. Cf. RA 613: nos. 202 and 203.
56 GA, *Keurboek* T: fo. 104 vs.
57 GA, *Keurboeken* M: fos. 197 vs. & 228 vs.; O: fo. 231: P, fo. 257: S: fo. 55; T: fo. 7.
58 GA, *Keurboeken* O: fo. 232; S: fo. 55 vs.
59 GA, *Keurboeken* S: fo. 143 vs.
60 One of the six smuggler-helpers was actually arrested for violently resisting a servant of justice on another occasion. He confessed to have rescued two women from impostmasters' servants three years earlier: GA, RA 607: no. 126.
61 GA, RA 605: 28 August 1699.
62 GA, *Keurboek* M: fo. 198 vs – 199; P: fo. 257.
63 In the seventh and eighth decades they make up 8 and 7%, respectively. In the remaining seven decades they never reach the 3% level.
64 In the entire series a fine as additional penalty occurs in 4.5% of the cases. Most of these are cases of smuggling.
65 GA, RA 323: fo. 260; GA, RA 330: fo. 239 vs; GA, RA 348: fo. 39 (also in GA, RA 605).
66 GA, RA 354: fo. 84 vs; GA, RA 378: fo. 105 vs.
67 Though one of them, a woman, with the sword over her head, thereby being the only woman getting this symbolic penalty. One spender of counterfeit money entered into the third sample. This person got an eternal banishment from Holland.
68 According to the editor, Bontemantel is not quite right in this.
69 Bontemantel, 1897: I, 63–5.
70 See bibliography, under Carpzovius. The text of the placard is to be found in *Placaetboek*, 1658: I, 491–4.
71 Carpzovius, 1752: II, 816.
72 Ibid., pp. 770–6.
73 Ibid., pp. 770–6.
74 GA, *Keurboek* P: fo. 208.

75 GA, *Keurboek* R: fo. 262. The penalty: 'public and corporal as the matter requires'.
76 GA, *Keurboek* S: fo. 88. The penalty: 'public in a rigorous way'.
77 GA, *Keurboek* R: fo. 72.
78 Cf., for instance, GA, RA 611: no. 201.
79 GA, RA 606: no. 82.
80 *Duyvelen*, 1682: 105–9.
81 The total of thumb-cuttings is five; four times combined with whipping, one time with branding. The branded one was also a swindler: GA, RA 583: fo. 178 vs. The non-swindling person who had his thumb cut off, had stolen with a false key and resisted his arrest with a pistol: GA, RA 592: fo. 40 vs.
82 Forty-four in the scaffold series; penalties: exposure (eight), whipping (twenty-seven), branding (nine). The first and second sample each contain one observation of banishment only.
83 Non-confessed violence offenses make up 1.2, 3.2 and 5% of the samples. Non-confessed authority offenses are rare. A confession mattered less in the morals group.
84 Hart, 1976.
85 Ibid.: 115.
86 Ibid.: 133.
87 GA, RA 395: fo. 88; GA, RA 395: fo. 241 vs. Compare Montyon's comment about the occupation of those tried in eighteenth-century France: 'Beaucoup de gens sans état se qualifient marchands, artisans, manouvriers et en effet l'ont été mais ne le sont plus au moment du crime.' Cf. Lecuir, 1974: 476.
88 '*Omlopers/omloopsters*'.
89 GA, RA 590: fo. 12.
90 GA, Raye ms.: 20 January 1753.
91 GA, RA 587: fo. 11 vs.
92 Hay, 1975: 37.
93 GA, RA 581: fo. 153.
94 GA, RA 613: no. 222.
95 Bongert, 1971: 74–6.
96 GA, RA 311: fo. 175.
97 GA, RA 325: fo. 217 vs.
98 GA, RA 375: fo. 19 vs.
99 GA, RA 311: fo. 62 vs.
100 GA, RA 581: fo. 116.
101 GA, RA 581: fo. 132.
102 GA, RA 584: fo. 96.
103 GA, RA 584: fo. 97.
104 GA, RA 595: fo. 159.
105 GA, RA 596: fos. 1 and 13 vs.
106 GA, RA 596: fo. 185.
107 GA, RA 596: fo. 190.
108 Mentioned in a new sentence from December 1718 when he was hanged. Cf. GA, RA 608, no. 426.
109 Bongert, 1971: 77–90.

110 GA, RA 609, no. 1.
111 Bontemantel, 1897: I, 74; GA, RA 583: fo. 111 vs.
112 GA, RA 581: fo. 238 vs.
113 GA, RA 581: fo. 241 vs.
114 GA, RA 582: fos. 4 vs and 6 vs.
115 GA, RA 582: fo. 102 vs.
116 GA, RA 582: fos. 179 and 179 vs.
117 GA, RA 583: fo. 159.
118 GA, RA 585: fo. 5.
119 GA, RA 585: fos. 15 and 230.
120 GA, RA 380: fo. 100. A year later the sentence of a woman banished for domestic theft explicitly mentions that she was 'excused from the scaffold', but gives no reason for it. Cf. GA, RA 381: fo. 204.
121 Cf. listing of prior trials in GA, RA 595: fo. 47.
122 GA, RA 324: fo. 57 vs.
123 GA, Raye ms. and Ra 639: 19 January 1771.
124 Hentig, 1962: 104. His argument concerning popular magical beliefs about the sanctity of pregnant women which explain the custom, seems unconvincing to me, certainly for the seventeenth and eighteenth centuries.
125 GA, RA 609: no. 143; GA, RA 628: 31 January 1722.
126 GA, RA 586: fos. 95 vs and 126 vs. Already in 1655 the judges had had doubts: a woman declared to be pregnant when led to the scaffold to be whipped. She was led back and confined in the spinhouse to await the next execution. She doesn't turn up again, so she may indeed have had a child: GA, RA 582: fo. 66.
127 GA, RA 321: fos. 114 and 152 vs.
128 Cf. list of prior trials in GA, RA 613: no. 133.
129 Hart, 1976: 120 and 185.
130 Eeghen, 1960; Sluys, 1940; Reijnders, 1969: 69–78; Braatbard, 1960: 69–93, 106–22, 151–2.
131 GA, RA 587: fo. 181 vs.
132 GA, RA 610: no. 225.
133 GA, RA 611: nos. 144 and 145. The sentences listed them both as High-German Jews, although Rebecca was obviously the Christian partner in the game. Both were born in Amsterdam.
134 The samples contain two, three and three cases, Jews as well as Christians, punished in varying ways except corporal.
135 In 1795 the Jewish community comprised 9.4% of the population. In the second quarter of the eighteenth century 3,000 persons were buried in Ashkenazic cemeteries. Burials amounted to 7,400 in the last quarter. Cf. Hart, 1976: 120. If we consider the percentage of 9.4 for 1795 and realize that the total population did but slightly increase during the period, we can conclude that the Jewish community made up about 4% of the population during the time covered by the third sample. This figure becomes the more plausible if we remember that Hart made an estimate of 3% for the first half of the eighteenth century.
136 Official language mostly spoke of German Jews. Sentences always designate an Ashkenazic Jewish prisoner by that name, but when an Ashkenazic Jew is

present in the stories of the crimes he is referred to as 'smous'. These stories generally adhere to popular language. Likewise they always designate other criminals by their aliases.

137 GA, *Keurboek* S: fo. 86 vs.
138 GA, RA 608: no. 419.
139 GA, *Keurboek* S: fo. 131 vs.
140 GA, RA 610: no. 222.
141 GA, RA 611: no. 81.
142 GA, RA 611: no. 111.
143 GA, RA 611: no. 151.
144 Braatbard, 1960: 125.
145 Ibid.: 50–1, 134–6.
146 GA, RA 608: no. 346.
147 GA, RA 392: fo. 98 vs.
148 GA, Raye ms., 24 January 1756.
149 GA, RA 323: fo. 152; GA, RA 589: fo. 158.
150 Former placards had already been issued in the sixteenth and early seventeenth centuries. Cf. Kappen, 1965: 367 *et seq.*
151 *Placaetboek*, 1658: IV, 509.
152 Ibid.: IV, 553.
153 Cf. Appendix B, no. 28.
154 GA, RA 610: no. 281.
155 GA, RA 605 (not numbered).
156 GA, RA 610: nos. 291, 295 and 308.
157 GA, RA 613: no. 191.
158 GA, RA 610: no. 285.
159 GA, RA 610: no. 321.
160 GA, RA 407: fo. 27.
161 Compare Kappen, 1965: 345 and 403.
162 GA, RA 608: no. 440.
163 Cf. Sewell, 1967: 210.
164 Bontemantel, 1897: II, 386–7.
165 Information on social processes in Amsterdam and the Republic is derived from the relevant chapters of my unpublished Ph.D. thesis ('Judicial Violence in the Dutch Republic. Corporal Punishment, Executions and Torture in Amsterdam, 1650–1750', Amsterdam, 1978) and from the literature referred to there.
166 All information on the process of aristocratization in the Dutch Republic from Spierenburg, 1981b.
167 Cf. Meinhardt, 1957: 226; Greenberg, 1976: 223. Greenberg notes an increasing severity in New York after 1750.
168 Hay, 1975: 22. See also Thompson, 1975.

6. THE DISAPPEARANCE OF PUBLIC EXECUTIONS

1 Among others: Gay, 1969: 423–47; Venturi, 1971: 95–116. These books are unreliable as far as information on judicial practice is concerned. Gay, for example, says that in the Dutch Republic 'the practice of torture was

abandoned at the beginning of the eighteenth century' (p. 425). In fact almost the reverse occurred.

2 Foucault, 1975; Ignatieff, 1978; Stekl, 1978; Perrot, 1980; Roth, 1981.

3 Cooper, 1974.

4 Foucault, 1975: 75–134 (especially pp. 77–96).

5 Ibid.: 94.

6 Puga, 1971: 269.

7 Jong, 1810: I, 81. See also Simons, 1974: 193–4 and 85–6.

8 Wagenaar, 1760: VII, 75.

9 Mieris, 1742: II, 385–6.

10 Beerenbrouck, 1895: 109–10. The scaffold had been used by the court of the Bishop of Liège.

11 Royaards, et al., 1961: 44–5; 58; plates 7, 12, 15, 16, 17.

12 'le plus vilain de tous les bastimens imaginables'.

13 All quotations from Huygens' letter are from Bake, 1929. Bake gives no reference and the original could not be traced.

14 Quoted in Huberts, 1937: 135.

15 ARA, Hof van Holland 5659: fo. 232 vs.

16 Meye, 1935: 39.

17 Which did not necessarily mean that he had not been tortured. It could just as well refer to a confession later repeated 'voluntarily'.

18 GA, RA 584: fo. 18.

19 GA, RA 582: fo. 93; 583: fo. 93 vs and 173 vs; 598: fo. 92 vs; 606: no. 39; 610: no. 337.

20 Mellor, 1961: 143.

21 Langbein, 1977: 65.

22 Grevius, 1624.

23 Heemskerk, 1647: 715–16 and *passim*. Van Heemskerk had already published a sketch of his book in 1637.

24 Jonctijs, 1650: *passim*.

25 Cf. Mellor, 1961: 128.

26 Cf. Heijnsbergen, 1925: 129.

27 Cf. Helbing, 1926: 330–1.

28 Langbein, 1977: 10; Hubert, 1897: 95–132; Weel, 1975: 356–7.

29 Huberts, 1937: 145–6.

30 Jelgersma, 1978: 20–1. Gonnet (1917: 18) says that the lords of Heemstede protested several times against the fact that Haarlem's gallows field was situated opposite to their dwelling. He mentions no date and gives no reference. No. 678a in the inventory of Haarlem's city-archive (A. J. Enschedé, *Inventaris van het Archief der Stad Haarlem*, vol. II, Haarlem 1866) is called 'Documents concerning the stone gallows of the city of Haarlem, under Heemstede, 1615–1631'. Unfortunately, this dossier has been lost since.

31 GA, Raye ms.: 8 May 1764.

32 Quoted in Mollema, 1933: 100–3. See also Bruijn, 1980: 78–80.

33 Quoted by Martin, 1927: 175.

34 Schuhmann, 1964: 68–9.

35 Ariès, 1974: 25.

36 Ibid.: 20–5, 55–82.
37 Vovelle, 1973: 106; Chaunu, 1978: 435–45. The situation in the churchyards was criticized also in the Dutch Republic, although a display of bones was not practiced there. Cf. Boer, 1976: 179–80.
38 Ibid.: 175. On the relationship between sense of hygiene and sensibility, see Goudsblom, 1979.
39 *Beschouwing*, 1773.
40 Ibid.: 4–5.
41 Rijk, 1796.
42 Ibid.: 3–4.
43 Ibid.: 11.
44 Ibid.: 15.
45 Quoted in Vanhemelrjck, 1964: 185. Similar expressions of revulsion were uttered at the failed hanging in Edinburgh in 1819, noted in chapter two. See the quotations in Laurence, 1960: 196.
46 Cf. Radbruch, 1950: 170–1.
47 Cf. Oppelt, 1976: 125.
48 Restif-de-la-Bretonne, 1960: 172–3 (326e, 'Nuit'). With a few deviations, the translation rendered is that which appears in Robert and Elborg Forster (eds.), *European Society in the Eighteenth Century*, London and Melbourne, 1969, pp. 388–9.
49 Compare the description of a service on the Sunday before the execution in Linebaugh, 1977: 251. 'The sheriffs shudder; their inquisitive friends crane forward.'
50 Leeuwen, 1827: II, 11.
51 Ibid.: I, 288.
52 Quoted by Cate, 1975: 138. For a similar view: Wind, 1827: 1–5.
53 GA, Bibliotheek: dossier no. J 1. 080. Original italics.
54 Cate, 1975: 157–60.
55 Quoted by Cooper, 1974: 99.
56 Ignatieff, 1978: 24.
57 Ibid.: 90.
58 Quoted by Ignatieff, 1978: 88. Ignatieff seems to argue that the events leading to the removal of executions to Newgate were a reaction to high numbers of executions caused by the 'crime wave' of the 1780s. But this crime wave was, as always in eighteenth-century England, the consequences of the aftermath of war. It only set in, as Ignatieff himself admits, after the end of the War of American Independence in 1783.
59 Linebaugh, 1975: 67. See also Chapman, 1980: 145.
60 Cooper, 1974: 148; Tobias, 1972: 138.
61 L. O. Pike, in Tobias, 1972: 139.
62 Cooper, 1974: 170–7.
63 Oppelt, 1976: 119, 123.
64 Chevalier, 1958: 78–81, 100.
65 Cate, 1975: 141; Perrot, 1980: 59.
66 Perrot, 1981: 37.
67 Oppelt, 1976: 120–1.
68 Perrot, 1981: 37; Rossa, 1966: 193–4.

69 Cf. GA, RA 626: fo. 239; 627: 68; 640: 12 December 1807 and 21 May 1808; 659: fo. 166 vs *et seq.*
70 On the guillotine: GA, Bibliotheek: dossier no. J 1. 086.
71 Cate, 1975: 146, 172.
72 Eeghen, 1955: 99–100.
73 Cooper, 1974: 159 *et seq.*

CONCLUSION: STATE FORMATION AND MODES OF REPRESSION

1 It is extensively discussed in Spierenburg, paper (see chapter two, note 22).
2 Elias, 1969.
3 Cf., for instance, Hubert, 1897: 106.
4 Foucault, 1975: 111 and 133.
5 The link between public executions and the personal element in wielding authority has also been noted by Blok (1979). He seems to consider this element as the only explanatory factor and does not pay attention to the degree of stability. As argued here, both elements were equally important as characteristics of the early modern states explaining the nature of repression.
6 Cooper, 1974: 1–26.
7 Cf. Elias, 1972. To be sure, Elias also takes the early modern state to be the dynastic state.
8 Elias, 1972: 280. Compare Mayer, 1981, who places the transition even later.
9 In this way we may argue that the emergence of liberal principles in general in the nineteenth century presupposes the preceding pacification and integration. Consequently the *raison d'état* represents a necessary stage of state formation processes. The early modern semi-centralized states would have been unable to survive without the relative arbitrariness of their systems of government. More liberal principles of law and authority would have left many loopholes for private challengers of the state's rule in particular regions. Such a situation was essentially a feature of Sicilian history from the middle of the nineteenth century. Blok (1974) analyzed it. The Italian state nominally took over an area actually made up of private domains of authority. Cherishing liberal principles it did not manage to impose its rule effectively there. When liberal principles were disavowed under fascism, *mafiosi* were beaten. Apparently this twenty-years' stage of *raison d'état* was too short for the stabilization of Italian rule, since *mafia* re-emerged after 1943. In most Western European states such stabilization was reached during the early modern era. To be sure, Blok himself does not discuss the implications of his analysis for early modern Western Europe, as noted here.
10 Cf. Roth, 1981: 161. In the Netherlands a few panoptic prisons were built next to a railroad.
11 Cf. Tobias, 1972: 140.
12 Cf. Philips, 1977; Davis, 1980; Gatrell, 1980.
13 Cf. Reenen, 1979: 50 *et seq.* Van Reenen considers the emergence of this impersonal system as a response to the rise of a workers' movement, but he admits that the beginnings of the former preceded the latter.
14 Ignatieff, 1978: 193–200; Roth, 1981: 299–307.

BIBLIOGRAPHY

Abbiateci (André), 'Les Incendiaires devant le Parlement de Paris: Essai de Typologie Criminelle (XVIIIe Siècle)' in A. Abbiateci et al., *Crimes et Criminalité en France sous l'Ancien Régime, 17e–18e Siècles* (Paris, 1971), pp. 13–32.

Achter (Viktor), *Geburt der Strafe* (Frankfurt am Main, 1951).

Amira (Karl von), 'Thierstrafen und Thierprocesse' in *Mitteilungen des Instituts für Oesterreichische Geschichtsforschung* 12 (1891), 545–601.

 Die germanischen Todesstrafen. Untersuchungen zur Rechts- und Religionsgeschichte in Abhandlungen der Bayerischen Akademie der Wissenschaften. Philosophisch-philologische und historische Klasse, XXXI, Band, 3, Abhandlung (Munich, 1922).

Andel (M. A. van), 'Onze collega de beul' in *Nederlands Tijdschrift voor Geneeskunde* 69 (1925) II, pp. 2,100–8.

Andrews (William), *Les Châtiments de Jadis: Histoire de la Torture et des Punitions Corporelles en Angleterre* (Paris, 1902).

Angstmann (Else), *Der Henker in der Volksmeinung* (Bonn, 1928).

Ariès (Philippe), *L'Enfant et la Vie Familiale sous l'Ancien Régime* (Paris, 1960).

 Western Attitudes toward Death: From the Middle Ages to the Present (Baltimore and London, 1974).

 L'Homme devant la Mort (Paris, 1977).

Avé-Lallemant (Friedrich Christian Benedict), *Das Deutsche Gaunerthum in seiner Social-Politischen, Literarischen und Linguistischen Ausbildung zu seinem Heutigen Bestande* (4 vols., Leipzig, 1858–62).

Backer (J. F.), 'Een Amsterdamsch Straf-proces in de Zeventiende Eeuw' in *Amsterdamsch Jaarboekje*, 1903, pp. 1–24.

Bake (C.), 'Huygens en het Schavot' in *Weekblad van het Recht*, no. 12,048 (1929), 8.

Becker (Marvin B.), 'Changing Patterns of Violence and Justice in Fourteenth- and Fifteenth-Century Florence' in *Comparative Studies in Society and History* 18, 3 (1976), 281–96.

Bée (Michel), 'La Société Traditionelle et la Mort' in *XVIIe Siècle* 106–7 (1975), 81–111.

Beerenbrouck (Charles Joseph Marie Ruysch de), *Het Strafrecht in het Oude Maastricht* (Maastricht, 1895).

Beik (William), 'Popular Culture and Elite Repression in Early Modern Europe' in *Journal of Interdisciplinary History* 11, 1 (1980), 97–103.

Bellamy (John), *Crime and Public Order in England in the Later Middle Ages* (London and Toronto, 1973).

Beneke (Otto), *Von Unehrlichen Leuten. Cultur-historische Studien und Geschichten aus Vergangenen Tagen Deutscher Gewerbe und Dienste, mit besonderer Rücksicht auf Hamburg* (Hamburg, 1863).

Bercé (Yves-Marie), *Histoire des Croquants: Etude des Soulèvements Populaires au XVIIe Siècle dans le Sud-Ouest de la France* (2 vols., Geneva, 1974).

Fête et Révolte: Des Mentalités Populaires du 16e au 18e Siècle (Paris, 1976).

Berigt, – aller-naauwkeurigst – of verhaal aangaande de gruwelyke moorden, geschied door Hidde van Grittinga aan Gerrit Avers en die van de huisvrouw van Avers aan de huisvrouw van Grittinga (Amsterdam, s.a.)

Berkhey (Johannes le Francq van), *Natuurlijke Historie van Holland*, vol. III (Amsterdam, 1776).

Beschouwing, – Aandoenlyke – over de ontzaggelyke rechts-pleeging geschied binnen Amsterdam op Zaturdag den 6 November, 1773 aan zeven kwaaddoenders (Amsterdam, 1773).

Bloch (Marc), *Feudal Society*, translated from the French by L. A. Manyon (London, 1965).

Blok (Anton), *The Mafia of a Sicilian Village, 1860–1960: A Study of Violent Peasant Entrepreneurs* (New York, etc., 1974).

'Theatrische Strafvoltrekkingen onder het Ancien Régime' in *Symposion* I (1979), 94–114.

Boer (Pim den), 'Naar een Geschiedenis van de Dood: Mogelijkheden tot Onderzoek naar de Houding ten Opzichte van de Dode en de Dood ten Tijde van de Republiek' in *Tijdschrift voor Geschiedenis* 89 (1976), 161–201.

Bongert (Yvonne), 'Délinquance Juvenile et Responsabilité Pénale du Mineur au XVIIIe Siècle' in A. Abbiateci et al., *Crimes et Criminalité en France sous l'Ancien Régime, 17e–18e Siècles* (Paris, 1971), pp. 49–90.

Bontemantel (Hans), *De Regeeringe van Amsterdam, soo in 't Civiel als Crimineel en Militaire (1653–1672)*, ed. G. W. Kernkamp (2 vols., 's-Gravenhage, 1897).

Boon (L. J.), 'De Grote Sodomietenvervolging in het Gewest Holland, 1730–1731' in *Holland* 8, 3 (1976), 140–52.

Bosch (Lambert van den), *Treur-toonneel der doorluchtige mannen of op- en ondergang der grooten* (3 vols., Amsterdam, 1698).

Braatbard (Abraham Chaim), – *De Zeven Provinciën in Beroering: Hoofdstukken uit een Jiddische Kroniek over de Jaren 1740–1752*, van – vertaald door L. Fuks (Amsterdam, 1960).

Bridenbaugh (Carl), *Cities in the Wilderness: The First Century of Urban Life in America* (New York, 1955).

Brucker (J.), – *Strassburger Zunft- und Polizei-Verordnungen des 14. und 15. Jahrhunderts: Aus den Originalen des Stadsarchivs ausgewählt und zusammengestellt von* – (Strasbourg, 1889).

Bruijn (J. R.) and E. S. van Eyck van Heslinga (eds.), *Muiterij: Oproer en Berechting op Schepen van de VOC* (Haarlem, 1980).

Brunner (R. J.), 'Het Gevangeniswezen te Batavia tijdens de Oost-Indische Compagnie' in *Tijdschrift voor Strafrecht* 42 (1932), 40–79.

Buchner (Eberhard), *Das Neueste von Gestern: Kulturgeschichtlich Interessante Dokumente aus Alten Deutschen Zeitungen*, vol. III (Munich, 1911).

Buijnsters (P. J.), *Levens van Beruchte Personen: Over de Criminele Biografie in Nederland gedurende de 18e Eeuw* (Utrecht, 1980).

Burke (Peter), *Popular Culture in Early Modern Europe* (New York, etc., 1978).

Buurspraecboeck. – *Het Utrechtse* – in *Archief voor Kerkelijke en Wereldsche Geschiedenissen inzonderheid van Utrecht*, uitgegeven door J. J. Dodt van Flensburg, vol. v (1846), pp. 55–119.

Carpzovius (Benedictus), *Verhandeling der lyfstraffelijke misdaden en haare berechtinge*, translated by Diderik van Hogendorp (2 vols., Rotterdam, 1752).

Castan (Nicole), 'La Justice Expéditive' in *Annales ESC* 31 (1976), 331–61.

Justice et Répression en Languedoc à l'Epoque des Lumières (Paris, 1980).

Castan (Yves), *Honnêteté et Rélations Sociales en Languedoc, 1715–1780* (Paris, 1974).

Cate (C. L. ten), *Tot Glorie der Gerechtigheid: De Geschiedenis van het Brandmerken als Lijfstraf in Nederland* (Amsterdam, 1975).

Cats (Jacob), *Alle de Wercken* (Amsterdam, 1655).

Chapman (Terry L.), 'Crime in Eighteenth Century England: E. P. Thompson and the Conflict Theory of Crime' in *Criminal Justice History* 1 (1980), 139–55.

Chaunu (Pierre), *La Mort à Paris: XVIe, XVIIe et XVIIIe siècles* (s. l., 1978).

Chevalier (Louis), *Classes Laborieuses et Classes Dangereuses à Paris pendant la Première Moitié du XIXe siècle* (Paris, 1958).

Cobb (Richard), *A Sense of Place* (s. l., 1975).

Cohn (Norman), *Europe's Inner Demons: An Enquiry inspired by the Great Witch-Hunt* (London, 1975).

Cooper (David D.), *The Lesson of the Scaffold* (London, 1974).

Coornhert (Dirck Volkertszoon), *Zedekunst dat is Wellevenskunste*, ed. B. Becker (Leiden, 1942).

Danckert (Werner), *Unehrliche Leute: Die Verfemten Berufe* (Berne and Munich, 1963).

Davis (Jennifer), 'The London Garrotting Panic of 1862: A Moral Panic and the Creation of a Criminal Class in mid-Victorian England' in V. A. C. Gatrell, Bruce Lenman and Geoffrey Parker (eds.), *Crime and the Law: The Social History of Crime in Western Europe since 1500* (London, 1980), pp. 190–213.

Dekker (R. M.), 'Oproeren in de Provincie Holland 1600–1750' in *Tijdschrift voor Sociale Geschiedenis* 9 (1977), 299–329.

Dekker (R. M.) (ed.), *Oproeren in Holland gezien door Tijdgenoten: Ooggetuigenverslagen van Oproeren in de Provincie Holland ten Tijde van de Republiek (1690–1750)* (Assen, 1979).

Dekker (Rudolf), *Holland in Beroering: Oproeren in de 17e en 18e Eeuw* (Amsterdam, 1982).

Dirksen (W.), 'Enige Opmerkingen over de Belastingheffing in de Republiek der Verenigde Nederlanden in de 17e en 18e eeuw, in het bijzonder over Inkomstenbelastingen in Zeeland' in *L'impôt dans le Cadre de la Ville et de l'Etat: Actes du Colloque International de Spa* (1966), pp. 235–61.

Droste (Coenraet), *Overblyfsels van Geheugchenis der Bisonderste Voorvallen*, ed. R. Fruin (Leiden, 1879).

Duyvelen, – Seven –, regeerende en vervoerende de hedensdaegsche dienst-maegden, door S.d.V. (Amsterdam, 1682).

Eeghen (I. H. van), 'De Beul te Amsterdam' in *Maandblad Amstelodamum* 41 (1954), 120–7.

'De Positie van de Scherprechters in Nederland in de 19e eeuw' in *Tijdschrift voor Rechtsgeschiedenis* 23 (1955), 93–100.

'De Gereformeerde Kerkeraad en de Joden te Amsterdam' in *Maandblad Amstelodamum* 47 (1960), 169–74.

Elias (Norbert), *Ueber den Prozess der Zivilisation: Soziogenetische und Psychogenetische Untersuchungen* (2 vols., 2nd edn Berne and Munich, 1969).

'Processes of State Formation and Nation Building' in *Transactions of the Seventh World Congress of Sociology at Varna, 1970*, vol. III (Sofia, 1972), pp. 274–84.

Erikson (Kai T.), *Wayward Puritans: A Study in the Sociology of Deviance* (New York, etc., 1966).

Esmein (A.), *Histoire de la Procédure Criminelle en France et Spécialement de la Procédure Inquisitoire depuis le XIIIe Siècle jusqu'a nos Jours* (2nd edn, Frankfurt am Main, 1969).

Evers (J. W. Staats), 'Curiositeiten uit de Lijfstraffelijke Regtspleging van den Ouden Tijd' in *De Oude Tijd* I (1869), pp. 130–4.

Fehr (Hans), *Das Recht im Bilde: Mit 222 Abbildungen* (Munich and Leipzig, 1923).

Feith (H. O.), 'Pardonbrief van den Scherprechter' in *Bijdragen tot de Geschiedenis en Oudheidkunde inzonderheid van de Provincie Groningen*, deel II (1865), p. 252.

Flandrin (Jean-Louis), *Families in Former Times: Kinship, Household and Sexuality* (Cambridge, etc., 1979).

Foucault (Michel), *Surveiller et Punir: Naissance de la Prison* (s. l., 1975).

Frederiks (K. J.), *Het Oud-Nederlandsch Strafrecht*, deel I (Haarlem, 1918).

Fruin (J. A.), 'Eene Crimineele Procedure en Executie uit het Einde der Achttiende Eeuw' in *Nieuwe Bijdragen voor Rechtsgeleerdheid en Wetgeving* nieuwe reeks, 6 (1880), 551–72.

Gatrell (V. A. C.), 'The Decline of Theft and Violence in Victorian and Edwardian England', in V. A. C. Gatrell, Bruce Lenman and Geoffrey Parker (eds.), *Crime and the Law: The Social History of Crime in Western Europe since 1500* (London, 1980), pp. 238–370.

Gay (Peter), *The Enlightenment, an Interpretation*, vol. II: *The Science of Freedom* (London, 1969).

Gernhuber (Joachim), 'Strafvollzug und Unehrlichkeit' in *Zeitschrift der Savigny-Stiftung für Rechtsgeschichte: Germanistische Abteilung* 74 (1957), 119–77.

Given (James Buchanan), *Society and Homicide in Thirteenth-century England* (Stanford, 1977).

Gonnet (C. J.), *De Meester van den Scherpen Zwaarde te Haarlem* (Haarlem, 1917).

Goudsblom (Johan), 'Zivilisation, Ansteckungsangst und Hygiene: Betrachtungen über einen Aspekt des europäischen Zivilisationsprozesses' in Peter Gleichmann, Johan Goudsblom and Herman Korte (eds.), *Materialien zu Norbert Elias' Zivilisationstheorie* (Frankfurt am Main, 1979), pp. 215–53.

Gough (Richard), *The History of Myddle*, ed. with an introduction and notes by David Hey (Harmondsworth, 1981).

Graaf (J. de), 'De Zutphense Scherprechter en diens Executies' in *Bijdragen en Mededelingen Gelre* (1952), pp. 143–69.

Greenberg (Douglas), *Crime and Law Enforcement in the Colony of New York 1691–1776* (Ithaca and London, 1976).

Grevius (Johannes), *Tribunal Reformatum* (Hamburg, 1624).

Hallema (A.), 'Strafbaarheid, Strafmaat en Straffeloosheid, alsmede de Verhouding tussen Gevangenis- en andere Straffen, blijkens Vonnissen van de Amsterdamse Schepenbank voornamelijk uit de Eerste Helft der 17de eeuw' in *Verslagen en Mededelingen van de Vereniging tot Uitgave van Bronnen van het Oud Vaderlands Recht* X (1952), pp. 570–646.

'Bestraffing van Huwelijksontrouw en Bestrijding van de Prostitutie te Amsterdam in de Jaren 1613–1621' in *Tijdschrift voor Strafrecht* 70 (1961), 321–40.

Hanawalt (Barbara A.), 'Violent Death in Fourteenth and Early Fifteenth-Century England' in *Comparative Studies in Society and History* 18, 3 (1976), 297–320.

Crime and Conflict in English Communities (Cambridge, 1979).

Handvesten, ofte privilegien ende octroyen mitsgaders willekeuren, costumen, ordonnantien en handelingen der stad Amstelredam (3 vols., Amsterdam, 1748).

Hart (Simon), *Geschrift en Getal: Een Keuze uit de Demografisch-, Economischen Sociaal-Historische Studiën op Grond van Amsterdamse en Zaanse Archivalia, 1600–1800* (Dordrecht, 1976).

Hay (Douglas), 'Property, Authority and the Criminal Law' in Douglas Hay et al., *Albion's Fatal Tree: Crime and Society in England in the Eighteenth Century* (New York, 1975), pp. 17–63.

Heemskerk (Johan van), *Batavische Arcadia* (Amsterdam, 1647).

Heijnsbergen (P. van), *De Pijnbank in de Nederlanden* (Groningen, 1925).

Helbing (Franz), *Die Tortur: Geschichte der Folter im Kriminalverfahren aller Zeiten und Völker*, neubearbeitet und ergänzt von Max Bauer (Berlin, 1926).

Hentig (Hans von), *Die Strafe* (2 vols., Berlin etc., 1954–5).

Studien zur Kriminalgeschichte, herausgegeben von Christian Helfer (Berne, 1962).

Hermesdorf (B. H. D.), 'Een Taaie Brit aan een Nieuwe Galg (1611)' in *Numaga* 11 (1964), 173–6.

Herwaarden (Jan van), *Opgelegde Bedevaarten. Een Studie over de Praktijk van het Opleggen van Bedevaarten (met name in de stedelijke rechtspraak) in de Nederlanden gedurende de Late Middeleeuwen, ca. 1300–ca. 1550* (Assen and Amsterdam, 1978).

His (Rudolf), *Das Strafrecht des Deutschen Mittelalters*, I: *Die Verbrechen und ihre Folgen im Algemeinen* (Leipzig, 1920).

Historie, van de wonderlijcke mirakelen die in menichte ghebeurt zijn ende noch dagelijcx ghebeuren binnen de vermaerde Coop-stadt Aemstelredam: In een plaets ghenaempt het Tucht-huys, ghelegen op de Heylighe-wegh (Amsterdam, 1612).

Hodne (Bjarne), *Personalhistoriske Sagn* (Oslo, 1973).

Hoerdom, –'t Amsterdamsch – Behelzende de listen en streken daar zich de hoeren en hoerewaardinnen van dienen (. . .) (Amsterdam, 1681).

Houten (B. A. van), *Crimineel proces tegen Hendrik Jansen, wegens moedwilligen* doodslag, aan zijne vrouw begaan; den 22sten Januarij 1803, te Amsterdam, te recht gesteld (Amsterdam, 1803).

Hovy (L.), 'Schikking in Strafzaken in Holland tijdens de Republiek' in Nederlands Acrhievenblad (1980), 413–29.

Hubert (Eugène), La Torture aux Pays-Bas Autrichiens pendant le XVIIIe Siècle (Brussels, 1897).

Huberts (Fr de Witt), De Beul en z'n Werk (Amsterdam, 1937).

Hufton (Olwen), The Poor of Eighteenth-Century France, 1750–1789 (Oxford, 1974).

Huizinga (Johan), The Waning of the Middle Ages: A Study of the Forms of Life, Thought and Art in France and the Netherlands in the Fourteenth and Fifteenth Centuries, translated by F. Hopman (Harmondsworth, 1976).

Huygens (Constantin), De Ledige Uren (Amsterdam, 1644).

Ignatieff (Michael), A Just Measure of Pain: The Penitentiary in the Industrial Revolution, 1750–1850 (New York, 1978).

Immink (P. W. A.), La Liberté et la Peine: Etude sur la Transformation de la Liberté et sur le Développement du Droit Pénal Public en Occident avant le XIIe siècle (Assen, 1973).

Jelgersma (H. C.), Galgebergen en Galgevelden in West- en Midden-Nederland (Zutphen, 1978).

Jonctijs (Daniel), De Pynbank Wedersproken en Bematigt (Amsterdam, 1650).

Jong (Cornelius de), Derde Reize naar de Middellandsche Zee, gedaan in de Jaren 1786, 1787 en 1788 (2 vols., Haarlem, 1810–12).

Kappen (O. van), Geschiedenis der Zigeuners in Nederland (Assen, 1965).

Keller (Albrecht), Der Scharfrichter in der Deutschen Kulturgeschichte (Bonn and Leipzig, 1921).

Koning (Jacobus), Geschiedkundige Aantekeningen betrekkelijk de Lijfstraffelijke Regtsoefening te Amsterdam, voornamelijk in de 16e Eeuw (Amsterdam, 1828).

Lachance (André), Le Bourreau au Canada sous le Régime Français (Quebec, 1966).

Langbein (John H.), Torture and the Law of Proof: Europe and England in the Ancien Régime (Chicago and London, 1977).

Laurence (John), A History of Capital Punishment (New York, 1960).

Lebrun (François), Les Hommes et la Mort en Anjou aux 17e et 18e Siècles: Essai de Démographie et de Psychologie Historiques (Paris and The Hague, 1971).

Lecuir (Jean), 'Criminalité et "Moralité": Montyon, Statisticien du Parlement de Paris' in Revue d'Histoire Moderne et Contemporaine 21 (1974) 445–93.

Leeuwen (J. van), 'Verhandeling ten betoge: dat de toenemende beschaving en de daaruit voortspruitende weldadige gevolgen eener meerdere verlichting, in zaken van hooge aangelegenheid, bijzonder in de hedendaagsche uitoefening van het lijfstraffelijk regt, blijkbaar zijn' in Liefde en Hoop, Tijdschrift over Gevangenen en Gevangenissen I (1827), pp. 287–304 and II (1828), pp. 3–19.

Linebaugh (Peter), 'The Tyburn Riot against the Surgeons' in Douglas Hay et al., Albion's Fatal Tree: Crime and Society in Eighteenth-Century England (New York, 1975), pp. 65–117.

'The Ordinary of Newgate and his Account' in J. S. Cockburn (ed.), Crime in England 1550–1800 (London, 1977), pp. 246–69.

Lofland (John), 'The Dramaturgy of State Executions' in Horace Bleackley and

John Lofland, *State Executions Viewed Historically and Sociologically: The Hangmen of England* (Montclair, NJ, 1977), pp. 275–325.

Lois (S.), *Cronycke ofte korte waere beschryvinge der stad Rotterdam* (The Hague, 1746).

Lonsain (B.), 'De Beul in Stad en Lande' in *Groningsche Volksalmanak* (1909), 56–83.

'Een Terechtstelling buiten de Heerepoort te Groningen' in *Groningsche Volksalmanak* (1917), 52–64.

Lottin (Alain), 'Les Morts Chassés de la Cité: "Lumières et Préjugés": les "Emeutes" à Lille (1779) et à Cambrai (1786), lors du Transfert des Cimetières' in *Revue du Nord* 60 (1978), 73–117.

Maes (Louis T.), *Vijf Eeuwen Stedelijk Strafrecht: Bijdrage tot de Rechts- en Cultuurgeschiedenis der Nederlanden* (Antwerp, 1947).

Malcolmson (Robert W.), '"A Set of Ungovernable People': The Kingswood Colliers in the Eighteenth Century' in John Brewer and John Styles (eds.), *An Ungovernable People: The English and their Law in the Seventeenth and Eighteenth Centuries* (London, etc., 1980), pp. 85–127.

Manen (I. J. van), and Vermeulen, K., 'Het Lagere Volk van Amsterdam in de Strijd tussen Patriotten en Oranjegezinden, 1780–1800'in *Tijdschrift voor Sociale Geschiedenis* 20 (1980), 331–56 and 21 (1981), 3–42.

Marin (P.), *Groot Nederduitsch en Fransch Woordenboek* (2nd edn, Dordrecht, 1730).

Martin (H.), 'De Galgenberg te Amersfoort' in *Jaarboekje van Oud-Utrecht* 4 (1927), 170–96.

Mattelaer (Johan), 'Le médionat – une tâche moins connue du barbier-chirurgien lors d'une exécution' in *Janus* 60 (1973), 137–47.

Mayer (Arno J.), *The Persistence of the Old Regime: Europe to the Great War* (London, 1981).

Meiners (W. J. F.), 'Onbekende Bijzonderheden van het Pachtersoproer te Amsterdam in Juni 1748' in *Maandblad Amstelodamum* 53 (1966), 224–32.

Meinhardt (Karl-Ernst), *Das Peinliche Strafrecht der Freien Reichsstadt Frankfurt am Main im Spiegel der Strafpraxis des 16. und 17. Jahrhunderts* (Frankfurt am Main, 1957).

Mellor (Alec), *La Torture: Son Histoire, son Abolition, sa Réapparition au XXe siècle* (Tours, 1961).

Meye (Albrecht), *Das Strafrecht der Stadt Danzig von der Carolina bis zur Vereinigung Danzigs mit der Preussischen Monarchie (1532–1793)* (Danzig, 1935).

Mieris (Frans van), *Beschryving der Stad Leyden (. . .)* (3 vols., Leiden, 1742–84).

Molhuijsen (P. C.), 'Aantekeningen uit de Geschiedenis van het Strafregt' in *Bijdragen voor Vaderlandsche Geschiedenis en Oudheidkunde* (1861), pp. 51–88 and 195–239.

Mollema (J. C.), *Een Muiterij in de Achttiende Eeuw* (Haarlem, 1933).

Mountague (William), *The Delights of Holland, or a Three Months Travel about that and the Other Provinces* (London, 1696).

Muchembled (Robert), *Culture Populaire et Culture des Elites dans la France Moderne, 15e–18e Siècles* (Paris, 1978).

Bibliography

Muinck (Bernard Ebo de), *Een Regentenhuishouding omstreeks 1700* ('s-Gravenhage, 1965).

Naamlijst, van alle personen die binnen Amsterdam door beulshanden zijn ter dood gebracht (Amersfoort, 1748, 2nd edn, 1766, 3rd edn, 1774).

Oldewelt (W. F. H.), 'Hollandse Voorlopers van de Pachtersoproeren' in *Jaarboek Amstelodamum* 50 (1958), 127–41.

'De Zelfkant van de Amsterdamse Samenleving en de Groei der Bevolking (1578–1795)' in *Tijdschrift voor Geschiedenis* 77 (1964) 39–56.

Oppelt (Wolfgang), *Über die Unehrlichkeit des Scharfrichters* (Antiquariat Traute Gottschalk) (Lengfeld, 1976).

Perrot (Michelle) (ed.), *L'Impossible Prison: Recherches sur le Système Pénitentiaire au XIXe Siècle: Debat avec Michel Foucault* (Paris, 1980).

'L'Affaire Troppmann (1869)' in *L'Histoire* 30 (Janvier 1981), 28–37.

Philips (David), *Crime and Authority in Victorian England: The Black Country, 1825–1860* (London, 1977).

Placaetboek, – Groot – vervattende de placaten (. . .) van de (. . .) Staten Generael (. . .) ende (. . .) Staten van Hollandt (. . .) mitsgaders (. . .) Staten van Zeelandt (10 vols., The Hague and Amsterdam, 1658–1797).

Poršnev (Boris) – Porschnew, B. F., *Die Volksaufstände in Frankreich vor der Fronde, 1623–1648* (Leipzig, 1954).

Porta (Antonio), *Johan en Gerrit Corver: De Politieke Macht van Amsterdam (1702–1748)* (Assen, 1975).

Puga (Pedro Herrera), *Sociedad y Delincuencia en el Siglo de Oro: Aspectos de la Vida Sevillana en los Siglos XVI y XVII* (Granada, 1971).

Quanter (Rudolf), *Die Leibes- und Lebensstrafen bei Allen Völkern und zu Allen Zeiten* (Dresden, 1901).

Racer (J. W.), *Overijsselsche Gedenkstukken: Zesde Stuk* (Kampen, 1787).

Radbruch (Gustav), *Elegantiae Juris Criminalis: Vierzehn Studien zur Geschichte des Strafrechts* (2nd edn, Basle, 1950).

Rechtspleeging, gehouden met Hendrina Wouters, wegens twee afschuwelyke moorden; op den 17 December 1746 binnen Amsteldam door Beuls handen ter Dood gebragt: Den vierden Druk, van veel Fouten gesuyvert (Amsterdam, s.a.).

Reenen (Piet van), *Overheidsgeweld: Een Sociologische Studie van de Dynamiek van het Geweldsmonopolie* (Alphen a.d. Rijn, 1979).

Reijnders (Carolus), *Van 'Joodsche Natiën' tot Joodse Nederlanders: Een Onderzoek naar Getto- en Assimilatieverschijnselen tussen 1600 en 1942* (Amsterdam, 1969).

Renger (Wilhelm), 'Hinrichtungen als Volksfeste' in *Süddeutsche Monatshefte* 10, 2 (1913), 8–21.

Restif-de-la-Bretonne (Nic.-Edme), *Les Nuits de Paris* (Paris, Hachette, 1960).

Rijk (G.), *Beschrijving van het laatste gedrag van Leenderd van Willigen (In Amsterdam op den 26sten van slachtmaand, des jaars 1796 op het schavot, voor het huis der gemeente, met de koorde gestraft). Ten betoge, dat eene zinsverandering in de laatste dagen van het leven, oprecht kan zijn* (Amsterdam, s.a.).

Rossa (Kurt), *Todesstrafen: Ihre Wirklichkeit in drei Jahrtausenden* (Oldenburg and Hamburg, 1966).

Roth (Robert), *Pratiques Pénitentiaires et Théorie Sociale: L'Exemple de la Prison de Genève, 1825–1862* (Geneva, 1981).

Royaards (C. W.), Jongens, (P.), Phaff, (H. E.), *Het Stadhuis van Haarlem: Algemeen Restauratieplan* (Haarlem, 1961).

Rudé (George), *Paris and London in the Eighteenth Century: Studies in Popular Protest* (s. l., 1970).

Rusche (Georg) and Kirchheimer (Otto), *Punishment and Social Structure* (New York, 1939).

Sanson, (H.), *Sept Générations d'Exécuteurs, 1685–1847: Mémoires des Sanson, mis en ordre, rédigés et publiés par H. Sanson* (6 vols., Paris, 1862–3).

Schuhmann (Helmut), *Der Scharfrichter: Seine Gestalt – seine Funktion* (Kempten, Allgäu, 1964).

Scott (George Ryley), *The History of Corporal Punishment: A Survey of Flagellation in its Historical, Anthropological and Sociological Aspects* (London, 1938).

Secretary, – Amsterdamsche – bestaende in formulieren van schepenen-kennissen, quijtscheldingen, schat-brieven, en andere, die gewoonlyk daar gebruikt werden (Amsterdam, 1700).

Sellin (J. Thorsten), *Pioneering in Penology: The Amsterdam Houses of Correction in the 16th and 17th Centuries* (Philadelphia, 1944).

Slavery and the Penal System (New York, etc. 1976).

Sewell (William H., Jr), 'Marc Bloch and the Logic of Comparative History' in *History and Theory* 6 (1967), 208–18.

Shorter (Edward), *The Making of the Modern Family* (New York, 1975).

Sickenga (Folkert Nicolaas), *Bijdrage tot de Geschiedenis der Belastingen in Nederland* (Leiden, 1864).

Simons (Constantijn Hendrik Frederik), *Marine Justitie* (Assen, 1974).

Slobbe (J. F. van), *Bijdrage tot de Geschiedenis en de Bestrijding der Prostitutie te Amsterdam* (Amsterdam, 1937).

Sluys (D. M.), 'Hoogduits-Joods Amsterdam van 1635 tot 1795' in *Geschiedenis der Joden in Nederland*, ed. H. Brugmans and A. Frank, vol. I (Amsterdam, 1940), pp. 306–81.

Spaan (Gerrit van), *Het koddig en vermakelyk leven van Louwtje van Zevenhuizen of het schermschool der huislieden* (Rotterdam, 1752).

Spierenburg (Pieter), 'De Sociale Functie van Openbare Strafvoltrekkingen' in *De Gids* 141 (1978), 510–23.

'De Dood op Bevel van de Rechter: Een Verkennende Historisch-Sociologische Beschouwing' in Geert A. Banck et al. (eds.) *Gestalten van de Dood: Studies over Abortus, Euthanasie, Rouw, Zelfmoord en Doodstraf* (Baarn, 1980), pp. 128–50.

(1981a) 'Theory and the History of Criminal Justice' in L. A. Knafla (ed.), *Crime and Criminal Justice in Europe and Canada* (Waterloo, Ont., 1981), pp. 319–27.

(1981b) *Elites and Etiquette: Mentality and Social Structure in the Early Modern Northern Netherlands* (Centrum voor Maatschappijgeschiedenis, vol. IX) (Rotterdam, 1981).

'Model Prisons, Domesticated Elites and the State', in Göran Rystad (ed.) *Europe and Scandinavia: Aspects of the Process of Integration in the 17th Century* (Lund, 1983), pp. 219–35.

Steinert (Heinz) and Treiber (Hubert), 'Versuch die These von der strafrechtlichen Ausrottungspolitik im Spätmittelalter "auszurotten": Eine Kritik an Rusche/Kirchheimer und dem Ökonomismus in der Theorie der Strafrechtsentwicklung' in *Kriminologisches Journal* 10, 2 (1978), 81–106.

Stekl (Hannes), *Österreichs Zucht- und Arbeitshäuser, 1671–1920: Institutionen zwischen Fürsorge und Strafvollzug* (Vienna, 1978).

Stenzel (Gustav Adolf) (ed.), *Scriptores Rerum Silesiacarum / Sammlung Schlesischer Geschichtsschreiber*, Band III (Breslau, 1847).

Stone (Lawrence), *The Crisis of the Aristocracy, 1558–1641* (Oxford etc., 1965). *The Family, Sex and Marriage in England, 1500–1800* (New York, 1977).

Styles (John), '"Our Traiterous Money Makers": The Yorkshire Coiners and the Law, 1760–83' in John Brewer and John Styles (eds.), *An Ungovernable People: The English and their Law in the Seventeenth and Eighteenth Centuries* (London, etc., 1980), pp. 172–249.

Thompson (E. P.), *Whigs and Hunters: The Origin of the Black Act* (New York, 1975).

Tilly (Charles) (ed.), *The Formation of National States in Western Europe* (Princeton, 1975).

Tobias (J. J.), *Nineteenth-Century Crime. Prevention and Punishment* (s. l., 1972).

Uffenbach (Zacharias Conrad), *Merkwürdige Reisen durch Niedersachsen, Holland, und Engelland*, Theil III (Ulm, 1754).

Unger (W. S.) (ed.), *Bronnen tot de geschiedenis van Middelburg in den landsheerlijken tijd*, deel I (The Hague, 1923).

Vanhemelrijck (F.), 'De Beul van Brussel en zijn Werk (XIVe–XIXe eeuw)' in *Bijdragen tot de Geschiedenis der Nederlanden* 19 (1964), 181–216.

Velius (D.), *Chroniick van Hoorn* (Hoorn, 1617).

Venturi (Franco), *Utopia and Reform in the Enlightenment* (Cambridge, 1971).

Volmuller (H. W. J.), *Het Oudste Beroep. Geschiedenis van de Prostitutie in Nederland* (Utrecht, 1966).

Vovelle (Michel), *Piété Baroque et Déchristianisation en Provence au XVIIIe Siècle. Les Attitudes devant la Mort d'après les Clauses des Testaments* (Paris, 1973).

Vries (Jan de), 'Histoire du Climat et Economie: Des Faits Nouveaux, une Interprétation Différente' in *Annales ESC* 32 (1977), 198–226.

Vries (Klaas de), *Bijdrage tot de Kennis van het Strafprocesrecht in de Nederlandse Steden benoorden Maas en Schelde vóór de Vestiging van het Bourgondisch Gezag* (Groningen and Djakarta, 1955).

Vries (W. de), 'Bossche Scherprechters en hun Familie' in *De Brabantse Leeuw* 8 (1959), 39–46.

Vrugt (M. van de), *De Criminele Ordonnantien van 1570* (Zutphen, 1978).

Wagenaar (Jan), *Amsterdam in zyne opkomst, aanwas, geschiedenissen, voorregten, koophandel, gebouwen, kerkenstaat, schoolen, schutterye, gilden en regeeringe* (13 vols., Amsterdam, 1760–68).

Walker (Nigel), *Crime and Insanity in England*, vol. I: *The Historical Perspective* (Edinburgh, 1968).

Walter (John), 'Grain Riots and Popular Attitudes to the Law: Maldon and the Crisis of 1629' in John Brewer and John Styles (eds.), *An Ungovernable People: The English and their Law in the Seventeenth and Eighteenth Centuries*

(London, etc., 1980), pp. 47–84.

Weel (A. J. van), 'De Nasleep van de Afschaffing van de Pijnbank' in *Verslagen en Mededelingen der Vereniging tot Uitgave der Bronnen van het Oud-Vaderlands Recht* 15, 2 (1975), 355–67.

Wiersum (E.), 'De Executie van een Doodvonnis in Schieland' in *Rotterdamsch Jaarboekje* (1941), 91–104.

Wind (S. de), *Bijzonderheden uit de Geschiedenis van het Strafrecht in de Nederlanden* (Middelburg, 1827).

Winslow (Cal), 'Sussex Smugglers' in Douglas Hay et al., *Albion's Fatal Tree: Crime and Society in Eighteenth-Century England* (New York, 1975), pp. 119–66.

Wirth (Louise Jeanne Thérèse), *Een Eeuw Kinderpoëzie, 1778–1878* (Groningen and The Hague, 1925).

Zetzner (Johann Eberhard) – *Aus dem Leben eines Strassburger Kaufmanns des XVII. und XVIII. Jahrhunderts – Reiss-Journal und Glücks- und Unglücksfälle – von – (1677–1735): Nach der Ungedruckten Originalhandschrift im Auszug mit Anmerkungen,* herausgegeben von Rudolf Reuss (Strasbourg, 1913).

INDEX